Annual selected Edition from **DETAIL** Review of Architecture

Architectural
Details 2003

Edition Detail · Institut für internationale
Architektur-Dokumentation GmbH & Co. KG
Munich

Architectural Press
Amsterdam · Boston · Heidelberg · London
New York · Oxford · Paris · San Diego
San Francisco · Singapore · Sydney · Tokyo

Editorial office: Christian Schittich (Editor-in-chief),
Andrea Wiegelmann (Project manager),
Sabine Drey, Andreas Gabriel, Frank Kaltenbach, Steffi Lenzen,
Julia Liese, Thomas Madlener, Edith Walter, Meike Weber, Heide Wessely
Freelance assistance: Christa Schicker

Translation German/English: Peter Green, Catherine Anderle-Neill
Drawings: Kathrin Draeger, Marion Griese, Nicola Kollmann, Emese Köszegie
DTP: Peter Gensmantel, Andrea Linke, Cornelia Kohn, Roswitha Siegler

1 604 46 105

This book is produced by
DETAIL – Review of Architecture
and distributed by Architectural Press – Elsevier Ltd.

British Library Cataloguing in Publication Data.
A catalogue record for this book is available from the British Library.

Printed on acid-free paper produced from chlorine-free pulp (TCF ∞).

Printed in Germany
Reproduction: Karl Dörfel Reproduktions-GmbH, Munich
Printing and binding: sachsendruck GmbH, Plauen

ISBN 0-7506-6375-8

9 8 7 6 5 4 3 2 1

Editorial

Over the past 43 years, DETAIL has occupied a top position
in international architectural publishing. Available in more than
80 different countries, DETAIL is one of the most widely read
reviews of architecture in the world and is to be found in most leading professional offices. With its unique concept, it contributes not
only to current debates in the world of construction; it also looks
behind the scenes, citing outstanding international projects as
examples of what is going on in architecture today. In ten issues
a year, the projects are presented with carefully researched information, newly drawn plans and coloured illustrations.

Details are more than just solutions to technical problems. They
have a major influence on the character and appearance of buildings, and they may also be used as a design tool. It has always
been one of the central aims of DETAIL to bring out these aspects.

For the first time, this yearbook for 2003 presents a summary of
the most important articles and buildings from a whole year's
publications in an exclusively English-language edition. The layout
of the book follows that of the journal itself. The building projects
contained in the "documentation" section are flanked by specialist
articles from the "discussion" and "technology" sections. In making
our selection, we have tried to include a representative cross-
section of the material covered in the course of the year –
representative in terms of building types and functions, materials,
forms of construction and geographical locations. As in every issue
of the journal, the editorial team seeks to present a sensible and
attractive mixture, especially in the choice of buildings.
The book contains a stimulating juxtaposition of well-designed
everyday structures – mostly by smaller, less-known offices – and
more spectacular projects by internationally renowned architects.

The yearbook is, therefore, an important reference work, full of
ideas and details that will help architects in their everyday planning
and practice.

Christian Schittich
editor-in-chief of DETAIL, Review of Architecture

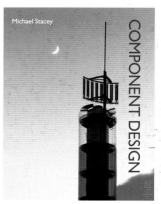

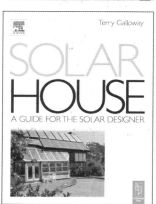
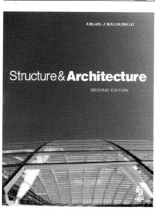

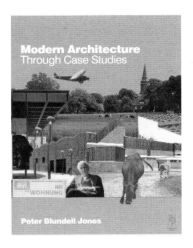

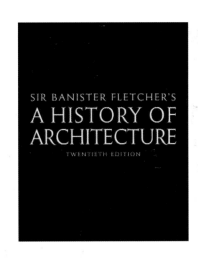

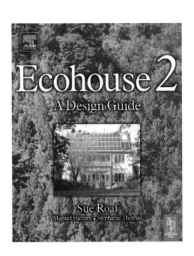

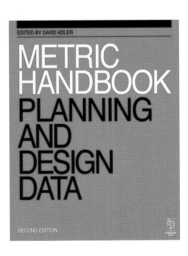
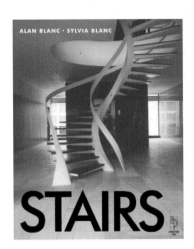

discussion

dokumentation

technology

appendix

discussion

Schools Are a Hobbyhorse of Mine – an Interview with Herman Hertzberger

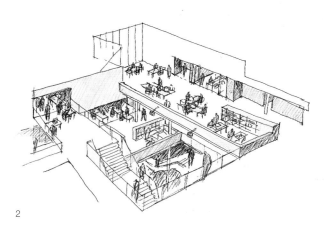

2

Detail: You have been building schools in the Netherlands since the 1960s. What educational developments have you seen in that time?
Hertzberger: In the field of education, one of the main political goals in the Netherlands today is to bring the various private and state schools in line with each other, to unify the complex educational system and reduce the large number of schools. It's not a bad idea, but it doesn't always make sense. Small schools are more comprehensible, for example, while larger schools can offer more facilities, such as media libraries.

How do you assess the conditions for school construction in the Netherlands?

We have witnessed a change since the 1990s. In the past, the Ministry of Education was the central authority responsible for schools and teaching. Seven or eight years ago, this responsibility was transferred to local authorities. The state now grants only basic funding. The rest has to be provided by the municipalities. Unfortunately, very few of them are interested in qualitative school building. Politically, the situation is problematic, but schools are a hobbyhorse of mine.

Is the lack of interest in building high-quality schools a socio-political problem?
Yes. We have to invest much more in edu-

cation in the Netherlands. We have to specialize and export knowledge. Schools should not be just a series of classrooms and corridors; they should provide a kind of home base. It's not enough just to learn mathematics and languages. In a multicultural society, it is important for children to learn to live together rather than attacking each other.

How do you implement your school concepts architecturally?
I believe a school should be a kind of polis, a microcosm. In my spatial concepts, therefore, I am particularly concerned with the zones outside the classrooms. Through

1

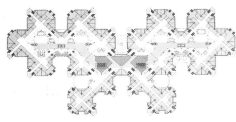

3

4

greater openness spatially, I ensure that corridors are not just circulation routes. In the Apollo School in Amsterdam, for example, just as many activities take place outside the classrooms as within them.

Maria Montessori was also concerned with space in her educational theory. Is your architectural approach related to this in any way?
No, not really. But I'm convinced that liberty can exist only within a certain framework. According to Montessori, pupils should be allowed as much latitude as possible within certain limits. I see my school architecture in that light: I provide the framework within which the pupils can develop freely.

To what extent does the age of the children affect the architecture?
Too much emphasis is placed on that aspect sometimes. People speak of finding the right scale for children, but they climb stairs just like adults. I'm not aware that children need smaller steps. Of course, things like tables and chairs will be lower for younger children, but other aspects like natural lighting, visual links and spaces for withdrawal are more important. In traditional school types, there are usually long corridors which serve solely as access routes. From the very outset, we wanted to develop a different type. In the Atlas College in Hoorn (2002–04), there will be study areas outside the actual classrooms – divided off by folding doors. In the De Eilanden School in Amsterdam (1996–2002), we used sliding doors for this purpose.

Do you involve teachers and pupils in the design process?
I always attempt to develop a school design in collaboration with the teachers and pupils. This helps to achieve a stronger sense of identity with the school. In the case of the Montessori College Oost in Amsterdam (see page 9), we sat down with 30 or 40 teachers every month. But that didn't prove to be very productive. For the most part, they fought for the interests of their own classes. They were concerned with having as many socket outlets as possible, hot water, light and so on.

Do the different nationalities of the pupils play a role in your design?
No. I am interested in fundamental forms: that's what Structuralism means to me today. I attempt to develop a common spatial programme for all pupils. There are two main aspects to this: enclosure or protection, and openness. In many cultures, space implies something enclosed, but to us as a seafaring nation, it can also mean something that extends over the horizon.

Can one trace your personal architectural development in your buildings?
As a rule, I design from the inside out. From the very beginning, I have provided a vertical link in all buildings that are more than two storeys high. In the Ministry of Social Affairs in The Hague (1979–90), I realized the concept of a large central hall, a space that links all parts of the building; but regrettably, I didn't take the idea to its logical conclusion. That building marks the end of a certain line in my design development. Since then, there has been a bolder gesture and a larger urban-planning element in my architecture.

Are there any differences between building in Germany and the Netherlands, particularly with regard to building regulations?
I have built schools only in the Netherlands, so I cannot make direct comparisons in that respect. German schools, which I admire very much, usually draw on a much bigger budget. As far as building regulations are concerned, they are analogous. We are building a large project in Germany at the moment, the Media Park Office Building in Cologne. Maybe I shouldn't say this, but I find the Dutch are more pernickety and stingier. People are more open in Germany. On the other hand, we don't have the notion that a building can bestow prestige and demonstrate power.

What is your favourite school project?
The most recent project I have worked on always means most to me, and that is the De Eilanden School. It was a difficult project, because the dwellings above the school

were not planned by us. Crazy conditions, but one invests a great deal of time in difficult projects and is always delighted at unexpected successes. It's the same as with one's children. DETAIL Konzept 3/2003

Herman Hertzberger was interviewed in Amsterdam by Sabine Drey and Gerard Bergers.

1 Apollo School, Amsterdam, 1980–83
2 Atlas College, Hoorn, 2002–04
3 De Eilanden School, Amsterdam, 1996–2002
4 Ministry of Social Affairs, The Hague, 1979–90: second floor layout
5 Polygoon Primary School, Almere, 1990–92
6 Primary school and kindergarten, Amsterdam, 1986

5

6

The Pioneering Age of Concrete Blocks – Frank Lloyd Wright's Textile-Block Houses

Edward R. Ford

"The universe," Ralph Waldo Emerson wrote, "is represented in every one of its particles. Everything in nature contains all the powers of nature. ... Each new form repeats not only the main character of the type, but part for part all of the details. ... Each one is an entire emblem of human life." This was a key tenet of American Transcendentalism, and it is understandable, therefore, that it should become a key tenet of the work of Frank Lloyd Wright. Throughout his career, Wright applied the concept of unifying geometric motifs, each representing both the part and the whole. Wright's motifs were often indifferent to scale and sometimes had the effect of blurring rather than articulating the qualities of materials; but this approach to design explains the constructional nature of Wright's architecture to a great extent. With few exceptions, his constructional methodologies originate in ornamental methodologies. Thus, the tree-like patterns of the art-glass windows of the Prairie houses became the tree-like concrete columns of the S. C. Johnson Building. By 1930, Wright's concept of plasticity had come to mean continuity of structure; and the grids of Louis Sullivan's ornamentation became the structural grid of Wright's buildings. This line of development is particularly evident in the textile-block system.

In the period from 1914 to 1925, in sharp contrast to the minimal ornament of the Prairie houses, Wright was working with repetitive, square, ornamental concrete blocks made with wood forms. The large frieze of Midway Gardens (1914) was constructed of blocks of site-cast concrete. The textile-block-like frieze of the Albert German Warehouse (1915) was actually cast in-situ. In neither case is the block used in a structurally unique way, but these were the origins of the gridded and repetitive ornaments Wright went on to apply to concrete masonry. After 1904, he used a grid for all his buildings, but the textile-block system was the first in which the grid was determined by the actual components: 16" × 16" × 3 1/2" blocks, forming 16-inch squares on plan

1

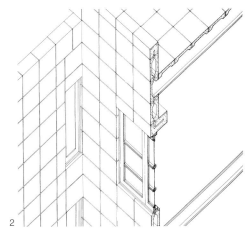

2

and in elevation and establishing a 4' 0"
structural module (three 16" blocks).
In the late 1920s, this grid became an ideology. It is always difficult to separate Wright's original thinking from his subsequent explanations, but in 1927 he proclaimed the textile-block system to be the appropriate response to "standardization" – in contrast to the large-module systems of Le Corbusier and Gropius. Wright's system was to be created by elevating an imprecise vernacular material – concrete blocks – into a mass-produced product of superior strength, standardized in its parts, precise in its manufacture and execution, and perfect in its performance – all accomplished with a minimum of skilled on-site labour.

The additional strength was provided by a grid of reinforcing bars between the edges of the blocks, while precision and standardization were achieved through the use of metal moulds to form blocks 1/8" smaller than the 16" module. The traditional 3/8" mortar joint was eliminated in favour of a semicircular groove at the edge of each block filled with grout to receive the reinforcement, leaving no visible face joint. The blocks and the walling were to be completely waterproofed. Wright's one concession to constructional imprecision was the double wall with a continuous cavity, which, according to the architect, had an insulating effect. The two layers were just as important for the accuracy of the construction, however. It would have been difficult to obtain the same precision with a single-thickness wall with two exposed faces, since the blocks vary slightly in width.

The first textile-block building to be completed was the Storer House (1923). This was followed by the Ennis House and the Freeman House (both 1924). Wright considered the Millard House (1923) to be a textile-block building, but it does not reveal the mature form of this kind of construction, since it lacks the grid of grouted reinforcing bars and uses a traditional 1/2" mortar joint reinforced with expanded metal.

Although the textile-block houses have received greater attention in recent years,

they have never achieved the popularity of the Prairie or Usonian houses. The increased mass and smaller areas of glazing of the early houses resulted in a greater monumentality and a regional appropriateness; but this was at the expense of domesticity and a relationship to the exterior. For many, the textile-block system represents a step backwards in terms of form and space, although this does not apply to the last of the series, the Freeman House with its dramatic glazed corners, which shows Wright at his best.

Like many of Wright's innovations, the textile-block system was not an economic success. The architect's grandson Eric, who has restored several of the houses, believes that grouting the joints between blocks (as opposed to filling them with mortar) drove the costs above a competitive level. Standardization proved equally illusory, since the actual number of block types required in a single building vastly exceeded the concept of a mass-produced standard unit. The Freeman House, for example, required 56 different blocks.

The waterproof wall proved to be even more problematic in the course of time. There is considerable debate about the causes of the leaking, spalling, cracking and general deterioration that have occurred in the houses.

Robert Sweeney argues that it is impossible to produce waterproof blocks with the extremely dry mixture that was necessary to form them in the complex metal moulds. By 1930, Wright seems to have acknowledged this himself.

Wright's concept consisted of a wall that was waterproofed on its outer face and contained an air space for insulation. Modern practice prefers a cavity wall in which water penetrates the outer skin and is then intercepted and drained to the exterior again, with additional insulation to meet modern energy standards. Wright's cavity wall intercepts water, but there is no means of draining the moisture to the outside again; and because of convection currents in the cavity, it does not provide as much insulation as

3

4

5

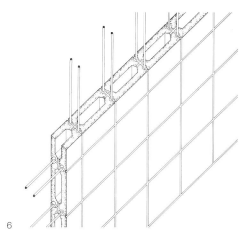

6   Constructional principles of textile-block
    system: double-skin concrete blockwork
    with an intermediate cavity to provide
    thermal insulation; a grid of horizontal
    and vertical reinforcement rods between
    the blocks; minimal mortar joint filling in
    preformed grooves

7   Freeman House, Pasadena, 1924: perforated
    blocks filter the ingress of light
8   Charles Ennis House, 1923–24, the largest of the
    four textile-block houses in Los Angeles
9   Millard Residence, La Miniatura, Pasadena,
    1923: garden facade, consisting of partly
    perforated concrete blocks

6

Wright claimed. Even so, this form of construction was common practice at the time. Furthermore, American standards of insulation were much lower than they are today. In fact, Wright's Usonian wall system of the 1930s contains no insulation at all.

Another problem is the action of moisture on the reinforcement over the years. This is particularly evident in the Ennis House. The cracking and spalling of the concrete blocks is undoubtedly the result of water coming in contact with the steel and causing it to rust, thereby breaking the bond with the concrete.

Wright's departure from California did not mean the end of his system. It was used subsequently in countless projects, including 15 houses and several larger buildings. In the unbuilt San Marcos in the Desert scheme (1929), Wright developed the block as a form for larger concrete columns and beams that would have made it an integral part of the frame.

In 1931, Wright's son Lloyd created a variation on the textile-block system in which the reinforcing bars are completely encased in grouting, and the inner face of the external skin is covered with a waterproof membrane. Frank Lloyd Wright adopted aspects of this system, but he nevertheless regarded these developments as detrimental compromises. The walls of the Arizona Biltmore Hotel (1928) are waterproofed on their inside face; and the Lloyd Jones House is waterproofed on the internal and external faces of the outer layer of blocks. The Florida Southern College buildings (1939–54) also made extensive use of the textile-block system, but much of the walling was covered with plaster, which is patterned in some areas to imitate the ornament of the adjacent blocks.

Just as the system seemed to have run its course, Wright invested it with new life. Faced with rising carpentry and masonry costs after the Second World War, he revised the system to create the Usonian "Automatic". While its technical details are

7

remarkably similar to the old system, its rationale was quite different – at least on the surface. The Usonian Automatic was not intended as an architectural form of standardization and assembly-line mass production; it was meant to enable the homeowner to do the work himself, fabricating and assembling the blocks without the need for skilled labour or heavy equipment. This was not accomplished by making the system any less precise or by eliminating its technical defects. The block was made larger (1' × 2'), but the tolerance was reduced to 1/16". (In comparison, the equivalent modern tolerance or allowable deviation is 1/8" – twice as great as that allowed by Wright in 1948.) The architect developed three wall types, two of which were based on a single-skin block wall. In the first of these, the inside face of the blocks was waterproofed, insulated and lined with plywood. In the second, there is no facing at all. The interior of the Adelman House (1951) is lined entirely with plywood, whereas the walls of the Tonkens House (1954) consist simply of a single thickness of concrete masonry exposed internally and externally and with no internal finishings. This series of houses was the first that Wright built wholly of concrete masonry units, including the roof.

Standardization again proved to be elusive. In *The Natural House,* Wright claimed that nine different block types would suffice, but the Pappas House required 25, and the Turkel House 37. Most of the houses also turned out to be just as expensive, if not more so, than comparable structures in timber or brick.

Donald Leslie Johnson and Robert Sweeney have argued that the textile-block system may have been invented by others – Walter Burley Griffin, William Nelson or Lloyd Wright. In 1934, the Portland Cement Association listed 40 similar unit forms of concrete masonry construction, including the Pancrete and Underdown systems, which bore a resemblance to Wright's solutions. None of them are any longer in use. Today, concrete masonry accounts for only about 10 per cent of single-family house-building in the US.

If Wright had been content to use the textile blocks as conventional masonry, many construction problems might have been avoided. The lack of success of this system, however, may have less to do with any inherent deficiencies than with the resistance of the American building industry to the use of anything other than the wood platform frame. The disparity between concept and performance in the textile-block systems is symptomatic of a broader disparity between Wright's ideas and the conventions of American building – not to mention the conventions of American society.　　DETAIL 4/2003

Bibliography:
Terry Patterson, *Frank Lloyd Wright and the Meaning of Materials*, New York, Van Nostrand Reinhold, 1994
Bruce Brooks Pfeiffer, *Frank Lloyd Wright Monograph*, 12 vols., Tokyo: A.D.A. EDITA, 1984–1988
Robert Sweeney. *Wright in Hollywood*, Cambridge: MIT, 1994
Frank Lloyd Wright, *The Natural House*, New York, Horizon, 1954
Portland Cement Association, *Report on Survey of Concrete House Construction Systems*, Chicago, PCA, 1934
Bruce B. Pfeiffer, *Frank Lloyd Wright, Selected Houses 8*, Tokyo, A.D.A. EDITA, 1991
David Gebhard. *Romanza, The California Architecture of Frank Lloyd Wright*, Chronicle Books, 1988
Edward R. Ford, *The Details of Modern Architecture*, MIT, 1990

Edward R. Ford is a professor at the School of Architecture of the University of Virginia.

Concrete – a Yearning for the Monolithic

Frank Kaltenbach

2

The strength of simplicity
Monolithic buildings radiate a sense of strength. The pervasiveness of a single material, in conjunction with only a few restrained details, creates an agreeable impression of archaic simplicity in our modern society. Stone huts in the Ticino Alps or adobe forts on the edge of the Sahara are not simply shelters; they are also abstract objects, ancient images of civilization in aggressive environments. These images still affect us today. If one seeks to achieve a unified design for structure, facade, pavings and other ancillary elements of a building in temperate climatic zones, the versatility of concrete makes it the ideal material.

Outside solid – inside hollow
Many different surface treatments are possible for the design of facades. In the Swiss embassy in Berlin, Diener and Diener sought to achieve a monolithic effect by avoiding all trace of working joints. The walls were concreted in a continuous process over a period of 26 hours (see Detail 6/2001). Sometimes the pattern of formwork ties may be exploited to lend the surface a certain structure. In the Schöller Bank in Vienna, however, Jabornegg and Pálffy used an elaborate expanding formwork technique to avoid precisely this effect. The monolithic outward appearance of a concrete building often results in internal complexity, especially in the building physics. An adequate solution can normally be achieved only through the creation of thermally separated inner and outer skins, in which case, care must be taken to avoid cracking caused by extremes of temperature. In the 16-metre-high exposed concrete facade of the Pinakothek der Moderne in Munich, which was executed without joints, flexible anchors were inserted between the two skins, and the external wall was prestressed. The slender columns of the building, which appear to have been constructed in a single pour, are, in fact, prefabricated hollow elements.

1

1 Housing on Zürichberg, 2000;
architects: Gigon/Guyer, Zurich
2 Stone imitation in housing development in
Fukuoka, Japan, 1997;
architects: OMA, Rem Koolhaas, Rotterdam
3 European Southern Observatory (ESO)
guest house, Cerro Paranal, Chile, 2001;
architects: Auer + Weber, Munich
4 Office building in Unterföhring, Munich, 2003;
architects: MVRDV, Rotterdam
5 Single-family house in Fläsch, Switzerland, 2001;
architects: Bearth and Deplazes, Chur

Yellow pollen

Monolithic structures may also be differentiated and given an individual character through the use of colour. In the housing group on the Zürichberg by Gigon/Guyer (ill. 1), the architects, working in conjunction with artist Adrian Schiess, applied mineral pigments to the surface of the concrete to create a matt, "pollen-like" texture. Concrete was also selected for the different floor surfaces: in-situ concrete for the living areas, precast sanded slabs in the ancillary spaces and unsanded slabs for the terraces. The principle of individualizing different building elements through colour is very effectively used by Peter Märkli. Although the single-family house in Erlenbach could hardly be referred to as monolithic, the technique of materializing the pink-coloured terrace screens suggests new concepts in the realization of monolithic forms of in-situ concrete construction. With its red-brown coloration, the guest house by Auer and Weber in Chile merges into the desert surroundings to become a monolithic relief in the landscape (ill. 3).

Jointing strategies

Different surface qualities may also be desired internally and externally. Precast concrete construction has two inherently different surfaces – the formwork face and the upper, finished face, which can simply be left as it is or treated as desired. The black memorial structure in Sachsenhausen by Schneider + Schumacher (see page 46) seems dematerialized externally by reflections of the surroundings in the long shiny walls. The rays of light entering through the glazed roof strips, however, highlight the rough-textured natural grey face of the internal skin, thereby augmenting the massive effect of the interior. Another method of circumventing the constraints of joints can be seen in an office building in Munich by MVRDV (ill. 4), where a series of U-shaped precast concrete elements were offset from storey to storey to develop a pattern of projections and recesses, creating the impression of a perforated solid cube.

Calculated illusion

The various forms of surface treatment that are possible with concrete also allow the simulation of naturally monolithic materials. Rem Koolhaas, for example, used the texture of traditional Japanese fortifications as a kind of collage in his housing development in Fukuoka (ill. 2). The multi-storey "Schaulager" from Herzog and de Meuron, also plays with illusion – the homogenous clay-like walls creating a false impression of monolithism.

A new simplicity?

With its 50 cm external walls, the house in Fläsch by Bearth and Deplazes (ill. 5) is truly monolithic. To achieve the necessary thermal insulation, a special type of expanded concrete was developed, foamed to form hollow pores in the material. This allowed not only the additives but also the concrete itself to act as an insulating material. Steel reinforcement was replaced with polypropylene fibres. The use of sawn vertical boarded formwork reduced the incidence of pockets and defects. The outer surface was treated with a water-repellent coating. The building is certainly experimental, but it also marks a step back to the original qualities of simple monolithic forms of construction, which hold a promise for the future.   DETAIL 4/2003

Between Fashionable Packaging and Responsive Skin: Trends in Modern Facade Design

Christian Schittich

Camouflage nets, plastic sheeting, green grass sprouting out of external walls, plastic beads sealed in transparent sheets, panels of stretched metal mesh, self-rusting steel and colourfully printed glass: leafing through international architectural magazines, one gains the impression that no building material, no form of application is too abstruse for facades. Today, buildings and their outer skins are more varied than ever before, exhibiting an often disparate juxtaposition of forms, materials and colours. Next to simple boxes one finds bizarre plastic compositions; multi-layered filigree structures alongside deliberately massive ones; multi-coloration next to monochrome design. With all this complexity and variety, architecture reflects our pluralist society, our fast-moving, media-dominated age. For the first time, there is no formally recognized style, but simply numerous parallel – sometimes just trendy – currents and movements.

Minimalism, Biomorphism or new sensitivity are name tags describing but a small cross section of today's spectrum. The vast majority of building design, of course, lies somewhere between these extremes; but the absence of a dominant style with its own theoretical basis (and without social relevance) can quickly lead to arbitrariness or formalism. Many present-day architectural stars, indeed, have a formal orientation and have tuned their own style into something like a trademark. In this respect, the facade, more than any other constructional element, often acts as the credentials of a building and its designer, conveying a certain image and serving as a vehicle for self-portrayal. This is the outcome of a development in which a central dictum of the Modern Movement has lost its validity: namely, that the external skin should express the internal life of a building; that form and function, interior and exterior should be in harmony with each other. On the one hand, the functions of buildings are less and less specific; on the other hand, the separation of the building skin from the structure has allowed the outer enclosure to become an independent curtain-like element – a real skin, in fact. Not surprisingly, therefore, attention has increasingly been focused on the surface, and one expression of this can be found in a new delight in ornamentation and decoration.

The desire for ornament and colour
The increased obsession with surfaces, together with technological innovation and the desire for ever new fashions, leads to a previously unattainable exploitation of ornament and decor. In an age when the senses are permanently bombarded with stimuli, architects are constantly constrained to create something new and spectacular in order to attract attention. Like nothing before it, the computer is changing not only the scope for design, but also our aesthetic sensibility and receptiveness. Colourful images can be sent around the world in seconds, infinitely copied and manipulated. This has inevitably had an influence on architecture. In addition, there is a host of new manufacturing processes and finishing techniques, especially in the production of glass and plastics, where new scope for coating and coloration exists. Colour now plays a more essential role. It is no longer used merely to accent forms, as in a solid coloured wall, for example. Today, it is likely to be implemented for its own intrinsic decorative value – to produce patterns.
Colour is one of the central stylistic features of the work of the architects Matthias Sauerbruch and Louisa Hutton in Berlin. In their

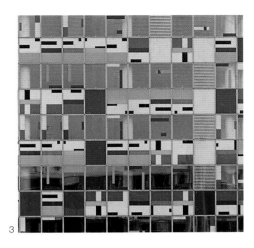

3

newly completed research building for the Boehringer Ingelheim concern in Biberach, Swabia (ills. 1, 2), they use glass printed in various forms to create a somewhat confusing pattern: an abstract, extremely magnified depiction of a molecular structure from the laboratory of this biochemistry company. The image covers the entire, evenly gridded external skin, resulting in a loss of all tectonic points of reference.

Apart from the decorative elements of the facade, the external panels of the double layered skin also provide protection against glare and solar gains. When lighting and insolation conditions permit, bands of vertically pivoting louvres can be opened to allow direct views out of the building. From the inside, seen against the light, the glass, although 70 per cent solid printed, is remarkably transparent. The surroundings are seen as if through an artificial, pastel-coloured veil. Viewed from the outside, however, the disconcerting pattern seems obtrusive.

The laboratory building in Biberach is a prime example of a box with more or less random decoration. Intentionally or not, it may also be seen as representative of our modern media world; for, in an opened position and in the appropriate light, the coloured glass louvres are remarkably photogenic. Whether or not the sensuous quality suggested by published photos can be experienced in reality is diffi-

cult to determine, as the building is located on an inaccessible, high-security company site. Will Alsop's equally colourful Colorium (ill. 3), prominently situated among an array of works by big international architectural offices in the new media harbour development in Düsseldorf, also cries out for attention. Alsop, too, covers his facades with a large-scale coloured pattern. Here, however, the individual panes of glass are not homogeneously coated as in the example by Sauerbruch and Hutton; they are printed with graphic images vaguely reminiscent of works by Mondrian. Seventeen different motifs are combined in various ways to create a pattern that is distinct from the structural order. In other words, the pattern is pure decoration, rather like fashionable wallpaper. Unfortunately the expensive glass panes cannot be changed as easily as wallpaper when fashions or trends change.

Layered construction – playing with transparency

A more subtle form of decoration is used by the Austrian architects Lichtblau and Wagner in their parish centre in Podersdorf on Neusiedler See (ill. 7). A glass wall with a spatially defining and integrating function is set in front of the group of buildings. It is printed with texts written by the children of the parish and with quotations from the Bible. In this way, the architects not only achieve interesting lighting effects on the buildings; they have also created a kind of media facade that conveys a message. Printing glass with words or pictures – with what are, in the first instance, aesthetic effects – remains the most common form of creating a media facade. Active building skins with moving images and changing messages are still restricted to advertising screens in big city centres.

Where the printed glass wall by Lichtblau and Wagner stands in front of other buildings, it forms part of a multilayered construction, resulting in various degrees of transparency and a fascinating interplay of light and shade. Playing with transparency is a major aspect of glass facades. By printing, etching or coating the surface, and by overlaying it with louvres,

4

5

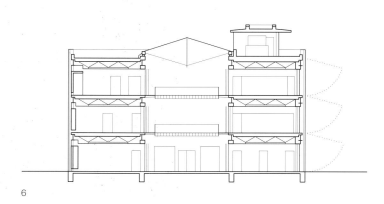

6

perforated sheet metal or metal mesh, a broad range of effects can be achieved between transparency and translucence. Despite the many fine examples that exist, such as Toyo Ito´s Mediatheque in Sensai, Peter Zumthor´s Bregenz Art Museum and Rafael Moneo´s Assembly Room in San Sebastian, one is ultimately forced to conclude that the usual impression communicated by glass facades is one of sterility. Possibly the coldness of translucent glazed facades will one day be seen as representative of our times, just as washed-concrete facades are typical of the 1960s. Although in everyday use, glass facades present a rather drab picture, there are examples where completely smooth glazed skins, reduced to a formal minimum, possess great aesthetic quality. Like many minimalist structures, they not only provide a response to the overstimulation of the senses. They are also a token of progress in glass technology; for today, most major functions of the facade, including solar screening, can be performed by the glazing itself.

The display of materials
Facade materials are no longer chosen simply for their appropriateness to a particular form of construction. In many cases, the material is the message, one might say. Today, ever greater importance is attached to the appearance of a particular material, its visual, substantial qualities, its colour effects and texture. The character of traditional materials such as stone, brick and clay is being rediscovered and put on show. Untreated timber that weathers to a grey colour – formerly confined to rural buildings – is now being used in the facades of prestigious inner-city developments. Exposed concrete surfaces no longer have to be as smooth as possible, in accordance with the standard set by Tadao Ando. Through the use of sawn formwork or subsequent fluting or bush-hammering, they can be lent a rough yet striking charm. The sculptural properties of the material are being accentuated again. Other effects can be achieved through the use of colour pigments and minerals. The

clay-like outer walls of the "Schaulager", an exhibition and storage structure in Basle by Herzog and de Meuron (ill. 5), can also be placed in this category.
In addition to traditional materials with their sensuous qualities, industrial products like plywood and fibre-cement sheeting, plastics and metals are finding widespread use in the facades of buildings, often presented in the manner of a set piece. The many innovations that can be observed are an expression of a strong urge to experiment. Every technical novelty is eagerly adopted and applied in building. Stainless-steel mesh is a prime example of this. As an industrial material for making sieves and filters, it was long neglected in the field of construction – until Dominique Perrault used it in the mid-1990s in the French National Library in Paris and for the velodrome in Berlin. Since then, it has enjoyed great popularity and can be found in the facades of many different types of building.

One could also see the Laban Centre by Herzog and de Meuron (ill. 8) as a successful staging of materials. In many of their earlier works, the Basle architects showed a profound understanding of the nature of artificial materials. Although adhering to this tradition, their new project occupies a special place in their oeuvre. Herzog and de Meuron are pioneers in the field of surface decoration and ornamentation. Viewed from the outside, however, what is striking about the Laban Centre is the use of materials in a pure form without further embellishment. Simple sheets of plastic are so ingeniously presented that the outcome is a noble, shimmering object. It adopts the volumetric forms and the scale of the surroundings, yet its outlines merge with the sky, resulting in an almost unrealistic, intangible appearance. The use of colour is particularly subtle, only the rear faces of individual triple-layer cellular slabs are colour coated, which accentuates the shimmering, pastel-like effect, evoking a range of subtle, iridescent

7

9

10

colour moods. The interaction with the second facade layer, consisting of translucent glass, produces an agreeable, airy atmosphere that is ideally suited to the needs of dance and the training spaces. In this respect, the Laban Centre differs from the above-mentioned Colorium in Düsseldorf, where the interior lighting suffers from the fashionable facade decoration.

Changeable facades
Changeable facades are nothing new. Traditional window shutters fall into this category as do modern fabric sunblinds. Elements of this kind not only have a functional purpose; they have always formed part of the visual design as well. Today, great importance is attached to the aesthetic effect of facades that are capable of change. Never before has the contrast between facades in an opened and closed state – achieved with folding, pivoting or sliding elements – played such a dramatic role in design. In this respect, one might cite the student hostel in Coimbra, Portugal, by Manuel and Francisco Rocha de Aires Mateus (see Detail 7/03), where a completely smooth, homogeneous wood-panelled surface can be transformed into an exciting, animated external wall simply by opening various elements. The same could be said of the bare, cubic metal box by Foreign Office Architects in Groningen (ill. 10), which can be turned into an articulated steel-and-glass structure – all the more striking when seen in conjunction with the minimalist architecture. In their housing development in Dornbirn (ill. 9), Baumschlager and Eberle also play with the visual changeability of the facade. Here, it is in the form of large obscured-glass elements that provide visual and solar screening for the dwellings within.
In terms of their appearance, the facades described here cover a broad spectrum, and the constant changes to which they are subject reflect the living patterns of the occupants. Other architects design entire sections of the facade as openable elements that can be swung upwards or aside. Examples of this can be found in Sean Godsell's weekend house in Australia (p. 98) and Shigeru Ban's

paper museum (ill. 6) with their upward pivoting, storey-height facade elements. One might see this as an extreme form of the large-scale horizontal louvres that are so popular at present and that not only provide sunshading, but, in a horizontal position, ensure a state of transparency and ideal, unobstructed lines of vision.

Whether plastic, glass or wood, whether changeable or minimal, brightly coloured or monochrome, the facade has acquired a versatility and potential that it scarcely possessed before. One observes a tremendous eagerness to experiment, to extend the boundaries of what is possible. Conventional visual habits are being questioned. New materials and concepts are being tried. Sometimes, however, there is a narrow dividing line between sensible innovation and a banal striving for effect. Furthermore, with increasing concentration on the surface, there is a danger of superficiality. When building skins

are conceived for their own sakes, basic architectural qualities are lost. Architects must take care that they do not surrender even more of the influence they have on the construction process; for there comes the point where they will be reduced to mere packaging artists.   DETAIL 7/8 2003

1,2 Pharmaceutical Research Centre in Biberach
      architects: Sauerbruch Hutton
3   Colorium in Düsseldorf
      architects: Alsop Architects
4   Innsbruck City Hall: sunshading elements
      architects: Dominique Perrault, Paris in collaboration with Reichert, Pranschke, Maluche Architects
5   "Schaulager" in Basle
      architects: Herzog & de Meuron
6   Paper Museum in Shizuoka
      architects: Shigeru Ban Architects
7   Parish Centre in Podersdorf
      architects: Lichtblau Wagner
8   Laban Centre in Deptford
      architects: Herzog & de Meuron
9   Housing Development in Dornbirn
      architects: B&E Baumschlager-Eberle
10   Hotel in Groningen
      architects: Foreign Office Architects

8

Industrial Building

Klaus-Dieter Weiß

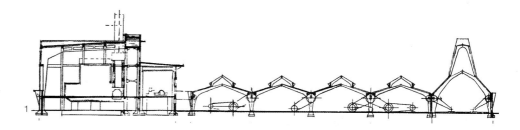

In the 19th century, the image of industrial building was dominated by huge factory structures in which the process of mass production was combined with a concentration of mechanical power. Today, our economic system is changing dramatically, with many of the actual production processes now taking place in Asia. Innovative concerns expect architects to provide holistic strategies rather than design details, and organizational structures based on communication and cultural needs rather than constructional refinements. More and more virtual concerns like Nike are dispensing with the actual production process to concentrate on product planning and marketing. The classical unity of time and place in which industrial activities were carried out in the past, and the kind of construction in which form reflected function are disappearing; but the transition to structures dominated by communications and intelligence is not reflected in the architecture. Quite the opposite, in fact, was previously seen in the East German "gold rush" and now in the economic opening of the developing industrial giant China to the West – where German architectural efforts are disturbing, rather than a recognition process being apparent. Where in the Shanghai office of Albert Speer, the "only German urban planner and architect successfully building in the entire world" (Frankfurter Allgemeine Zeitung), decisions are made by the most efficient rather then the most thoughtful architects as to the fate of an internationally sized industrial city of gabled cottages.

Where a central railway station of the 21st century is modelled after an ancient chinese palace. One may ask – shouldn't the architectural contribution of the nation where the modern movement has its roots, and industrial building a fine heritage, be more thoughtfully and intelligently considered, and more responsibly implemented?

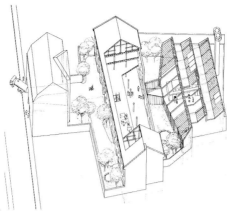

3

4

1   Hat factory, Luckenwalde
    architect: Erich Mendelsohn, 1922
2   Glazed factory, Dresden
    architect: Gunter Henn, 2000–2002
3   Zollverein Colliery, Essen
    architect: Fritz Schupp, 1928
4   Rischart´s Bakery, Munich
    architects: Kiessler + Partner, 1983
5   A. Borsig locomotive assembly hall, Berlin Tegel
    architect: C. Metzmacher, 1841
6   Fiat factory, Turin
    architect: Giacomo Matté-Trucco, 1915–21

The working city

When the German Architecture Museum in Frankfurt produced an exhibition of 20th century architecture with reference to the German Architectural Review, the section entitled "Industrial Building" was more harmlessly renamed "increased productivity", the architects represented, being Peter Behrens, Hugo Häring, Fritz Schupp und Martin Kremmer, Rudolf Lodders, Egon Eiermann, James Stirling and Thomas Herzog – with only a sub-note on Walter Gropius and Adolf Meyer, Philipp Jacob Manz, Peter C. von Seidlein and the architects of the Vitra Works in Weil – gained their credentials through the historical and also through the architectural chronology of events.

It is not easy to formulate a precise and acceptable definition of industrial building. One set of guidelines for industrial construction lists "buildings or parts of buildings that serve the production, processing or storage of products and goods". Under the same heading, the Brockhaus encyclopedia (1989) includes buildings for industrial production and research, together with ancillary administration and social structures, with the Fiat Works in Turin (ill. 6) and Stirling's Olivetti Training Centre in Haslemere serving as illustrations. By this definition even Tadao Ando's Conference Pavillion in the Vitra plant conforms to the idea of an industrial building, as a place of productive energy and innovation.

Detypologizing

For a long time, one of the most questionable goals of planning has been to detypologize industrial building by neutralizing the layout and thus the form of structures. In the long term this implies the elimination of the historical dimension of architecture, the loss of future building monuments and the dissolution of the close links that exist between building types and the urban fabric. Even the distinctions between industry, commerce and handwork trades blend. The Brockhaus definition of industry includes assembly and repair work. The Bu-

reau of Statistics in Germany, however, uses the term "productive commerce" rather than industry, thereby including productive trades. The final point of assistance from the Bureau of Statistics is the size of the company – the minimum number of employees being twenty – creating a separation between industry and commerce based purely on size. In his "History of Building Types", Nikolaus Pevsner confines his treatment of industrial structures largely to factories of a certain size in which products are manufactured in great numbers, as well as to warehouses, market halls and exhibition structures. Applying this simple definition, one could include Rischart's Bakery in Munich (1982) by Uwe Kiessler – at the time, a much admired example of an industrial building in an inner-city location (ill. 4). For Gunter Henn, the architect of the glazed manufacturing works in Dresden (ill. 2), design potential lies not only in the solution, but in the brief. By making the flow of communications legible (netgraphing) as well as the goals and concepts (programming), the design work is translated to a meta-plane of great complexity.

Complex aesthetic

Pevsner soon stretches his own definition, however, to include the steam-turbine house erected for the fountains of Sanssouci. Built in 1842 by Ludwig Persius, a pupil of Schinkel, the building is in the form of a mosque in Moorish style. Erich Mendelsohn's Einstein Tower is a similar case. Adolf Behne cited this structure in his analysis of the Modern Movement, in "Der moderne Zweckbau", which appeared in 1926, as a workshop structure with the qualities of a historical monument. It is really nothing more than an expressionistic or "neotechnical" (Paul Virilio) tower telescope with underground laboratories. The representational image of atomic physics reduced to merely an industrial building? Is it even practical to use titles to define and describe industrial buildings when industry itself is changing to such a degree? Is it not too shallow to consider industrial buildings

from purely aesthetic points of view? In the catalogue to the exhibition "The Useful Arts" staged in Berlin in 1981, Roland Günter argued that "architecture and art studies have to learn to understand the processes of this world in all their complexity instead of reducing them to a string of beads"; i.e. the presentation of facades like a sequence of pictures. This would allow factory architecture to reflect economic history instead of being classified according to stylistic expressions that are devoid of content. This philosophy has not yet succeeded, otherwise our conceptual definitions would have developed further. It appears as if the architect is totally over-

5

6

7   Schlumberger research building, Cambridge,
    architects: Michael Hopkins and Partners, 1984
8   Renault works, Swindon,
    architects: Foster Associates, 1983
9   Inmos microprocessor factory, Newport,
    South Wales,
    architects: Richard Rogers Partnership, 1982

whelmed by this challenge. Architecture, a profession that seemed predestined to participate in the design of future developments, leaves roughly 40 per cent of all built areas to trend researchers, brand designers and other self-appointed "experts". Among the few exceptions to this in Germany are the Cologne architects Gatermann + Schossig, who are known for their long-term planning strategies with an urban orientation (e.g. the Micropolis commercial park in Dresden, 1999 – ills. 11, 12); and the Hamburg architect Carsten Roth. Through a subtle process of complementing and extrapolating existing structures, Roth has helped to introduce the element of architectural and urban spatial complexity that is lacking in most industrial and commercial developments. An example of this is his Synopharm Laboratory in Barsbüttel, Hamburg (1998).

With an eye on the profits
The problems outlined here are compounded by a paucity of more scholarly literature on the subject of industrial building. The "Industriebau" catalogue edited by Kurt Ackermann for an exhibition in 1984 (republished in a fourth edition in 1994) is still an indispensable standard work today, although its perspective inevitably lies quite a long way in the past. With all due respect to the standpoint adopted in this work, it documents the stagnation of a profession "whose social and ecological responsibility seems out of all proportion to the ignorance it reveals in the face of social and ecological challenges", as the "Frankfurter Rundschau" wrote on the 100th anniversary of the founding of the professional institution for architects. The scientific analysis of complex planning work that Christopher Alexander presented 40 years ago with the title "Notes on the Synthesis of Form" is now in its 17th edition, but it does not seem to have had much effect on industrial building in practice. Uli Zech, who was head of the civic planning department of Munich, once heroically urged that building permis-

sion should be denied to investors who submitted schemes that were as "ugly as sin". His call, supported as early as thirty years ago by Rolf Keller in "Agglomerations- und Wegwerflandschaften", has been largely ignored, however, by industry. On the contrary, by pandering to commercial interests with an eye to trade-tax revenue, local authorities have completely degraded large areas of our cities, as Meinhard von Gerkan remarked in 1995. "Sometimes, one has the impression that we live in a purely residential, not a working, society," Kurt Ackermann wrote, arguing that the factory is also part of the habitable environment – and not just in the form of

abandoned structures that can be converted into youth centres and homes for the arts, or requisitioned for residential communities. Public attention should also be called to the location of the workplace rather than continually only to its form. Was it inappropriate, then, for the Federation of German Architects (BDA) to mark its 100th anniversary with a display of historical projects, beginning with the AEG Turbine Hall and ending with the almost 100-year-old grain store in Würzburg, which the architects Brückner & Brückner had sensitively converted into an aesthetically pleasing museum? In 1996, Helmut C. Schulitz warned that architects were enamoured of

9

form and were neglecting the technical aspects of building, especially new concepts related to content and space. As a result, architects were losing ground in the race with industry, which was demoting them to the role of packaging decorators. Even in the automobile industry, where one expects innovation and exploration, high quality and technically exciting designs are indeed to be found, but without formal relevance – in sharp contrast to Gunter Henn's, unfortunately shelved, Auto-Uni Wolfsburg. As Kenneth Frampton once said, architecture is neither technology nor art.

Architecture without an audience
Most industrial building takes place without any relation to the surrounding city and the population at large. A factory can be more than just a provider of workplaces for production, though. It can also make a contribution to the cityscape and the urban image. It can help to create urban spaces. It can reduce the noise from a traffic artery far more effectively than acoustic screening walls. With the proper layout and landscaping, it can have a positive effect on urban climate. Solar energy can be generated and stored on its large roof areas, or additional parking spaces can be made available at weekends for leisure activities. Sensitive industrial building offers, in fact, a last chance for the repair and further development of the city fabric. The present "grey zones" of handyman centres, enormous car yards and giant furniture showrooms, together with storage facilities and light industrial plants, demonstrate the failure of our built environment to integrate wholly into homogenous built cities as demanded in the past by Alexander Mitscherlich, Christopher Alexander[9], Frederic Vestner[10] and Walter Henn[11]. "For generations, in the face of urban concentration, environmental damage, traffic chaos and mass consumption, a solution was seen in the separation of functions," the Berlin Senate noted in a presentation for the International Building Exhibition in 1978. As a result, the concepts of connec-

tivity and plurality have been lost, even though they offer the chance of mutual enrichment between habitation and workplace. In 1965, Alexander Mitscherlich was the first to speak out against this ideology, which was proclaimed in the Charter of Athens in 1943. "When production, administration, leisure and dwelling realms are strictly separated, what holds urban life together?" he asked. Partial needs may be satisfied, but at the expense of the whole.

Logic of chaos
By linking industrial buildings with other areas of urban life, more problems could be solved than would be caused by mutual disturbance. With the development of cleaner, more compact technology, industry has created the conditions in which a rethinking process is necessary. Even cities with a great architectural awareness, like Hamburg, have an antiquated approach in this respect, as is shown by the recently extended building of the lamp designer Tobias Grau (ill. 10). In spite of efforts by the company over many years to secure a city location, the architects Bothe Richter Teherani were finally obliged to conceal their spectacularly frugal spacecraft-like design for the works – the operation of which causes no environmental disturbance – behind an embankment in a commercial zone in Rellingen. The publicity this building has managed to attract has, in fact, been entirely due to self-advertising and the electronic medium of the Internet – a solution of necessity, the interpretation of which negates the very essence of a city. Such acts of exclusion challenge the city as a collective phenomenon in which human history is reflected. Gunter Henn's glazed factory in Dresden set the standard in this regard.

The city of knowledge
The more short term and "unimportant" products really are to our lives, the more effort the manufacturers expend on their publicity and the seduction of clientele. Com-

panies like Volkswagen and Siemens avail themselves of urban metaphors to keep the loyalty of their clientele or as a reference point for innovative processes (e.g. "the revitalization of the polis"). In this way, urban qualities are exploited to create a synthetic surface that rouses emotions and sparks innovation. Helmut Volkmann's miniaturized "city of the future" – Xenia, made by Siemens – is a "studio for innovators" (in reality nothing more than an open plan office) set in Neuperlach, a suburb of Munich, but it would have been better located in real urban surroundings. Rather like the Palais Royale in Paris 200 years ago, the Xenia project was conceived as a means of exploring the pressing problems of our age through an exchange between technology and the arts, between the working city and the city as a place of human intelligence. The regeneration of the civilian community offers the best prerequisites; the argument of the Siemens management in Munich had a chance of success. "Nothing is more effective than human interaction, the visitor and user receives information he wasn't originally searching for, but will have use for anyway." [14]
It's not so very surprising that Siemens prefers to advertise itself using the Berliner Bogen from BRT than its own Xenia product.

Modern industrial culture
A century ago, the composer Maurice Ravel marvelled at the ironworks in Duisburg, speaking of palaces of flowing metal, glowing cathedrals, a wonderful symphony of whistles and terrible hammer-blows. A glimpse behind the scenes of our modern epoch-making "cathedrals of labour" and "corporate identity" is less satisfying than enthusing over the highlights of building history. Nevertheless, it is strange that the term "industrial culture" is used mainly in a historical context, rather than the largely unrecognized term "industrial archeology", and not to describe the future potential of modern architecture; the history of technology, the social history of labour, the architectural history of factories and collieries,

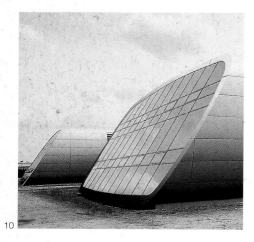

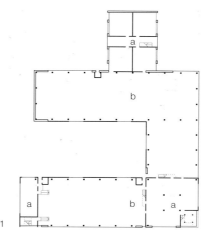

10

11

together with the historical development of industrial zones and towns. The main sites of industrial tourism are memories of the past, to be found in the new "industrial museums" and in the conservation of important industrial buildings from the "good old days". For example, the former textile producing town of Lowell, Massachusetts, with a population of 70,000, has been designated a national park.

Ghost towns
The German equivalent of this would be the UNESCO World Heritage Sites where the industrial culture of the Saarland and the Ruhr area can be seen. Our passion for the past and our pessimistic view of civilization is unbroken. If one is to believe the advocates who reject all things modern and embrace the reconstruction, replication and "retro-aesthetic" of past eras, then Schinkel is the most important German architect of the 19th century, and the rebuilt Berliner Bauakademie the most architecturally influential building of its time. Together with the Zollverein Colliery in Essen (ill. 3), representing the 20th century, we are expected to believe 200 years of industrial architecture to be satisfactorily covered. Admittedly, in contrast to Switzerland, the preservation of historical monuments in Germany is not equated with an absolute ban on further development. But does the immense

volume of disused industrial fabric in urban situations (the listed Siemens works in Berlin alone covers an area of 500,000 sq.m) genuinely serve as a catalyst for a new understanding of a working city? A waterworks with its romantic background may be transformed into a parliamentary assembly, a transformer station into a design museum, a car factory with a test track on the roof may be converted into an art gallery, trade fair centre, hotel, university and shopping palace; but no company aware of its corporate identity is willing to attire itself in second-hand clothing. "History is more or less bunk. It's tradition. We don't want tradition," the car manufacturer Henry Ford said in 1916; built an entire city based on the automobile in the Soviet Union and created a sense of freedom not felt since the French revolution. With his modern concepts of financing, advertising, repair and friendly service, Ford was far ahead of his time, and he demonstrated this architecturally, too – with the aid of his company architect, Albert Kahn (1869–1942). A similar developmental leap would be conceivable for modern industry if it were to abandon its strongholds and integrate itself in a dynamic European city environment stripped of retrospective tendencies and open to experiment. "More quality of life through the revitalization of the polis," as Siemens says. And the architects?   DETAIL 9/2003

Klaus-Dieter Weiß is an author and critic who works with international publishers and architectural journals. His numerous publications on industrial building are an important focus of his work.
www.klausdieterweiss.de

10 Tobias Grau building, Rellingen, architects: Bothe Richter Teherani, 2001
11 Commercial park, Dresden, architects: Gatermann + Schossig, 1999 Floorplan showing functions
    a Leasable office space
    b Leasable production space
12 Commercial park, Dresden, architects: Gatermann + Schossig, 1999

References:
[1] Romana Schneider, Winfried Nerdinger, Wilfried Wang (ed.): Architektur im 20. Jahrhundert. Deutschland, Munich/London/New York, 2000
[2] Nikolaus Pevsner: Funktion und Form. Die Geschichte der Bauwerke des Westens (1976), Hamburg 1998, p. 273
[3] Roland Günter: Fabrik-Architektur, in: Tilmann Buddensieg, Henning Rogge (ed.): Die Nützlichen Künste, Berlin, 1981, p. 175
[4] Klaus-Dieter Weiß (ed.): Gatermann + Schossig. Bauten für Industrie und Technik (architypus 1), Braunschweig/Wiesbaden, 1996
[5] Frankfurter Rundschau 20.06.03, p. 10
[6] Rolf Keller: Bauen als Umweltzerstörung (1973), Zürich, 1977
[7] Kurt Ackermann: Industriebau, Stuttgart, 1984, p. 41
[8] Helmut C. Schulitz: Die unvollendete Moderne, in: Schulitz + Partner. Bauten und Projekte, Berlin, 1996, p. 21
[9] Christopher Alexander: Notes on the Synthesis of Form, Cambridge, USA, 1964, cf.: A City is not a Tree (1965)/Eine Stadt ist kein Baum, Bauen + Wohnen, 7/1967
[10] Frederic Vester: Ballungsgebiete in der Krise (1976), Munich, 1983
[11] Walter Henn: Optischer Umweltschutz – Verpflichtung des Architekten, db deutsche bauzeitung, 4/1979
[12] Alexander Mitscherlich: Die Unwirtlichkeit unserer Städte (1965), Frankfurt, 1970, p. 116
[13] Klaus-Dieter Weiß: Industrie, Architektur und Stadt. Plädoyer für eine stadtbezogene Industriearchitektur, in: architypus 1, note 4
[14] Helmut Volkmann: Wandel der Innovationskultur mit der »Stadt des Wissens als Stätte der Begegnung«, Henn Akademie, 1/1998, p. 60/61 (cf. Gabler-Magazin No. 3/1995, p. 25–29)
[15] Susanne Hauser: Ephemeres und Monumentales. Versuch über Materialität und Architektur im 20. Jahrhundert, in: Wolkenkuckucksheim, September 2001
[16] cf. Friedrich Achleitner: Dieses Haus stammt aus dem 8. Jahrhundert, erbaut 1898, in: Konrad Paul Liessmann (ed.): Die Furie des Verschwindens, Vienna, 2000

12

documentation

Media Library in Vénissieux

Dominique Perrault, Paris

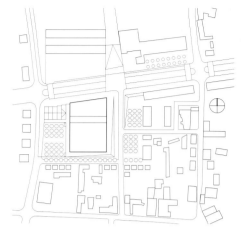

Situated on the southern outskirts of Lyons, Vénissieux is one of the suburbs of the city that was subject to social unrest in the 1990s. The present media library, erected opposite the 1970s' town hall, was conceived as a new centre with an integrative function for the local population and visitors from neighbouring communities. The various sections of the library are laid out at ground level over a roughly 3,200 m² area. Resembling a large market hall, the space is divided into different thematic zones solely by furnishings, bookshelves, and wood and glass partitions. The administration, stores and special spaces are housed in a three-storey tract above the east-west circulation strip. The load-bearing struc-ture of this large hall consists of a simple steel space frame with a ribbed sheet-metal roof. The roof is supported by 16 exposed concrete shear walls, which are integrated into the overall layout. Extending round the building between the inner functional area and the facade is a three-metre-wide periph-eral circulation space that affords access to the various departments from all sides, there-by obviating the need for additional routes that would disrupt the internal activities.

The facade forms one of the special attrac-tions of the design. By day, the building has the appearance of a completely opaque, gleaming aluminium box externally, while from the inside – depending on one's position – there is an almost clear view out. At night, when the media library is illuminated internally, the effect is reversed. This play of light was made possible by a double skin of glazing, with perforated, horizontal, U-shaped aluminium sheeting elements in-serted in the intermediate space to provide sunshading and visual screening. As a result of the perforations (35 per cent of the area), the sheeting is permeable to light. Slightly angled and offset in depth, the elements es-tablish a mystical interplay with the transpar-ent facade. The intermediate space between the layers of glazing also allows the circu-lation of air and thus serves the air condition-ing of the hall.   DETAIL 1/2 2003

Site plan
scale 1:5000
Section
Ground floor plan
scale 1:500

1 Entrance
2 Entrance hall
3 Adult library and reading room
4 Children's library
5 Auditorium

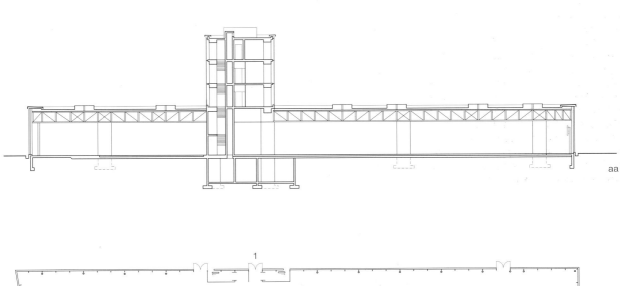

aa

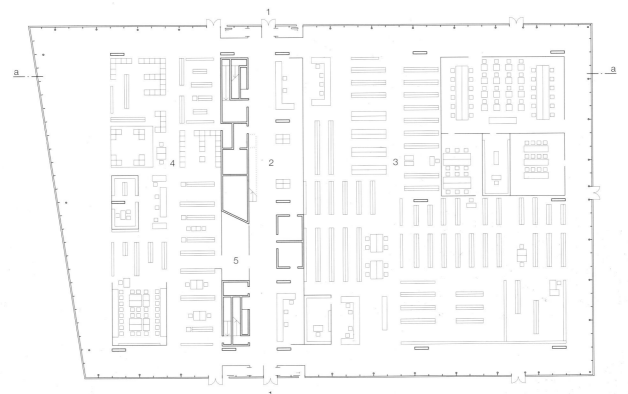

Vertical section
Horizontal section at corner
scale 1:5

1	0.75 mm galvanized 镀锌 sheet-steel covering
2	90/5 mm steel connecting plate
3	100/50/3 mm steel RHS
4	steel I-section 100 mm deep
5	11 mm lam. safety glass

6	8 mm toughened glass
7	perforated, castellated sheet aluminium
8	50/50 mm alum. SHS rail with Ø 8 mm locking bolt
9	115/50 mm aluminium RHS post
10	metal grating

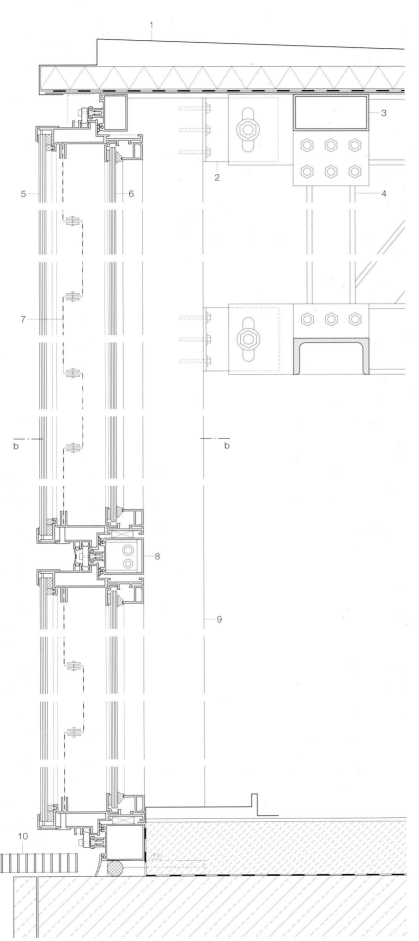

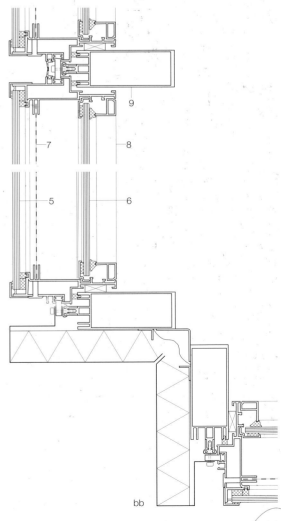

bb

Museum in Kalkriese

Annette Gigon, Mike Guyer, Zurich

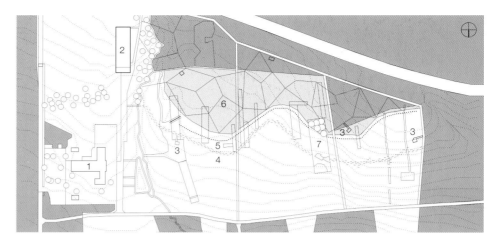

In 1987, a British amateur archaeologist found evidence that helped to locate the scene of the legendary Battle of the Teutoburg Forest, which was fought over an area of nearly 30 km². Here in AD 9, Hermann (Arminius), the leader of the Cherusci, inflicted a crushing defeat on the Roman legions of Publius Quincitilius Varus. Although no remains of buildings were found, numerous objects and a revetment were excavated. An exhibition park, with three pavilions and a museum structure, has now been created on the site. The route taken by the Romans along the revetment is marked by large iron plates, while the winding paths of the Germans through the forest are indicated by small pieces of wood. The line of the former German revetment is articulated with iron stakes. Only a small section of the terrain at a lower level has been reconstructed. The area is retained by sheet-steel piling that forms a striking enclosure. The three small pavilions, in contrast, leave more to the imagination of visitors and were designed to heighten the sense of perception. Together with the designers Ruedi Baur and Lars Müller, the architects conceived the pavilions on a thematic basis related to vision, hearing and questioning. The pavilion for questioning forms a bridge to the present, with slits on one side that afford a view of the battlefield, while on the other side, video films provide information on modern warfare. Rising above everything is an almost 40-metre-high museum tower that commands a view over the entire battlefield. At its base, the tower is intersected by a flat cubic structure containing the exhibition spaces. The pavilions and the museum are clad in sheet steel. All the new elements, therefore, form a homogeneous whole. Steel is, indeed, the dominant material of the scheme, used not only for the exposed skeleton-frame structure of the tower, but for the wall and soffit cladding and the stakes, ground plates and piling that form the field markings. Externally, the sheeting has a rough rusted texture. Internally, the wall and ceiling panels have a finer, non-rusted finish.   DETAIL 1/2 2003

Site plan
scale 1:5000
Sections · Floor plans
scale 1:750

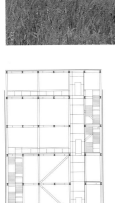

aa

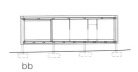

bb

cc

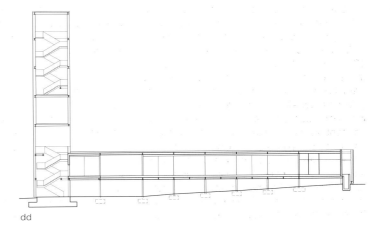

dd

Levels 2–6

19

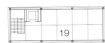
17

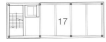
18

18   17

Level 1

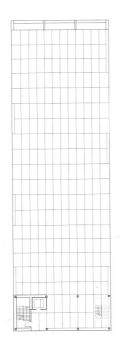

Level 0

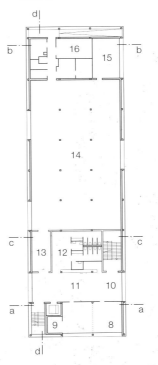

16   15

14

13 12

11   10

9   8

Level -1

1   Visitors' centre
2   Museum
3   Pavilions
4   Route of Romans
5   Earth revetment
6   Paths of Germans
7   Reconstruction
    of historic site
8   Lecture room
9   Store
10 Entrance area
11 Shop
12 Cloakroom
13 Lobby
14 Exhibition area
15 Teaching space
16 Ancillary space
17 Void
18 Platform
19 Terrace

33

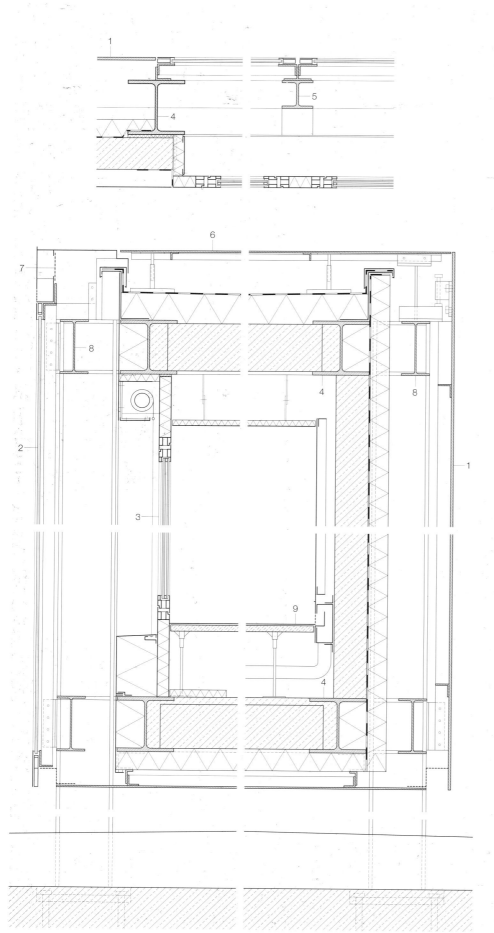

Horizontal section
Vertical section
scale 1:20

1   15 mm oxidized-steel facade
    sheets 3100/5900 mm with blasted
    surface, chamfered horizontal
    edges and 20 mm joints
    100 mm mineral-fibre thermal
    insulation
    vapour-retarding layer
    175 mm precast aerated
    concrete unit
    3 mm steel sheets 120/400 mm,
    hot rolled or pickled, with
    transparent varnish finish,
    4 mm joints and 100 mm rear cavity
2   15 mm toughened glass in steel
    frame: 90/60/8 mm angles and
    90/5 mm flats
3   double glazing: 10 mm lam. safety
    glass (2× 5 mm) + 8 mm float glass
    65 mm steel frame, welded to
    foam-filled sheet-steel extension
    frame
4   steel I-beam 300 mm deep
5   steel I-beam 160 mm deep,
    double coated at works, with
    in-situ finishing coat
6   6 mm oxidized-steel sheet
    3100/1500 mm with blasted surface
    laid to falls on 40/40 mm steel
    angles
    three-layer bituminous seal
    with root-proof layer
    165 mm (av.) foamed-glass
    insulation
    220 mm precast aerated
    concrete unit
    30 mm fibreboard insulation
    2 mm perforated sheet-steel
    panels 1200/600 mm
7   perforated sheet-metal ventilation
    outlet
8   steel I-beam 300 mm deep
9   3 mm stainless-steel sheets
    1200/600 mm with 3 mm adhesive-
    fixed protective matting
    33 mm lightweight concrete
    bearing slab
    40 mm concrete topping
    200 mm precast aerated
    concrete unit
    120 mm mineral-fibre insulation

1 10 mm sheet-steel roof element
   double-coated at works,
   with in-situ finishing coat
2 steel I-beam 300 mm deep
3 15 mm oxidized-steel facade sheeting,
   with blasted surface
4 horizontal fixings:
   6 steel angles per sheet
5 vertical fixings with set bolts: 2× per sheet
6 10 mm sheet-steel landing element double-

coated at works, with in-situ finishing coat;
quartz sand non-slip coating in areas
for foot traffic; surface coating in same
colour as load-bearing structure
7 100/100/12 mm steel angle raising pieces
   to landing
8 Ø 37 mm tubular steel handrail
9 10 mm sheet-steel stairs with welded strings and
   ribs, quartz-sand non-slip coating; surface coating
   in same colour as load-bearing structure

Staircase tower: levels 3–6
Vertical sections • Horizontal section
scale 1:100
Vertical sections • Horizontal section
scale 1:20

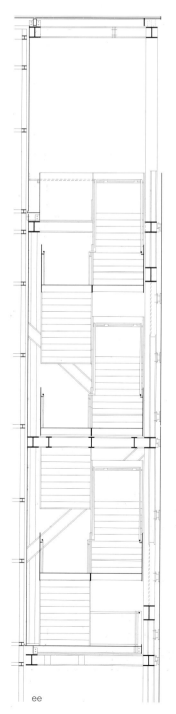

ee

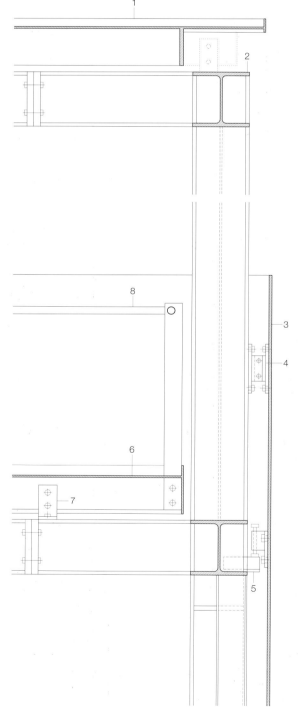

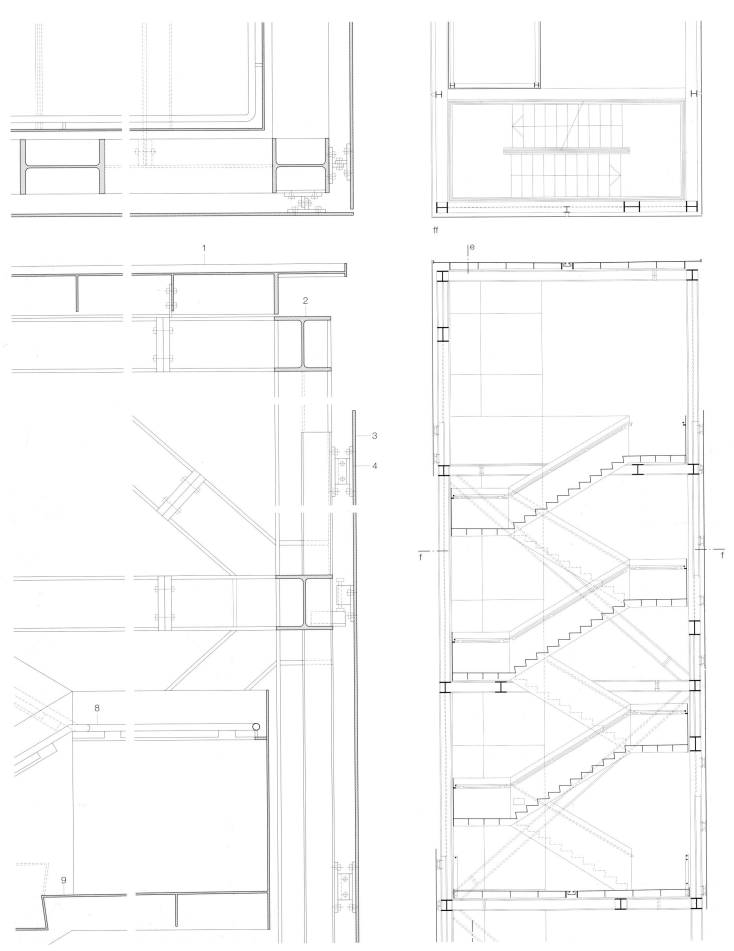

Secondary School in Vienna

Henke and Schreieck Architects, Vienna

The school building is situated in suburban surroundings on the outskirts of Vienna and introduces a new urban dimension to the small-scale structure of the area. The complex comprises a series of single- and two-storey tracts laid out around a large courtyard. Here, the atrium type assumes a special form. Large areas of glazing lend the building a quality of transparency on all sides. Approaching the school from the road to the north, one is confronted by a single-storey structure raised on slender steel columns. Access to the slightly elevated courtyard is via a gently rising flight of steps flanked by a low concrete wall and a ramp that divide off the teachers' entrance. Within the courtyard, the various tracts have different facades. On the two long faces, there are wood-strip canopies cantilevered out at different heights. The southern end of the atrium is marked by a thin, dematerialized glass skin, behind which is the assembly hall. The view extends through this entire space to the sunken sports hall beyond. One scarcely notices that the western tract of the building contains three storeys. Here, the ground level has been lowered externally to allow the special classrooms on the lower floor to receive natural lighting. The various groups of rooms are clearly articulated in the layout, with classrooms set out on the north, east and west faces. The wide corridors, which afford views to the courtyard, can also be used as recreational spaces. The only central corridor in the raised tract receives daylight from above. At the southern end, there is a glazed library with access to a roof terrace over the sports hall. The many staircases linking the different levels of the school provide alternative routes through the building. The lightweight partitions along the corridors are separated from the soffits by clerestory strips. In the well-lighted rooms, the various materials enter into an engaging dialogue. For the most part, they are used in a carefully worked natural state. Over the main staircase in the assembly hall is a large roof light with sunshading fins, the form of which is continued by the wood strips of the canopy roof.   DETAIL Konzept 3/2003

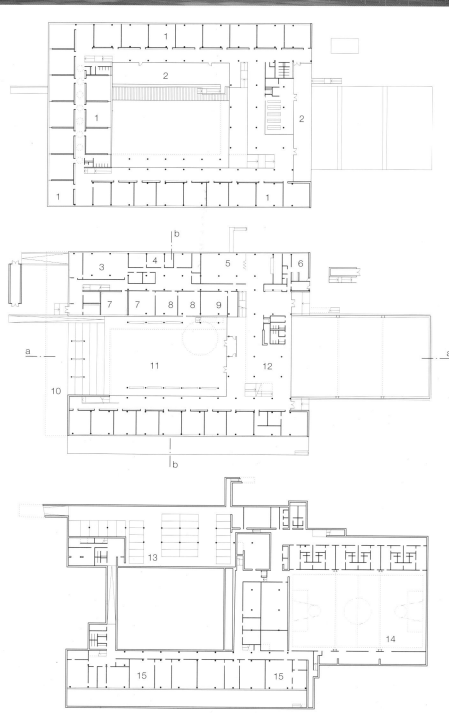

Floor plans · Sections   scale 1:1250

1 Classroom
2 Terrace
3 Teachers' room
4 Administration
5 Multi-purpose space
6 Caretaker's flat
7 Computer room
8 Recreation area
9 Music room
10 Forecourt
11 Playground
12 Assembly hall
13 Garage
14 Sports hall
15 Special teaching spaces

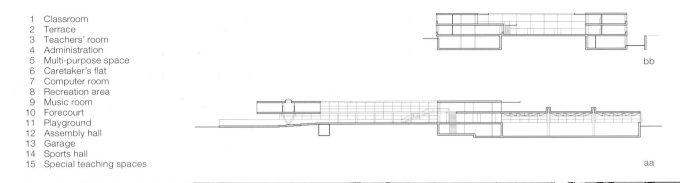

bb

aa

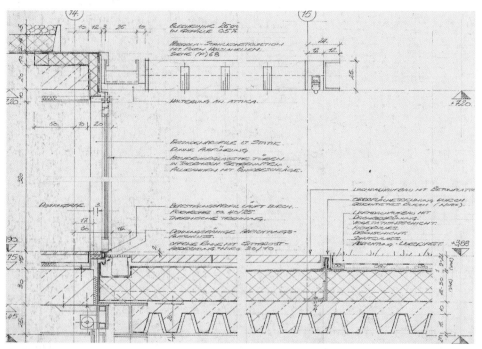

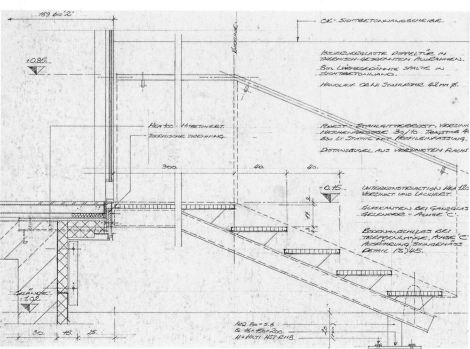

Construction planning

Drawing by hand still plays a central role in the work of Henke and Schreieck. Without computers, the office would not be at a loss for a means of expression. As part of the construction planning for the secondary school in Heustadelgasse, Vienna, drawings were prepared to a scale of 1:100, using CAD, but the details – to scales of 1:20, 1:10 and 1:5 – were drawn by hand in pencil.

At the beginning of the construction planning stage, the main points to be detailed were precisely drawn in pencil and submitted for approval to the planning team, which consisted of architects, structural engineers and specialists for mechanical services and building physics. Isometric pencil drawings were made to clarify abutments and junctions; and spatial situations were investigated in part by means of hand-drawn studies, including perspectives. Important points were investigated by developing alternatives. For example, in determining the sunshading system for the facade, the architects explored solutions using external blinds, as well as printed panes of glass that could be raised and lowered by means of chains within the frame sections. A mock-up facade was built, and the client expressed approval of the proposed solution. Unfortunately, although the specified thickness of the glass was adequate technically, the bending deflection exceeded the limits allowed by building regulations. Since thicker glass would have been considerably heavier and more expensive, the architects finally opted for a design solution with external blinds.

Office supervision of the school building was the responsibility of a project architect and an assistant architect. Henke and Schreieck themselves, however, continued to develop and articulate the project with their own drawings, and the two partners were involved in the scheme at all times. Certain architectural services, such as the preparation of bills of quantities and other tender documents, are farmed out, so that the office is not encumbered with extraneous work.

Sectional details   scale 1:20

1   50 mm layer of gravel
    filter mat
    rigid-foam thermal insulation
    elastomer-bitumen roof sealing layers
    450–330 mm reinforced concrete roof slab
    32 mm mineral-wool insulation
    18 mm perforated veneered composite
    wood sheeting
2   double curtain track
3   low-E glazing (U = 1.1 W/m²K)
4   double glazing, colour printed
    90 mm sheet-metal panel with thermal insulation
    25 mm mineral-wool insulation
5   Ø 300 mm reinforced concrete column
6   18 mm Vittorio verde serpentine paving
7   20/160 mm laminated larch beam
8   3 mm sheet-aluminium covering
9   200 mm reinforced concrete wall
    80 mm rigid-foam core insulation
    200 mm reinforced concrete wall

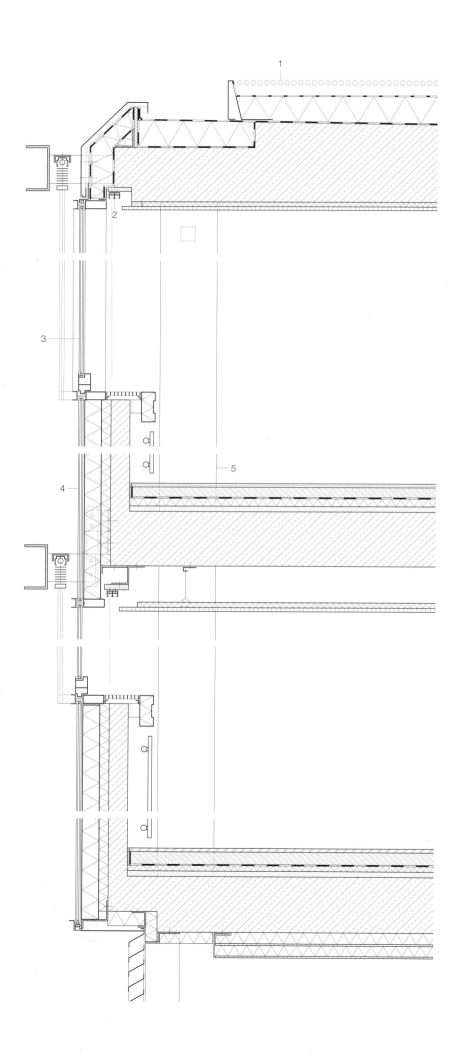

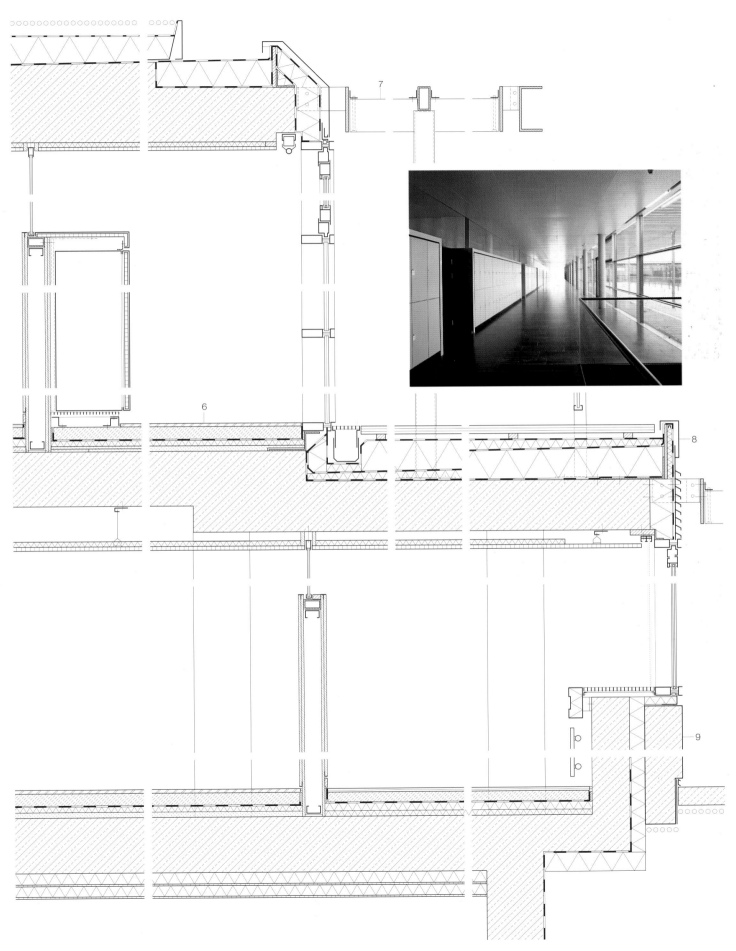

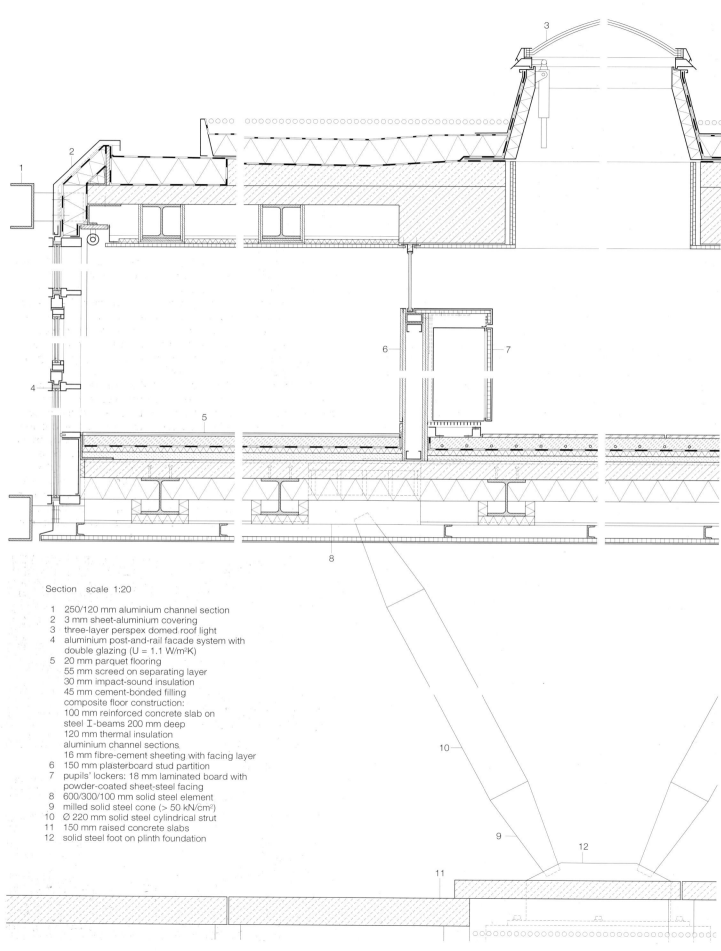

Section   scale 1:20

1   250/120 mm aluminium channel section
2   3 mm sheet-aluminium covering
3   three-layer perspex domed roof light
4   aluminium post-and-rail facade system with
    double glazing (U = 1.1 W/m²K)
5   20 mm parquet flooring
    55 mm screed on separating layer
    30 mm impact-sound insulation
    45 mm cement-bonded filling
    composite floor construction:
    100 mm reinforced concrete slab on
    steel I-beams 200 mm deep
    120 mm thermal insulation
    aluminium channel sections
    16 mm fibre-cement sheeting with facing layer
6   150 mm plasterboard stud partition
7   pupils' lockers: 18 mm laminated board with
    powder-coated sheet-steel facing
8   600/300/100 mm solid steel element
9   milled solid steel cone (> 50 kN/cm²)
10 Ø 220 mm solid steel cylindrical strut
11 150 mm raised concrete slabs
12 solid steel foot on plinth foundation

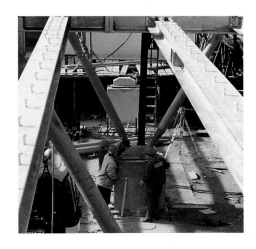

The authors:
Manfred Gmeiner, Dipl.-Ing., born in 1957
Martin Haferl, Dipl.-Ing., born in 1963
In 1989, they founded a joint engineering office for
structural planning and building physics in Vienna

Structural planning concept

It is important for us as structural engineers to be drawn into the planning process as early as possible. Projects that proceed from a competition, as was the case in the present development, can often be implemented in a more purposeful manner, since a number of alternative solutions will already have been investigated. The architectural design sets the parameters for the load-bearing structure. The structural planning, in turn, stimulates new design ideas. In this way, an interactive process between the architect and the structural engineer is set in motion. A minimalized structure, with carefully designed details that take account of manufacturing and assembly constraints, will considerably enhance the cost efficiency of the construction.

In the case of a school, which has clear functional needs, the structure is likely to be subordinated to spatial aspects. In the present project, a slender skeleton-frame construction was required with a minimum number of solid walls in order to facilitate a flexible layout.

The "floating" cross-wall structure over the entrance is raised on pairs of V-shaped columns and cantilevered out on both sides. Differential forces resulting from asymmetrical loading are transmitted to the adjoining building structure via the floors.

Composite steel slabs 10 cm thick were used to minimize the dead load. At 3 kN/m², this form of construction achieves a 60 per cent reduction in weight compared with comparable reinforced concrete slabs (7.5 kN/m²). This, of course, has a major effect on the design of the columns. They consist of Ø 220 mm steel cylinders with milled conical ends in special high-strength steel that taper in diameter to 80 mm.

Calculating the dimensions of such elements requires a much greater amount of work than providing proof of the load-bearing capacity of standard columns. Despite the complex demands of the structure, especially in respect of the combination of steel and reinforced concrete elements, it was possible to avoid virtually any cracking in the concrete.

The classroom tracts are mainly in reinforced concrete construction with point-supported flat-plate floors and only a few reinforced concrete cross-walls to provide horizontal stiffening. The high quality specified for the exposed concrete surfaces required precise planning of the working joints, formwork, abutments, openings, etc. A visually satisfying and economic solution was achieved by using a hybrid form of shuttering, consisting of a steel framework and large-area panels.

Museum of Soviet Special Camp in Sachsenhausen

Schneider + Schumacher, Frankfurt

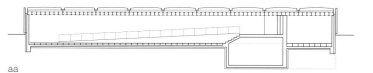

Site plan
scale 1:7500

Section · Floor plan
scale 1:400

1 Museum
2 Cemetery of Soviet
  special camp
3 Detention camp huts
4 Watchtower

5 Wall around
  former concentration
  camp
6 Monument
7 Exhibition space

8 Media room
9 Staff room
10 Services
11 Entrance
12 Lecture room

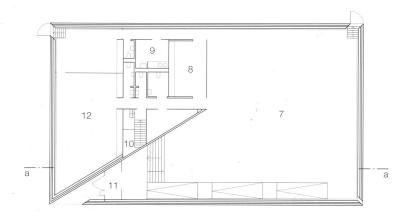

aa

Between 1945 and 1950, 60,000 people were interned in the Soviet Special Camp 7/1, which stood on the site of the former Sachsenhausen concentration camp near Berlin. Roughly 12,000 of those detained there by the Soviets died of hunger or disease. The victims are now commemorated in a museum erected on the site at the end of 2001. Located between the former camp huts and the external cemetery, the single-storey museum was sunk into the ground in order not to overtop the existing low-height buildings. Outwardly restrained in form, the cubic structure has smooth, shiny-coated concrete walls externally that mirror the dismal surroundings. The recessed entrance was created by folding back the outer wall on the diagonal at one corner; and there are glass slits at two of the other corners. Otherwise, the outer walls are completely closed. From a recessed lobby, visitors descend via a ramp or steps to the column-free exhibition space sunk one metre below ground level and divided from the seminar and information areas by glass walls. The 660 m² interior is dominated by the effect of the closely spaced steel beams overhead. The 15 cm slits between the beams are closed with strips of cold-tensioned glass, through which daylight enters, creating an oppressive spatial effect, as if one were looking up to the sky through the bars of a prison. The impression of confinement within a solid structure is heightened by the finishes to the precast concrete load-bearing double-skin walls. In contrast to the shiny, seemingly immaterial outer face, the inner skin is left in a rough, irregular state. To obtain this texture, the formwork was coated with a contact-retarding agent, and the cement surface was washed out before it had finally set. The joints between the elements are clearly visible internally and reflect the grid of beams. Larger elements (6.64 × 2.75 m) were used externally to reduce the number of joints. These are visually minimized by silicone strips, thus further accentuating the monolithic nature of the building. The two-layer construction also facilitated a precise, sharp-edged execution of the external skin.   DETAIL 4/2003

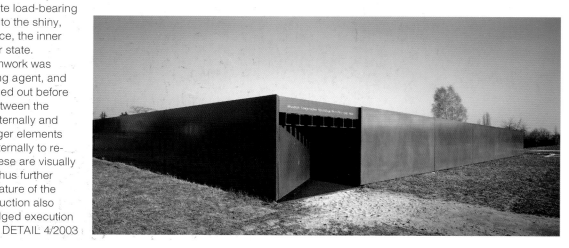

Vertical and horizontal sections
scale 1:20

1 140 mm precast concrete facade
   element 6.64/2.75 m with water-
   repellent finish
   150 mm polystyrene rigid-foam
   insulation
   polythene sheet sealing layer
   250 mm precast concrete wall
   element 3.60/3.48 m with acid-
   treated surface
2 low-E double glazing: 10 mm
   toughened glass + 12 mm cavity
   + 2× 20 mm lam. safety glass
3 120/80/8 mm steel angle
4 plastic sealing layer
   60 mm mineral-wool insulation
   8 mm sheet-steel gutter section

5 200/310/8 mm steel T-section
6 fabric sunblind, cable operated
7 140/75/8 mm steel angle
8 180/220/20 mm steel T-section
9 steel I-beam 320 mm deep
10 8 mm toughened glass, black
   screen printed
11 8 mm sheet-steel surround
12 8 mm toughened glass + fire-
   resistant glazing in steel frame
13 2 mm sheet steel, painted black
14 33 mm concrete slabs on
   adjustable raising pieces
   200 mm reinforced concrete
   polythene sealing layer
   100 mm polystyrene rigid-foam

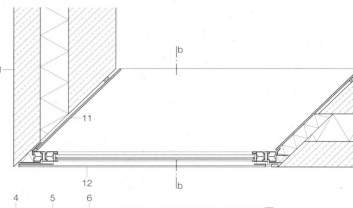

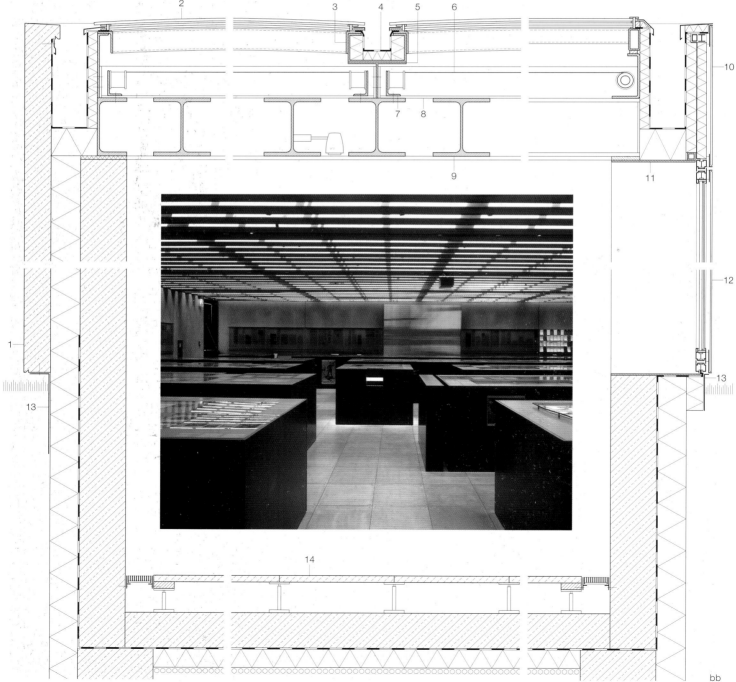

bb

Laboratory Building in Utrecht

UN Studio, Amsterdam

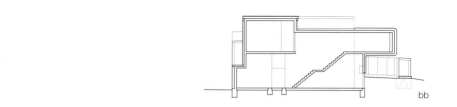

The university campus is situated on the outskirts of Utrecht and was first developed in the 1960s. A new master plan drawn up in 1986 by Rem Koolhaas formed the basis for a number of further buildings, including the "Minnaertgebouw" by Neutelings and Riedijk; a university for economics and management by Mecanoo; dining halls by OMA; and a library by Wiel Arets.

A new structure has now been added to this complex: the Nuclear Magnetic Resonance Research Centre by the Ben van Berkel office in Amsterdam. In this building, the molecular structures of DNA will be investigated with the aid of electromagnets. It is hoped that the outcome of this research can be used, among other things, in the fight against the HIV virus.

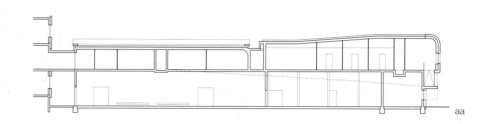

The form of the building and the materials used are directly based on the experimental processes that take place there. The trials are centred about eight electromagnets with a field strength of up to 500,000 times that of the earth's gravitational force. Any outside influences that might affect this magnetic field are screened off by the reinforced concrete casing, which is in the form of a clearly legible strip wrapped round the two central, windowless laboratories. With a series of further convolutions, the exposed concrete enclosure also accommodates the various ancillary spaces required in the development. This wrap-around structure continues from floor to wall, from wall to roof, from roof to facade and back again. The ramp drawn round the building is similar in nature and forms a spatially defining link between the different levels. There is no lift in the building, since this would have interfered with the sensitive magnetic fields of the centre's trial facilities.

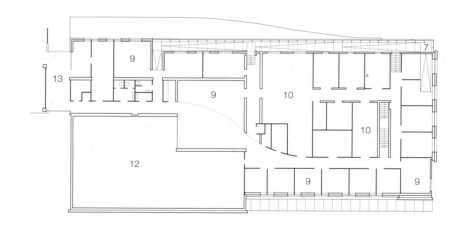

Wherever possible, areas of glazing – covered with a screening grid of dots – were installed between the concrete elements. The end faces of the concrete strip reveal the constant thickness of the material and make its special features legible. One of the most striking aspects is the high degree of plasticity evoked by the petrified curvature of the structure. DETAIL 4/2003

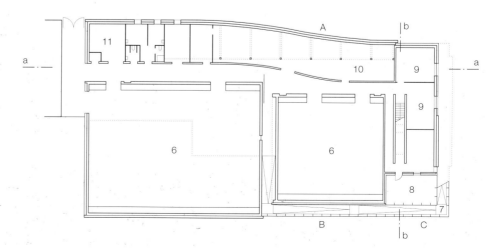

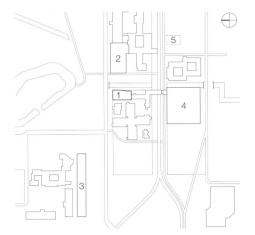

Site plan
scale 1:10,000
Sections · Floor plans
scale 1:500

1 NMR Research Centre
   by UN Studios

2 Dining halls by OMA
3 "Minnaertgebouw" by
   Neutelings Riedijk
4 University for Economics and
   Management by Mecanoo
5 Library (under construction) by
   Wiel Arets
6 Laboratory with electromagnets

7 Ramp
8 Outdoor area
9 Office
10 Operations room/
   Laboratory
11 Staff room
12 Void
13 Link to existing building

Sections
scale 1:50

 预浇制

1 200/600 mm precast concrete edge strip
2 rendering
50 mm thermal insulation 绝/隔热材料
80 mm thermal insulation
150 mm sandlime brickwork n 石明砖
3 point-fixed lam. safety glass with screen printing as solar filter
4 glass fin supporting construction, screw fixed with aluminium angles
5 lam. safety glass fixed ventilating louvre
6 aluminium grating over perforations in concrete slab for natural ventilation
7 12 mm fibre-reinforced cement-bonded slab
90 mm thermal insulation
150 mm sandlime brickwork
8 aluminium cladding
ventilated cavity
80 mm thermal insulation
300 mm reinforced concrete wall
9 services space behind aluminium construction
10 linoleum
500 mm reinforced concrete floor slab bedded on insulators to avoid vibration
11 louvred sunblind
12 drainage channel to falls
13 sheet aluminium cladding
14 precast concrete element
15 suspension for walkway with turnbuckle, adjustable internally
16 80/80 mm aluminium angle

A

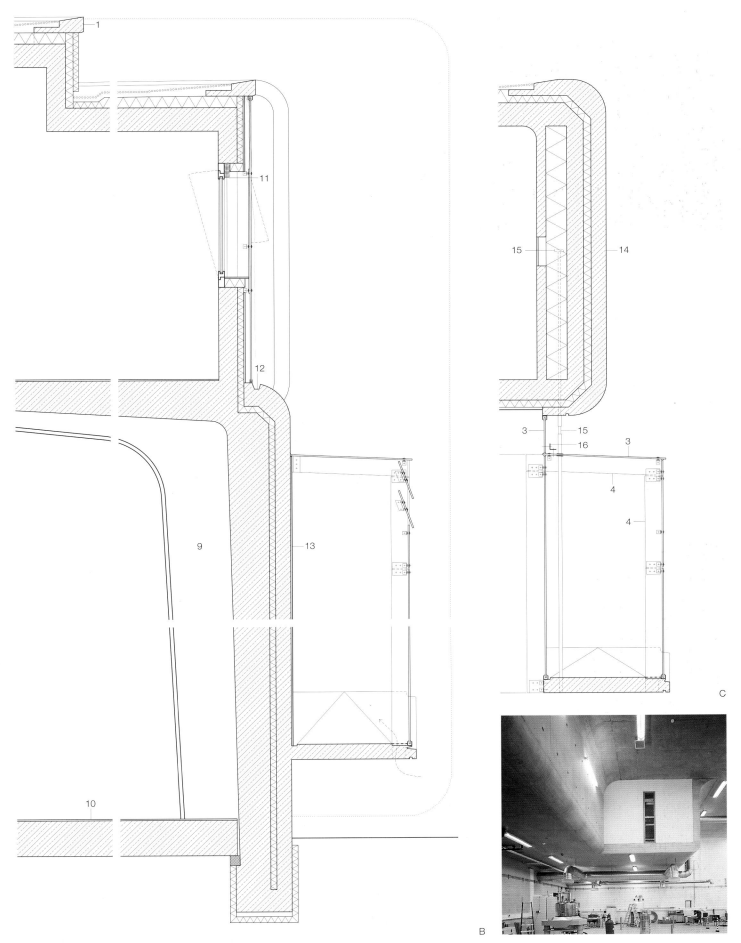

B

C

Primary School in Au

Beat Consoni, Rorschach

After deciding to extend the existing school in Au, the primary school board commissioned ten architectural practices to prepare studies. Beat Consoni won the competition with a proposal to demolish the existing building and to replace it with a strikiing new structure in exposed concrete. The development responds sensitively to the surrounding topography. The unadorned, minimalist, cubic form follows the contours of the sloping site and is linked to a series of outdoor spaces. Varying in design according to their aspect, the facades accentuate the contrast between the open view over the Rhine Valley to the south and that to the steep slope on the northern side. A covered forecourt was created by cantilevering the two upper storeys out over the entrance. An undivided window strip in the south facade extends over nearly the entire length of the building. The ground floor corridor to the rear provides access to the teachers' rooms, WCs and a multi-purpose space with a stage. This space can be opened over its full width to the corridor. Single-flight staircases at the end of the access route lead down to the basement – containing a workroom and ancillary spaces – and up to the classrooms on the first and second storeys. On these two floors, which have an identical layout, the circulation route runs along the north side, while the classrooms are oriented to the south through continuous window strips. The access corridors along the north face receive daylight through narrow clerestory glazing and through a number of window slits near the work tables integrated into the cloakroom cupboard units. At the end of the building, the classrooms are turned to face west, with strip windows over the entire width of the narrow facade. The structure consists of in-situ concrete cross-walls and prestressed concrete floors. The double-skin external walls, with an intermediate layer of insulation, were cast without joints and have no metal coverings, which serves to heighten the monolithic appearance of the school. The noble expression of this restrained building reflects the high quality of the workmanship that went into it.   DETAIL 4/2003

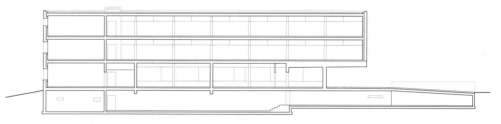

aa

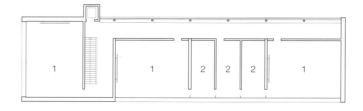

First floor plan

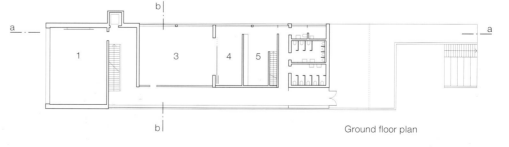

Ground floor plan

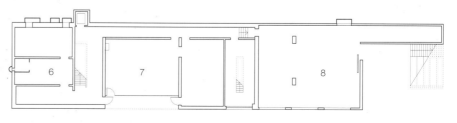

Basement plan

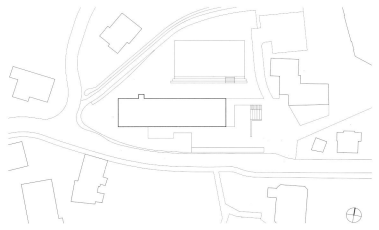

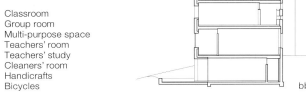

Site plan   scale 1:1500
Sections • Floor plans   scale 1:500

1   Classroom
2   Group room
3   Multi-purpose space
4   Teachers' room
5   Teachers' study
6   Cleaners' room
7   Handicrafts
8   Bicycles

bb

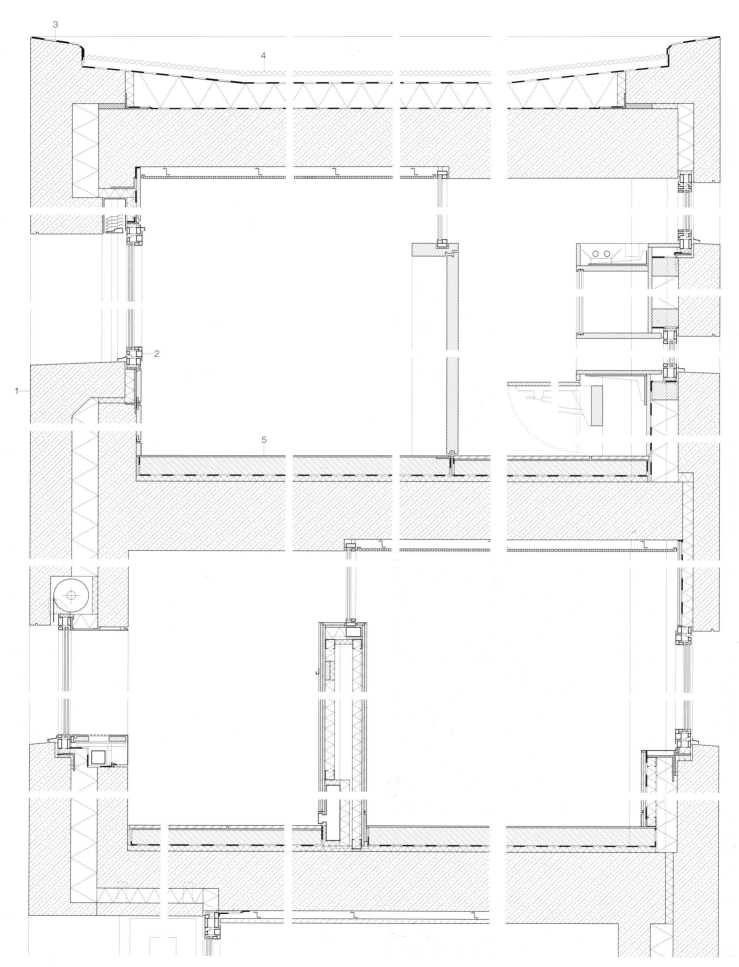

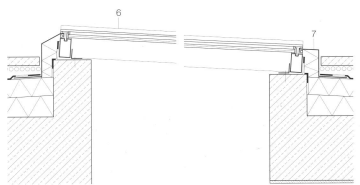

Sectional details
Section through roof light
Sections through stairs   scale 1:20

1   220 mm reinforced concrete wall
    140 mm polystyrene rigid-foam
    200 mm reinforced concrete wall
    20 mm plasterboard
2   steel window frame painted
    with wet look
3   liquid-plastic seal
4   50 mm layer of gravel
    separating mat
    two-layer bituminous
    membrane
    140 mm polyurethane foam
    vapour barrier: bituminous sealing
    layer laid in hot bitumen
    320 mm reinforced concrete roof
    perforated plasterboard
5   3 mm linoleum

    105 mm anhydrite screed
    polythene sheeting
    30 mm mineral-fibre impact-
    sound insulation
6   stepped double glazing: 10 mm
    toughened glass + 15 mm cavity
    + 18 mm lam. safety glass
7   2 mm stainless-steel sheeting
8   330/110 mm prec. conc. tread
9   60/60/8 mm stainless-steel angle
10 impact-sound insulation
11 opening grouted with mortar
12 20 mm stone paving
    90 mm anhydrite screed
    polythene sheeting
    impact-sound insulation
    30 mm mineral-fibre insulation

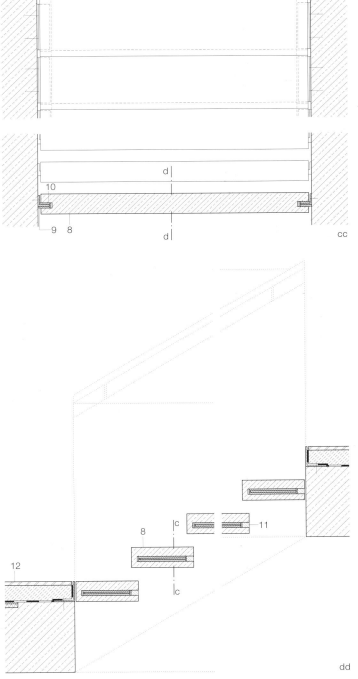

Restaurant in Brighton

dRRM, London

In creating this sushi bar for a London restaurant chain, a new 14 × 14 × 3.5 m box-like enclosure was superimposed over an existing single-storey, octagonal, domed pavilion dating from the 1980s. The fact that the building now bears a certain resemblance to an oriental lantern is attributable to the choice of materials and the quality of transparency that was achieved. The pre-fabricated, lightweight facade construction consists of translucent fibreglass elements reminiscent of Japanese paper screens. Standing on a raised deck, it seems to float above a transparent, glazed plinth zone. The building is crowned by a strip of green-patinated copper panels. This facade construction encloses the restaurant on nearly all sides. On the east face, it is divided into three segments, which can be pushed aside into a steel frame next to the entrance, allowing the internal space to be opened over its full width and the wood flooring to extend out to an external terrace. In this way, a transition is created between indoors and outdoors. Internally, the finely dimensioned, hand-made seating, which flows around a series of fixed benches, appears to be folded from a single sheet and almost to float above the wood flooring. Overhead, the soffit is painted in a luminous-red tone, which radiates out at night through a cruciform central roof light, bathing the space around the restaurant in a reddish glow.

DETAIL 5/2003

Site plan
scale 1:750

Floor plan
Section · East elevation
scale 1:200

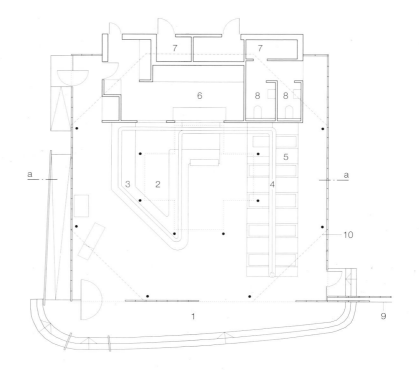

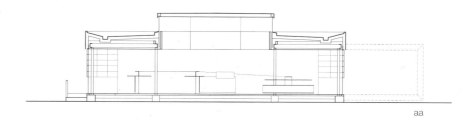

aa

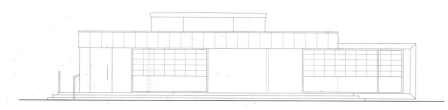

1 Terrace
2 Sushi preparation
3 Sushi bar
4 Sushi conveyor
   strip
5 Sitting area
6 Kitchen
7 Store
8 WC
9 Parking frame for
   sliding facade
10 Former octagonal
   pavilion dating from
   the 1980s
11 Administration building
   and hotel complex
   dating from the 1980s
12 Neoclassical civic hall

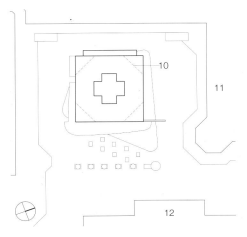

Sections   scale 1:20

1   3.2/31.7 mm aluminium flat
2   28 mm redwood boarding with inlaid
    rubber strips
3   70 mm prefabricated fibreglass
    facade panel
4   12 mm toughened glass, point-fixed
    to 70/12 mm angle frame, consisting
    of steel flats
5   Ø 114 mm tubular steel column
    replacing previous structure
6   existing reinforced concrete strip
    foundations
7   28 mm redwood strip flooring,
    black-stained
8   50/50 mm battens/underfloor
    heating system
    18 mm impregnated plywood
    50/225 mm existing timber joists
9   15 mm plasterboard, painted
    fluorescent red
10 89/178 mm existing peripheral steel
    channel
11 50/125 mm existing timber rafters
12 0.7 mm prepatinated copper fascia
    element with 18 mm plywood backing
13 plastic roof sealing layer adhesive fixed
    to thermal insulation on
    12 mm plywood
    63/150 mm timber rafters
14 12 mm composite wood board,
    painted fluorescent red
15 6 mm glass mirror adhesive fixed to
    composite wood board, with aluminium
    angle to lower edge
16 fluorescent tube
17 12 mm toughened glass raised roof light
18 bamboo matting on
    18 mm combustion-modified plastic
    sponge foam
    2× 4 mm flexible bent MDF
    supporting structure
19 18 mm plywood
20 24 mm black-coated solid-core laminate

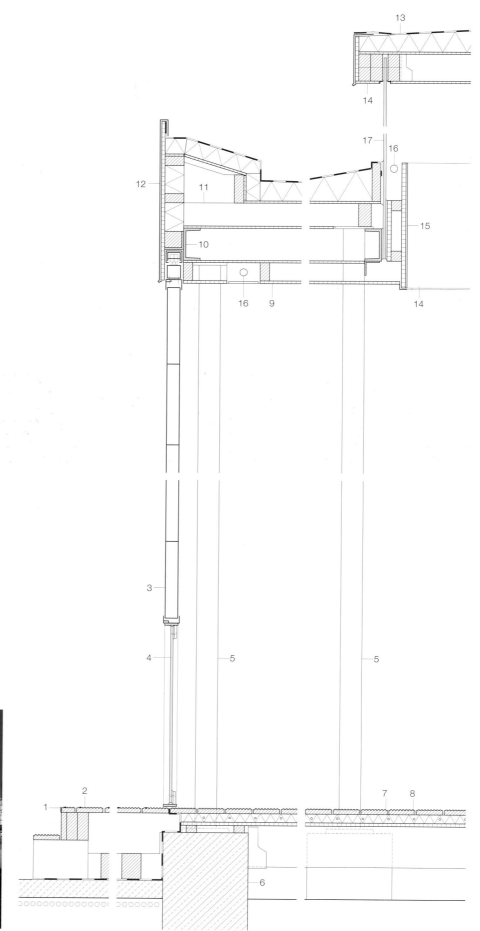

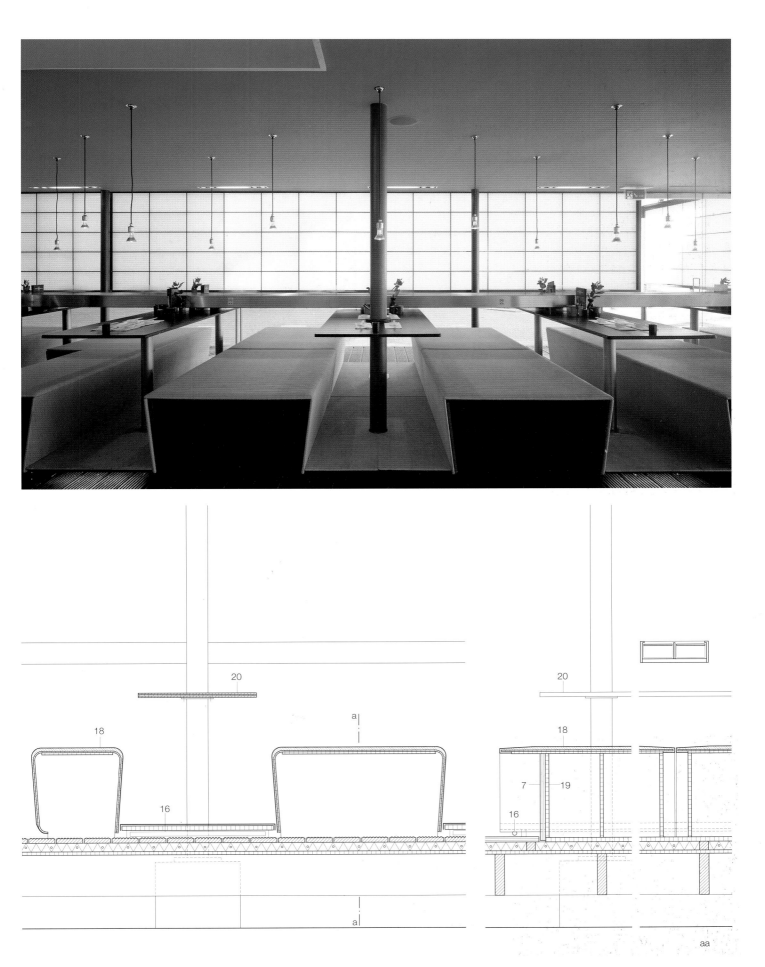

Wine Tavern in Fellbach

Christine Remensperger, Stuttgart

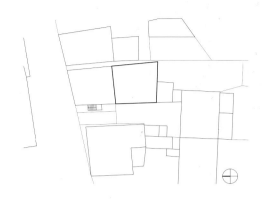

Prior to its conversion, this timber-framed house dating from 1805 was used for wine-making, and the vaulted cellar was the scene of many wine festivals. On the ground floor, which has a room height of only 2.05 m in part, a sales area has been created with a space for tasting the small but select range of self-produced wines. The building was gutted, and the sales spaces were laid out around a central timber structure. Internally, the walls are lined with panelling, shelving and cupboard units, which serve to even out irregularities in the surface. The principal material used for the furnishings and fittings is oiled oak – a reference to the old wine casks made of the same wood. The floor is uniformly finished with a polished screed, which accentuates the flowing, harmonious nature of the sequence of spaces – from the tall shop in the entrance area, up a broad flight of steps over the cellar vaulting to the lower-height tavern. Thanks to the purist quality of the design, the wine bottles remain the focus of attention.   DETAIL 5/2003

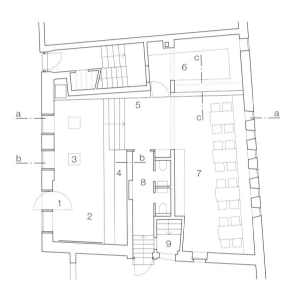

Site plan
scale 1:1000
Ground floor plan
Cross-section
scale 1:200

1   Entrance
2   Shop
3   Movable counter
4   Wine racks
5   Fitted cupboard
6   Kitchen
7   Wine-tasting
8   WCs
9   Stairs to vaulted
    cellar

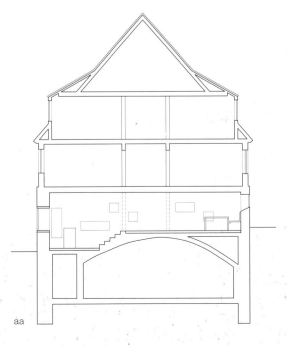

1   25 mm mineral plaster
    500–700 mm existing brick/
    sandstone external wall
2   top-hung casement with
    double glazing
3   40/700 mm oak window surround
    oiled with hard wax
4   sales counter:
    25 mm oak-veneered MDF oiled
    with hard wax
5   drawers:
    25 mm oak-veneered MDF
6   flush flap:
    25 mm oak-veneered
    MDF with stainless-steel
    ironmongery
7   60 mm (av.) polished screed with
    coloured pigments and
    Ø 8–12 mm pebbles
    polythene sheeting
    heat-conducting metal sheeting
    underfloor heating
    35 mm polystyrene sheeting
    80 mm thermal insulation
    50–200 mm lean-mix screed

8   180/270 mm step:
    50 mm polished screed with
    coloured pigmentation
    reinforced concrete
    supporting structure on
    vaulted stone arch
9   25 mm oak-veneered MDF
    adhesive fixed to concrete
    plinth
10 wine racks:
    25 mm oak-veneered MDF
    oiled with hard wax,
    with glued joints and con-
    cealed mechanical fixings
11 labelling system:
    20/5 mm anthracite MDF flush
    strips; prices chalked on
12 6 mm oak-veneered MDF
    vertical divisions
    let into grooves
13 50/50 mm wood batten
14 2× 12.5 mm plasterboard on
    wood bearers between
    timber soffit beams
    120 mm mineral-wool insulation

Vertical section
scale 1:20

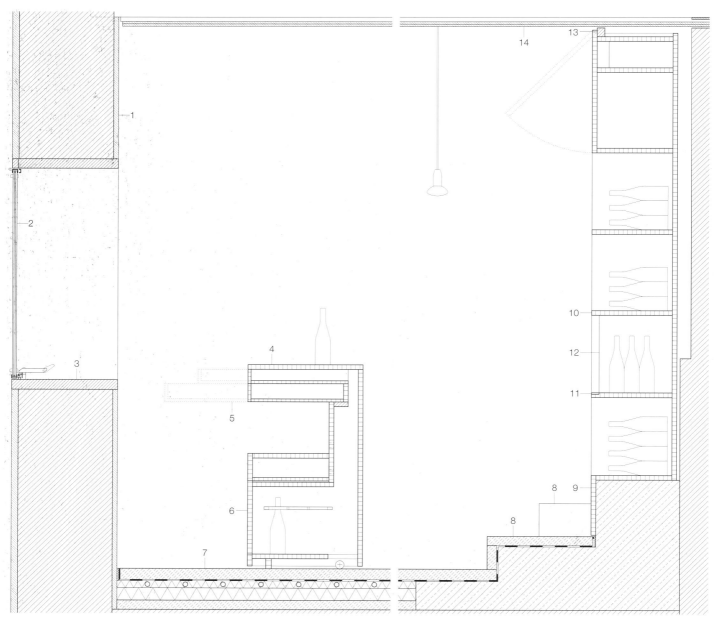

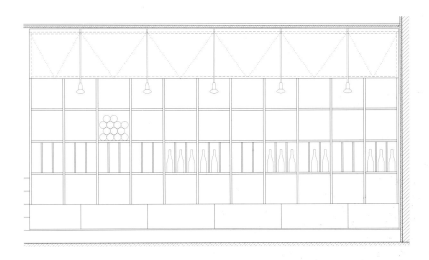

Section/Elevation of wine rack
scale 1:50

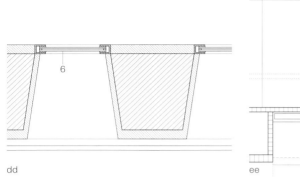

dd

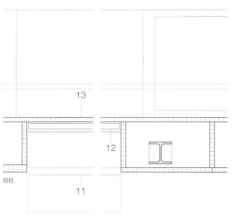

ee

The benches fixed to the external wall are veneered with oiled oak – an allusion to the former wine casks in the same wood.

Horizontal section · Vertical section
scale 1:20

The fitted cupboards conceal steel I-members inserted in place of internal walls, while the integrated showcases allow the display of bottles of fine wine.

Horizontal section · Vertical section
scale 1:20

1 40/50 mm wood batten
2 seat back: 25 mm oak-veneered composite wood board oiled with hard wax

3 30/30 mm steel channel support, screw fixed
4 seat: 40 mm oak-veneered composite wood board

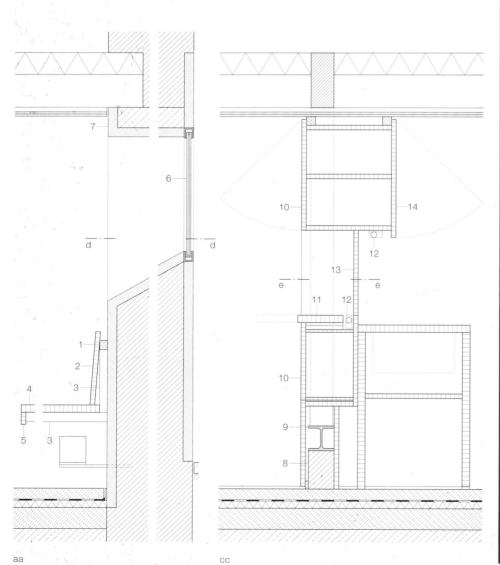

aa

cc

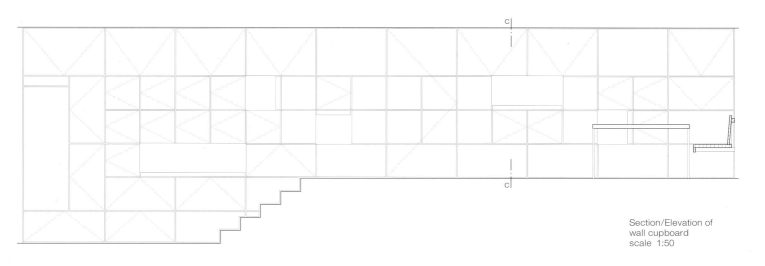

Section/Elevation of
wall cupboard
scale 1:50

5	composite wood board fascia strip, glued to seat		section frame, plastered in	9	steel I-beam 140 mm deep as bearing for vertical I-section supports 120 mm deep	10	25 mm oak-veneered MDF flap/lining oiled with hard wax		pull-out shelf with rear lighting		veneered MDF back of showcase
6	30 mm double glazing in 35/35 mm aluminium channel-	7	25–50 mm mineral plaster			11	40 mm anthracite-coloured MDF	12	concealed fluorescent lighting in recess	14	matt-coated MDF flap to hatch with aluminized surface
		8	240 mm existing brick wall					13	25 mm oak-		

Pedestrian Bridge in Boudry

Geninasca Delefortrie SA,
Architects FAS SIA, Neuchâtel

Spanning the River Areuse in Switzerland, the bridge leads from a steeply rising bank on one side to a large open space on the other. The different situations at the two ends are reflected in the cross-sectional dimensions of the structure, which increase along its length – a gesture that is accentuated by the sinuous curve of the bridge on plan. The dynamic formal language and the simple means of construction reveal a confident yet respectful approach to the surroundings. Proceeding along the bridge, one experiences a play of light through the open wood bars and the steel sections of the enclosing structure. The spatial impression is never constricting.

One has a sensation of wandering beneath a shady avenue of trees. In spite of the simple details and the use of only a few materials, the bridge has a relatively complex structure. It is in the form of a box girder that transmits bending and torsion loads to the strip foundations at the ends. The structure consists of 12 steel frames, the walls, roof and base of which all form part of the load-bearing system. The individual steel frames are connected internally by diagonal compression and tension members that are scarcely visible from the outside and that heighten the impression of a filigree form of construction. In view of the difficult access to the site, three prefabricated elements

were delivered by helicopter, provisionally held in position and secured, and then welded together. After two days, the bridge was self-supporting. Finally, the horizontal wood strips were fixed to the steel structure. They serve as an additional means of reinforcement.   DETAIL 6/2003

1   150/27 mm fir planks
2   200/100/10 mm steel RHS
3   Ø 60.3/14.2 mm steel tube
4   Ø 25 mm steel diagonal bracing rod
5   120/80/10 mm steel RHS
6   100/65/7 mm steel angle
7   100 mm bed of gravel
8   1 mm separating mat
9   150/100/10 mm steel RHS
10 1 mm perforated ribbed metal sheeting
    59 mm deep

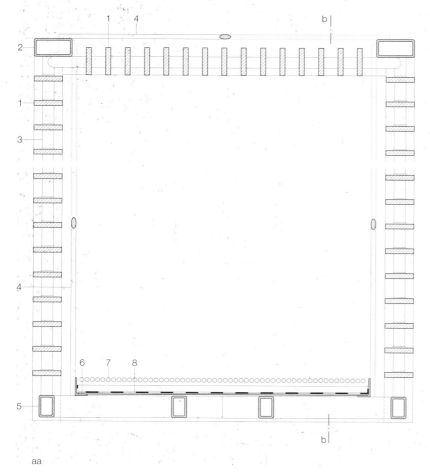

aa

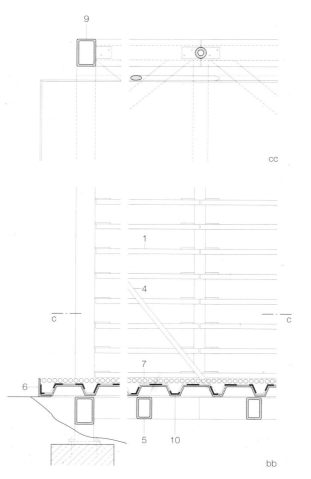

bb

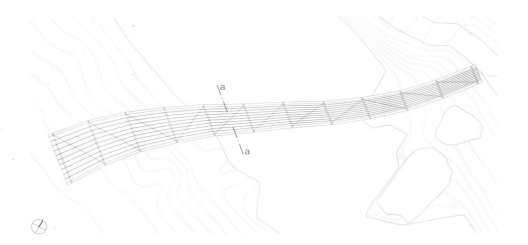

View from above
scale 1:250

Vertical sections
Horizontal section
scale 1:20

Hotel in Groningen

Foreign Office Architects, London
Alejandro Zaera Polo, Farshid Moussavi

In 2001, an architectural event with the title "Blue Moon" was held in the Dutch town of Groningen under the direction of Toyo Ito. The programme included the erection of a number of temporary structures in various locations, as well as the creation of permanent buildings like the Aparthotel, which stands in a little square in a district noted for its small docks, warehouses and guest houses. In a closed state, the hotel resembles a plain storage structure. In use, however, as the various shutters and doors are opened, the facade is transformed in appearance. The outer skin also undergoes a change at night. The finely perforated corrugated metal sheeting that seems opaque by day shimmers when the lights are turned on inside, revealing something of the life within the building. The erection of a hotel with a café and bar has created a new social venue in the district and achieved a successful revitalization of the square. From the roof terrace, hotel guests enjoy a view over the old town centre around them. DETAIL 6/2003

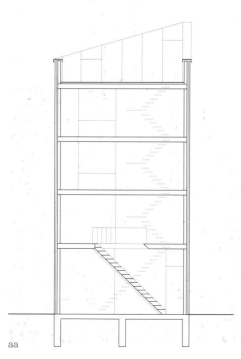

aa

Site plan
scale 1:2000
Section
Floor plans
scale 1:200

1   Café
2   Access to apartments
3   Guest apartment
4   Bathroom
5   Roof terrace
6   Services space

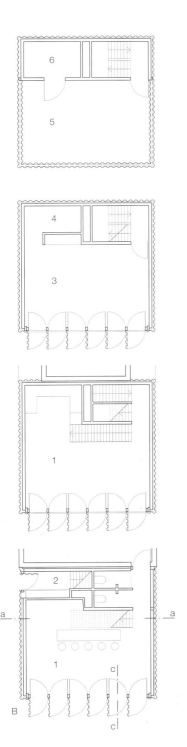

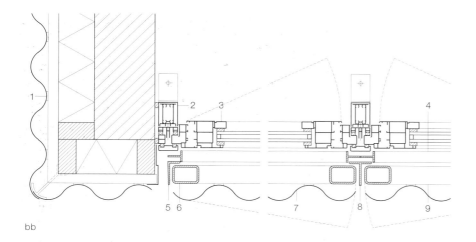

bb

Horizontal section · Vertical section
scale 1:10

1. wall construction:
   aluminium-zinc corrugated sheeting
   160/40 mm
   30/20 mm steel RHS supporting structure
   90 mm thermal insulation
   150 mm sandlime brickwork
2. 140/50 mm aluminium post
3. aluminium casement with double glazing:
   8 + 8 mm laminated safety glass
4. 30/30/3 mm steel T-section
5. 65/30 mm steel angle
6. 70/50 mm steel RHS
7. perforated aluminium-zinc corrugated
   sheeting 160/40 mm
8. 60/60/3 mm steel T-section
9. 50/50 mm steel SHS
10. roof construction:
    30 mm concrete paving slabs
    bituminous sealing layer
    60 mm thermal insulation
    vapour barrier
    200 mm reinforced concrete roof slab
11. steel bracket for fixing hinge
12. 30/50 mm steel RHS safety rail
13. 25 mm composite wood board
14. 15 mm thermal insulation
15. 18 mm reconstructed stone paving
16. precast concrete plinth

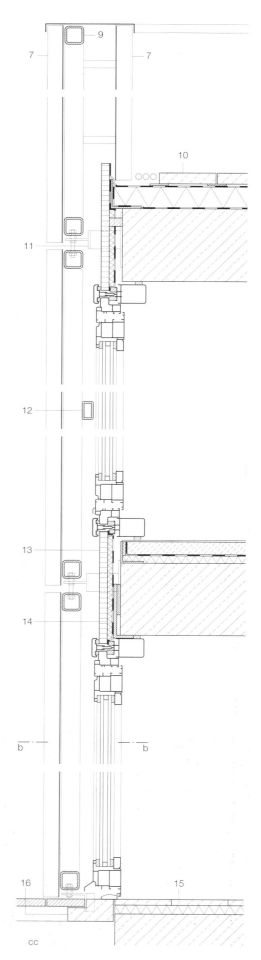

cc

House in Dortmund

Archifactory.de, Bochum

Situated in a suburban street in Dortmund, this house stands in stark contrast to the neighbouring developments. Its shimmering silver-grey larch cladding forms a homogeneous skin in which large glazed openings are set flush with the facade. The larch boards are cut to mitre at the corners, so that nowhere is their thickness evident. As a result, the house has a monolithic appearance; and there are no projecting canopies, eaves or gutters to diminish this effect. The present scheme comprises an extension of the existing building on the site. The main access to the house is located directly next to the garage. From the entrance, the eye is drawn upwards, via a flight of stairs, to the open living area on the level above. This double-height room conveys a feeling of spaciousness, and the split-level layout evokes a sense of flowing transitions. An external flight of concrete steps connects the main living space with the garden. In contrast to the sense of openness created by the large areas of glazing in the facade, the roof terrace is screened from prying eyes by storey-height wood enclosing walls. As well as ensuring the requisite degree of privacy, they create an introverted outdoor space. If desired, the rooftop facade can be opened by means of two doors that allow a view out to the surroundings, but that, in a closed position, are scarcely visible.   DETAIL 6/2003

Sections
Floor plans
scale 1:250

1   Garage
2   Living area
3   Kitchen
4   Void over living
    area
5   Living area/
    Study
6   Bedroom
7   Roof terrace

aa

bb

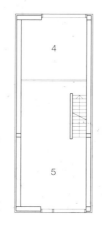

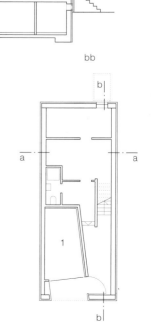

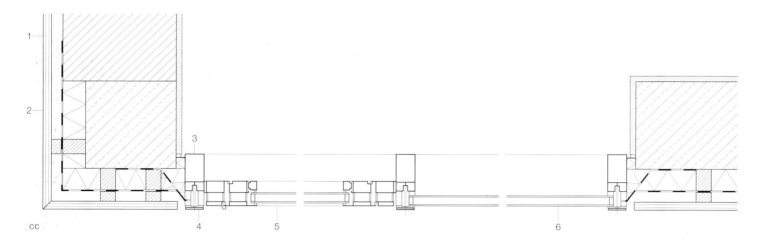

1
2
3
4   5   6
cc

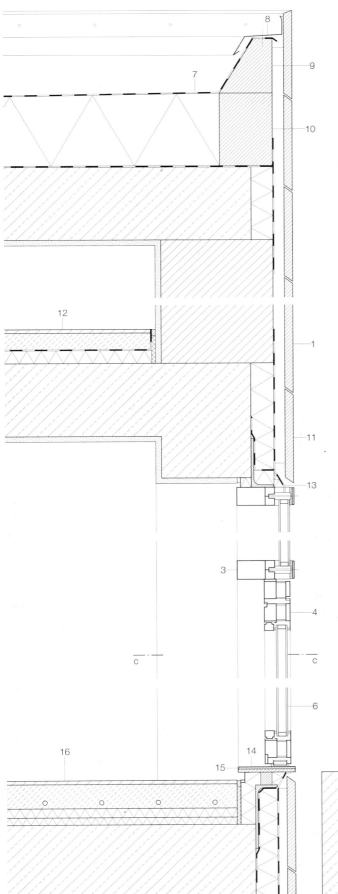

Horizontal section
Vertical section
scale 1:10

1 22/214 mm sawn larch boarding
   with 6 mm open joints
   50/30 mm batten
   ventilated cavity
   300 mm aerated concrete wall
   15 mm white gypsum plaster
2 22/214 mm sawn larch boarding
   50/30 mm batten
   ventilated cavity
   moisture-diffusing waterproof
   membrane
   60 mm mineral-fibre thermal
   insulation between
   50/60 mm batten
   240 mm reinforced concrete wall
   15 mm white gypsum plaster
3 aluminium post-and-rail
   construction
4 aluminium cover strip with visible
   screw fixings
5 door: aluminium frame with
   double glazing
6 double glazing: 4 mm toughened
   glass + 16 mm cavity + 4 mm
   float glass
7 two-layer bituminous sealing
   membrane
   140–200 mm thermal insulation
   finished to falls with surface
   coating
   welded bituminous sheet
   vapour barrier
   bitumen undercoat
   200 mm reinforced concrete
   filigree beam floor
   15 mm white gypsum plaster

8   0.8 mm sheet titanium-zinc
    covering, bent to shape
9   140/150 mm timber plate,
    splay cut
10 140/200 mm timber plate
11 22/214 mm sawn
    larch boarding
    50/30 mm batten
    30 mm ventilated cavity
    moisture-diffusing waterproof
    membrane
    60 mm thermal insulation
    concrete lintel
12 10 mm shiny anthracite
    terrazzo
    45 mm cement-and-sand
    screed
    polythene separating layer
    35 mm impact-sound insulation
    200 mm reinforced concrete
    filigree beam floor
    15 mm white gypsum plaster
13 windproof layer
14 2 mm sheet stainless steel
15 neoprene sealing strip
16 10 mm shiny anthracite
    terrazzo
    65 mm screed around
    underfloor heating
    25 mm rigid-foam thermal
    insulation
    20 mm polystyrene thermal
    insulation
    200 mm reinforced concrete
    filigree beam floor
17 exposed concrete stairs

bb

Vertical sections
through roof terrace
Horizontal section through flap
scale 1:10

1   door to roof terrace: aluminium
    frame with double glazing
2   aluminium fascia on
    30/30/3 mm galvanized steel
    RHS frame with
    20 mm rigid-foam insulation
    windproof layer

3   22/214 mm sawn larch
    boarding
    50/80 mm wood bearers
    wood firrings
    two-layer bituminous sealing
    membrane
    140–200 mm thermal
    insulation finished to falls,
    with surface coating
    bituminous vapour
    barrier
    bitumen undercoat

    200 mm reinforced concrete
    filigree-beam floor
    15 mm white gypsum plaster
4   22/234 mm sawn larch
    boarding with 6 mm open
    joints
    50/30 mm wood battens
    140/140 and 200/140 mm
    timber framing
    50/30 mm wood battens
    22/234 mm sawn larch
    boarding with 6 mm open joints

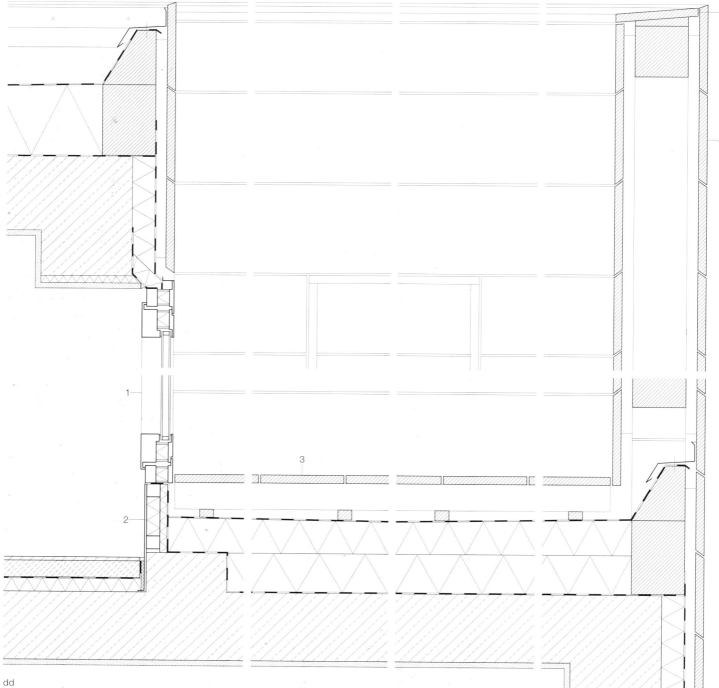

5   larch cover strip
6   opening flap: steel RHS frame, mitre cut and welded, covered on both faces with larch boarding
7   Ø 30 mm tubular galvanized steel safety rail
8   140/140/8 mm steel plate with steel sleeve welded on
9   Ø 8 mm galvanized steel rod welded to steel frame
10   Ø 8 mm steel rod for fixing opening flap at 90° angle

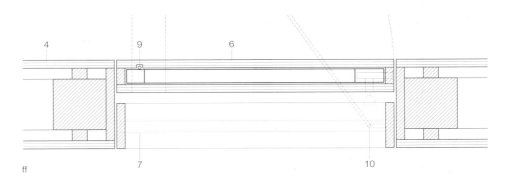

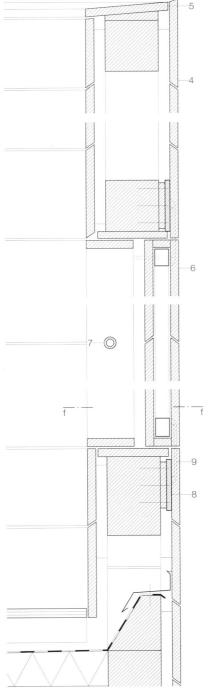

Store and Studio in Hagi

Sambuichi Architects, Hiroshima
Hiroshi Sambuichi

Each of the storage spaces in this warehouse, which belongs to a well-known Japanese ceramics firm, is related to a stage in the production process. There are spaces for raw materials, semi-finished products and fired wares, as well as a studio for painting and glazing. The positive/negative principle underlying the forming of ceramics is also reflected in the construction of the concrete elements. Central aspects of the design are the relationship between formwork and poured concrete, and the idea of re-using the shuttering as a construction material. The dimensions of the concrete surfaces were, therefore, carefully coordinated with those of openings and other elements

of the building. Standardized boarded formwork to the walls, for example, was subsequently used to make floor-height shutters to windows and doors. The internal formwork was recycled to create lightweight partitions or inbuilt fittings, and the shuttering to the soffit on the upper storey was reused as the floor finish. The surfaces of these two quite different materials – concrete and wood – resemble each other, with the grain of the wood recurring in the faces of the concrete walls. In the course of time, there is also a greater correspondence in the coloration: externally, the initially fresh, light brown of the untreated wood weathers to a natural grey close to that of the concrete.

DETAIL 6/2003

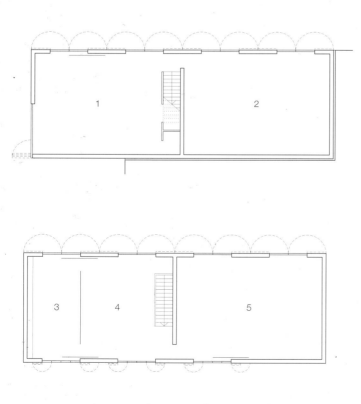

Site plan
scale 1:2000

Floor plans
scale 1:250

1 Semi-finished
  products
2 Raw materials

3 Studio area
4 Finished products
5 Fired wares

Section   scale 1:20

1   6 mm sheet stainless-steel
    covering
2   roof construction:
    extensive planting
    50 mm topsoil
    2 mm bituminous sealing layer
    30 mm thermal insulation
    250 mm reinforced concrete
    roof slab
3   formwork wall panels reused as
    pivoting shutters:
    12 mm cedar boarding
    50/30 mm wood bearers
    12 mm cedar boarding
4   sliding door:
    stainless-steel frame with 8 mm
    laminated safety glass
5   floor construction:
    12 mm cedar board
    soffit formwork reused as
    flooring
    50/30 mm wood bearers
    sole plate:
    105/45 mm and
    100/40 mm wood scantlings
    250 mm reinforced concrete
    floor slab
6   100 mm precast concrete
    paving slab
7   gravel bed
8   floor construction:
    350 mm reinforced
    concrete slab
    50 mm cement-and-sand
    screed
    40 mm thermal insulation
    150 mm bed of gravel
    polythene sheeting
9   concealed stainless-steel hinge

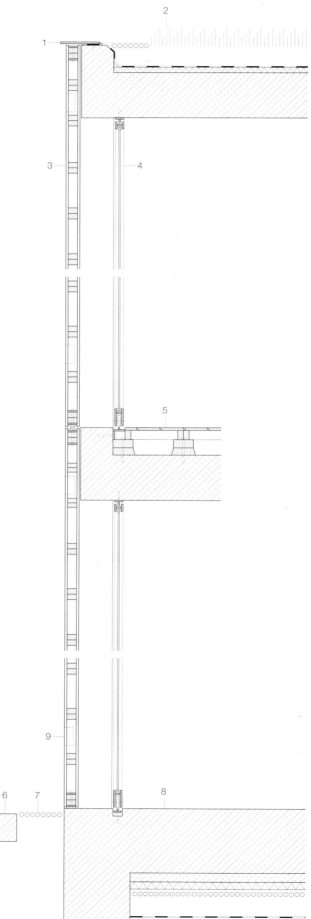

Housing Development in Dornbirn

B&E Baumschlager-Eberle, Lochau

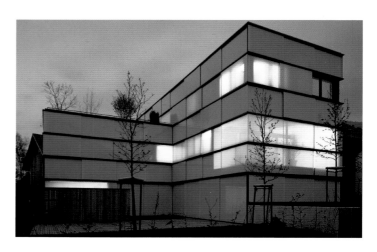

This new housing development is located on the densely populated outskirts of Dornbirn in Austria. It stands out from the traditional pitched-roof building fabric by virtue of its unusual volumetric form and facade design. Two tracts, one three storeys high, the other two storeys high, are offset to each other in a way that helps to integrate the structure into the small-scale surrounding developments and to define new external spaces. To ensure a maximum exploitation of the site, the dwelling block was erected as close to the neighbouring house as possible. Access to the basement garage is, in fact, beneath the existing building. The architects responded to the dense local settlement pattern not only in the form of this development, but in the facade design.

Containing nine dwellings, the complex resembles a white glazed cube in which the surroundings are reflected. In this way, a series of visual links and new spatial relationships were established. The white glazed facade is articulated horizontally by black guide tracks. Set out in three planes, the sliding glazing elements lend the smooth surface a subtle sense of depth and varied reflecting qualities. Concealed behind the outer layers of glazing is a timber stud construction lined with laminated boarding. The surroundings are reflected in the glass skin in different ways: as clearly defined images in the rectangular windows, which are set in the wall behind the outer layer; or filtered and diffused in the white surface glazing. The appearance of the facade also varies according to weather conditions and the time of day. Residents can regulate to what degree they wish to communicate with the surrounding environment. The screen-printed facade elements shield not only the interior, but also the loggias, from the prying eyes of neighbours. At the same time, they do not impede views out of the building. When two panes of glass are slid in front of each other, however, the view out is obscured. This variability is an essential feature of the uniform facade system. DETAIL 7/8 2003

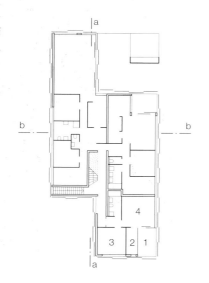

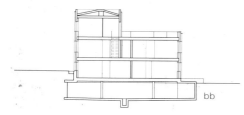

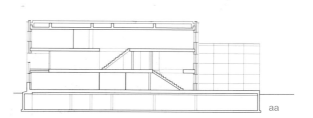

Site plan
scale 1:2500

Floor plans · Sections
scale 1:500

1 Loggia
2 Kitchen
3 Bedroom
4 Living room
5 Roof terrace

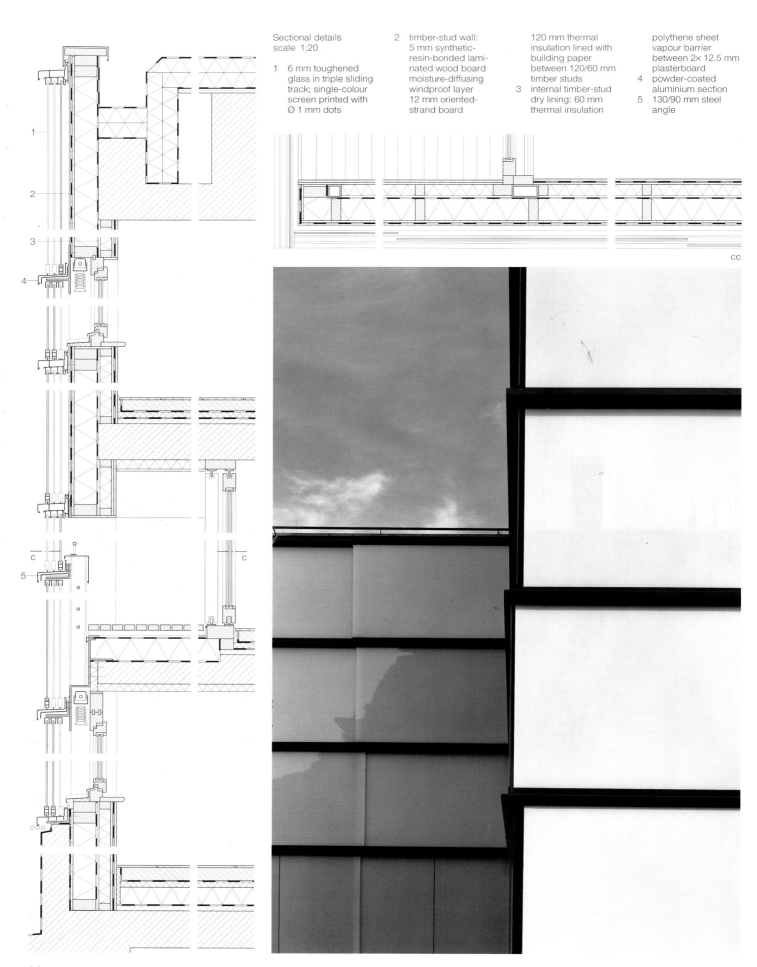

Sectional details
scale 1:20

1   6 mm toughened
    glass in triple sliding
    track; single-colour
    screen printed with
    Ø 1 mm dots

2   timber-stud wall:
    5 mm synthetic-
    resin-bonded lami-
    nated wood board
    moisture-diffusing
    windproof layer
    12 mm oriented-
    strand board

    120 mm thermal
    insulation lined with
    building paper
    between 120/60 mm
    timber studs

3   internal timber-stud
    dry lining: 60 mm
    thermal insulation

    polythene sheet
    vapour barrier
    between 2× 12.5 mm
    plasterboard

4   powder-coated
    aluminium section

5   130/90 mm steel
    angle

cc

University for Applied Design
in Wiesbaden

Mahler Günster Fuchs Architects, Stuttgart

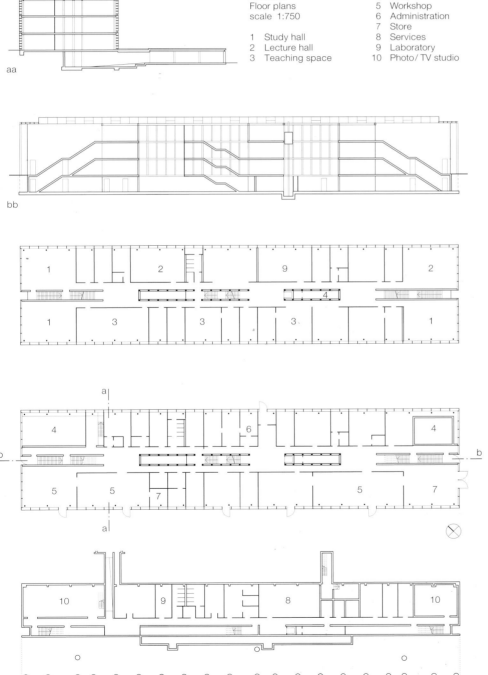

Sections
Floor plans
scale 1:750

1 Study hall
2 Lecture hall
3 Teaching space

4 Void
5 Workshop
6 Administration
7 Store
8 Services
9 Laboratory
10 Photo/ TV studio

The new university for applied design in Wiesbaden is well integrated in the neighbouring faculty developments. A grove of oak trees on the site of a former film production company is reflected in the glazed facades of the new structure, which responds to the trees in other ways as well. To protect their roots, for example, the basement extends under only half the building area; and the surrounding ground is not sealed off. Similarly, account is taken of the existing environment in the choice of materials and the form of the slenderly dimensioned, transparent wood-and-glass facades. Constructionally, the long faces of the building are contrasted with the end faces. The long north and south facades, set in front of load-bearing composite columns, consist of 40-centimetre-deep posts and rails with double glazing fixed on the outside. The system not only forms a kind of structural shelving where various objects can be placed or exhibited; on the south face, it also serves to shade the building, in conjunction with the trees. Room-height flaps facilitate the cross-ventilation of the structure. A special feature of the end faces is the intermediate space between the layers of glazing. At the suggestion of the architects, a finely dimensioned grid of Malaysian meranti was inserted in the cavity to filter incoming light, while still allowing a view out to the magnificent oak trees. DETAIL 7/8 2003

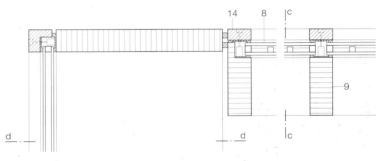

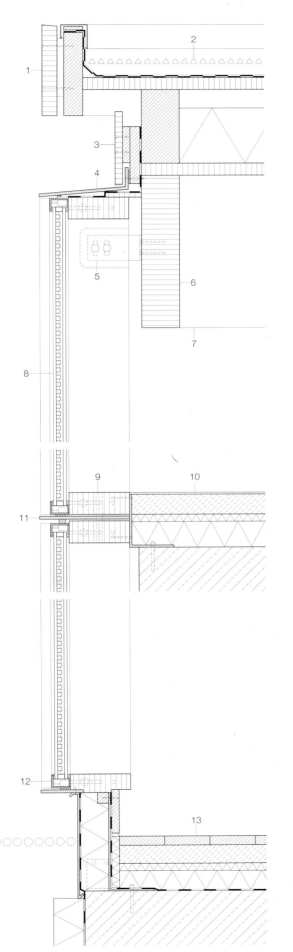

Vertical section
Horizontal section
scale 1:10

1 40/250 mm Douglas fir fascia
2 50 mm broken glass topping
   two-layer bituminous sealing
   membrane
   33 mm laminated timber sheeting
   ventilated cavity and
   150 mm thermal insulation between
   100/200–320 mm softwood joists
   to falls
   30 mm three-ply laminated sheeting
3 20 mm three-ply laminated sheeting
4 8 mm sheet-aluminium covering on
   moisture-diffusing sealing layer
5 150/70/6 mm steel fixing bracket
6 100/420 mm laminated Douglas
   fir beam
7 160/420 mm laminated Douglas
   fir beam
8 double glazing:
   2× 8 mm toughened glass with
   dark-red meranti grille in
   18 mm cavity (11/11 mm horizontal

bars with 9 mm spacings;
10/10 mm vertical bars with
500–600 mm spacings)
9 60/160 mm laminated Douglas
   fir beams with
   Ø 24 mm aluminium connectors;
   fixed with dowels
10 5 mm linoleum
    55 mm screed
    20 mm impact-sound insulation
    70 mm insulation slab
    320 mm reinforced concrete
    floor slab
11 240/8 mm aluminium plate
12 45/35/4 mm aluminium angle
13 25 mm parquet
    50 mm screed
    20 mm impact-sound insulation
    50 mm thermal insulation
    5 mm bituminous sealing layer
14 62/30 mm Douglas fir fixing strip
    treated with resin oil

cc

Vertical section
scale 1:10

1 50 mm broken glass topping
two-layer bituminous sealing
membrane
33 mm laminated timber
sheeting
ventilated cavity and
150 mm thermal insulation
between
100/200–320 mm softwood
joists to falls
30 mm three-ply laminated
sheeting
100/420 mm laminated
Douglas fir beams
2 160/150 mm softwood plate
3 8 mm sheet-aluminium
covering on
moisture-diffusing sealing
layer
4 440/50 mm laminated
Douglas fir rail
5 380/70/6 mm steel fixing
bracket
6 160/420 mm laminated
Douglas fir beam
7 Ø 194/10 mm tubular steel
column filled with concrete
8 double glazing:
2× 6 mm toughened glass
+ 16 mm cavity
9 380/40 mm laminated
Douglas fir rail treated
with resin oil
10 70/8 mm aluminium flat
11 40/150 mm three-ply Douglas
fir fascia strip
12 45/35/4 mm aluminium angle
13 top-hung glazed flap:
95/95 mm Oregon pine frame
treated with resin oil
14 2 mm aluminium sheeting
50/34 mm battens
sealing membrane
16 mm three-ply laminated
sheeting

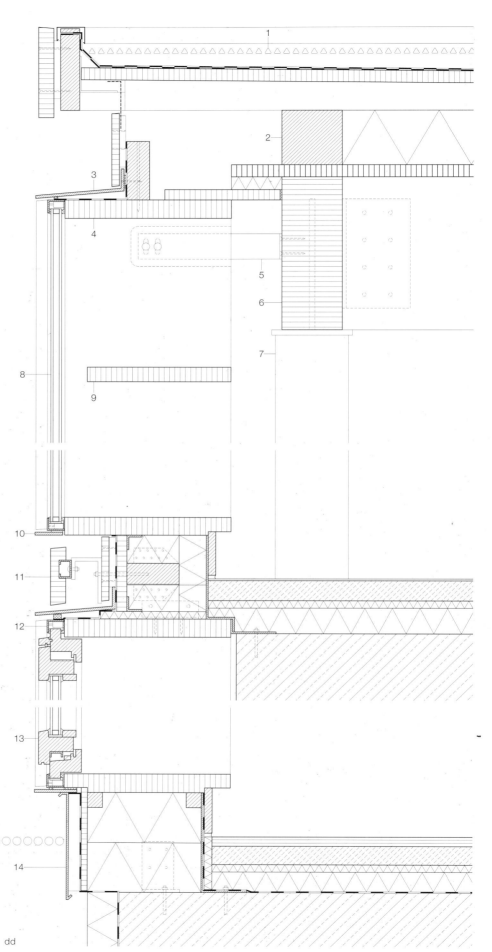

dd

Laban Centre in London

Herzog & de Meuron, Basle

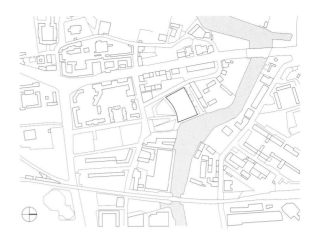

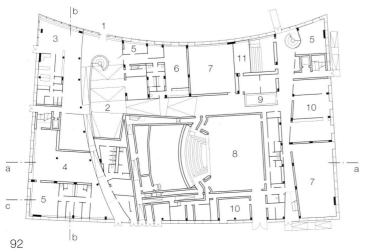

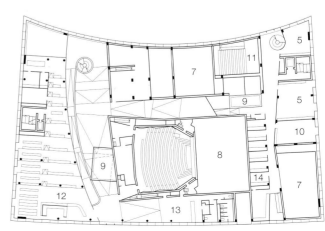

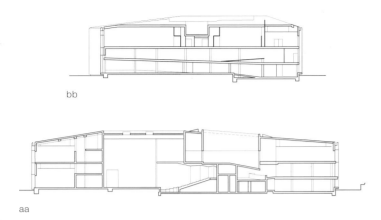

bb

aa

Site plan
scale 1:10,000

Floor plans · Sections
scale 1:1000

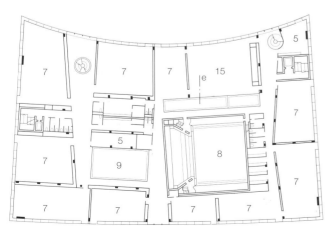

1 Entrance
2 Foyer
3 Café
4 Therapy
5 Office
6 Staff room
7 Studio
8 Theatre
9 Light well
10 Workshop
11 Lecture hall
12 Library
13 Bar
14 Teachers' room
15 Studio theatre

The Laban Centre is one of the largest institutions for modern dance in Europe. Named after Rudolf Laban, the famous choreographer and pioneer of dance, it is situated among warehouses and workshops on a tributary of the Thames in Deptford, southeast London. The large volume of the building is well integrated into its surroundings, although the somewhat unreal, floating quality lent by the shimmering facades distinguishes the centre from the neighbouring developments. The structure is enclosed in a double-skin facade with a 60 cm ventilated cavity between the two layers. The outer skin, which provides thermal insulation and acts as a visual screen, consists of polycarbonate sheeting – either transparent or in different colour tones. The coloured coating was applied to the rear face of the inner layer, lending this skin a pastel-like, three-dimensional effect. The inner skin consists largely of translucent double glazing. Movement and communication, two central aspects of the dance centre, are also themes of the architecture. The concave, curved entrance facade seems to embrace the external space in a sweeping gesture. Internally, too, the building suggests a state of movement. Ramps and circulation routes lead through the complex layout of rooms and broaden into open spaces. Light wells allow daylight to penetrate into the deep volume of the building and establish visual links through the centre. The transparent and translucent walls have more of an articulating than a separating function. Within this open "cityscape", the colours form a visual aid to orientation. Walls and inbuilt fittings in the corridors are coloured bright turquoise, green and magenta. In contrast, the dance studios have a more restrained design. Here, panes of obscured glass filter the incoming light. A single room-height window in each studio space allows a view out to the surroundings. The double-skin facade creates a subtle reciprocity between inside and outside: the colours of the facade panels shimmer internally, while externally, one sees the shadowy forms of the dancers in the evening. DETAIL 7/8 2003

1 plastic roof sealing layer
50 mm polyurethane thermal
insulation
2 anodized aluminium ventilation
louvres
3 2 mm anodized alum. sheeting
4 triple-layer transparent
polycarbonate hollow cellular
slabs (40/500 mm) with
coextruded coloured rear face
5 55/80 mm anodized
aluminium frame for 4

6 50/50/4 mm aluminium SHS
anti-suction anchor
7 60/60/4 mm steel angle
8 100 mm rock-wool thermal
insulation, grey coated
9 80/80/4 mm galvanized
steel SHS rail
10 80/80/4 mm galvanized
steel SHS post
11 50/120 mm aluminium
RHS post
12 50/60 mm aluminium RHS rail

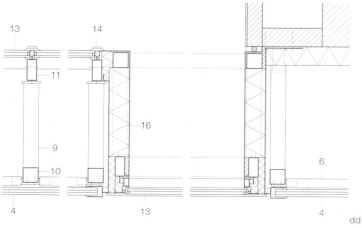

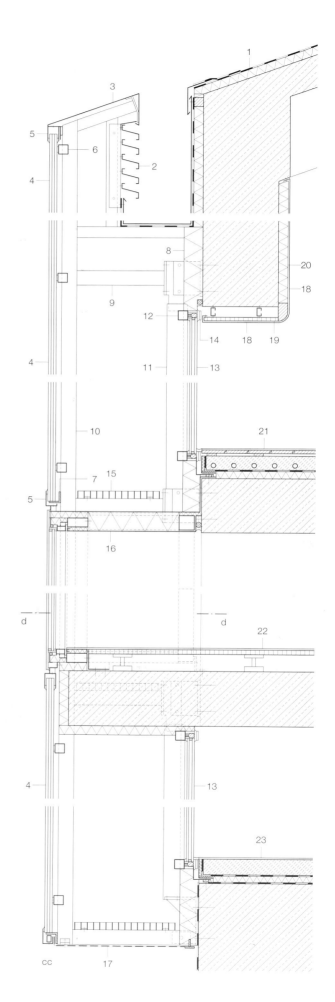

dd

cc

13 double glazing:
    10 mm toughened glass +
    16 mm cavity + lam. safety
    glass (2× 6 mm) with
    matt film
14 Ø 60 mm aluminium clamping
    plate
15 40 mm galvanized steel grating
16 100 mm insulated
    aluminium panel
17 2 mm perforated aluminium
    sheeting

18 fabric wall lining
19 20 mm plywood
20 50 mm sound insulation
21 studio floor construction:
    5 mm vinyl flooring
    2× 9 mm plywood sheeting
    20 mm elastic bearers
    77 mm screed around
    underfloor heating
    separating layer
    40 mm impact-sound
    insulation

22 library floor construction:
    10 mm carpeting
    18 mm plywood sheeting
23 office floor construction:
    10 mm carpeting
    85 mm cement-and-sand
    screed
    separating layer
    25 mm polystyrene insulation
    sealing layer
24 50/165 mm aluminium RHS
25 rainwater channel

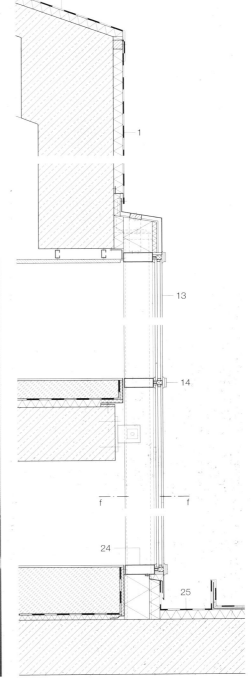

ee

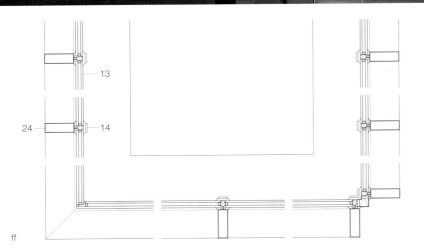

ff

With the aid of aluminium framing, it was possible to set the outer face of the double glazing to the windows flush with the surface of the polycarbonate sheets, which are coloured on the rear face. In conjunction with the inner skin of translucent insulating glazing, a two-layer ventilated facade was created.

The courtyards, or light wells, with conventional double-glazed, post-and-rail facades, allow daylight to penetrate to the interior of the building.

Horizontal sections • Vertical sections
South facade
Courtyard facade
scale 1:20

Horizontal sections
scale 1:5

1 double glazing: 10 mm toughened
   glass + 16 cavity + lam. safety
   glass (2× 6 mm) with matt film
2 Ø 60 mm aluminium clamping plate
3 50/120 mm aluminium RHS post
4 80/80/5 mm galvanized steel SHS
5 40 mm galvanized steel grating
6 Ø 6 mm steel cable
7 50/50/4 mm aluminium SHS
   anti-suction anchor
8 80/80/5 mm galvanized steel SHS
   post
9 5 mm transparent perspex sheet,
   bent to shape and adhesive
   fixed to 10

10 3 mm transparent perspex sheet,
    bent to shape
11 triple-layer transparent
    polycarbonate hollow cellular slabs
    (40/500 mm) with coextruded
    coloured rear face
12 80/40/7 mm steel T-section
13 5 mm sheet steel
14 2 mm anodized aluminium sheeting
15 aluminium section reinforced with
    2× 23/172 mm steel sections
16 double glazing: 10 mm toughened
    glass + 16 mm cavity + lam.
    safety glass (2× 6 mm) adhesive
    fixed with silicone

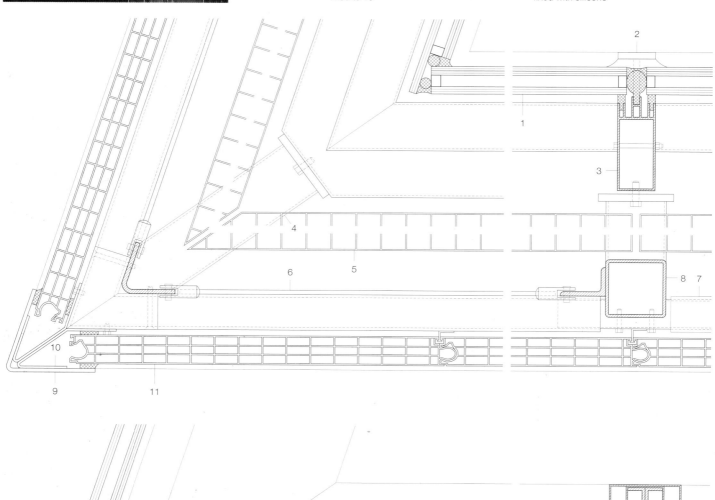

1:16

Weekend House in Australia

Sean Godsell Architects, Melbourne

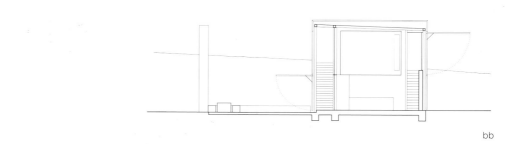

bb

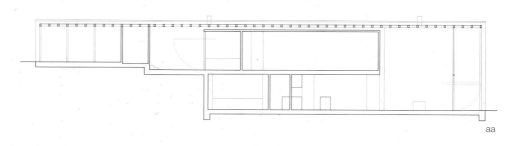

aa

Situated in the midst of natural surroundings, this weekend house stands on a hillside site on the south coast of Australia. At first glance, the structure has the appearance of a simple box with a homogeneous wood-strip facade. Only on closer investigation does it reveal its complexity. Set within the timber skin is a steel-and-glass volume. On the north and east faces, the space between the core structure and the outer enclosure is used as a covered veranda. Here, the house can be opened by sliding aside glass doors and pivoting up large areas of the wood skin into a horizontal position.

The spatial programme is as simple as the geometry of the building, with the living room, the bedroom and the library forming the main spaces. The two-storey living room is completely glazed on its north side and is thus open to the sunshine over its full height. The lower part of this face can be raised in an up-and-over movement like a garage gate. The bedroom is a closed cube suspended over the living room, thus echoing the idea of a space within a space. Hard native jarrah was used for the outer wood strips, which are of very slender cross-section, so that the enclosing skin appears virtually transparent from a certain angle. At the same time, it serves to filter the incoming light; and with the changing position of the sun, interesting lighting effects are created both internally and externally. DETAIL 7/8 2003

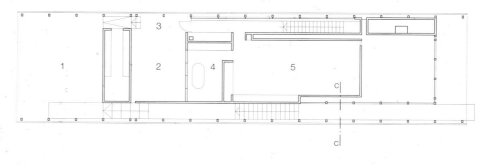

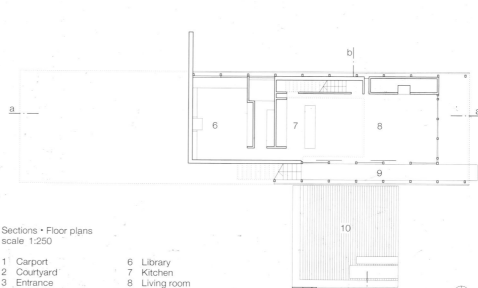

Sections · Floor plans
scale 1:250

1 Carport
2 Courtyard
3 Entrance
4 Bathroom
5 Bedroom
6 Library
7 Kitchen
8 Living room
9 Veranda
10 Terrace

98

Horozontal section
Vertical section
scale 1:20

1 35/10 mm sawn jarrah strips
2 30/30 mm galvanized steel SHS
3 10 mm toughened glass
4 100/150 mm preoxidized steel RHS
5 8 mm laminated safety glass
6 bedroom wall construction:
   10 mm plasterboard
   70 mm glass-wool thermal insulation between
   90/45 mm timber studding
   10 mm plasterboard
7 steel I-beam 300 mm deep
8 floor construction:
   70/19 mm ash boarding, adhesive fixed
   100 mm reinforced concrete floor slab
   bed of gravel
9 terrace construction:
   70/19 mm pine boarding on bearers
   80 mm reinforced concrete slab
   bed of gravel
10 wall construction:
    1.2 mm preoxidized steel sheeting
    25/40 mm battens
    190 mm concrete hollow block walling
    (390/190/90 mm)
    25/40 mm battens
    1.2 mm preoxidized steel sheeting

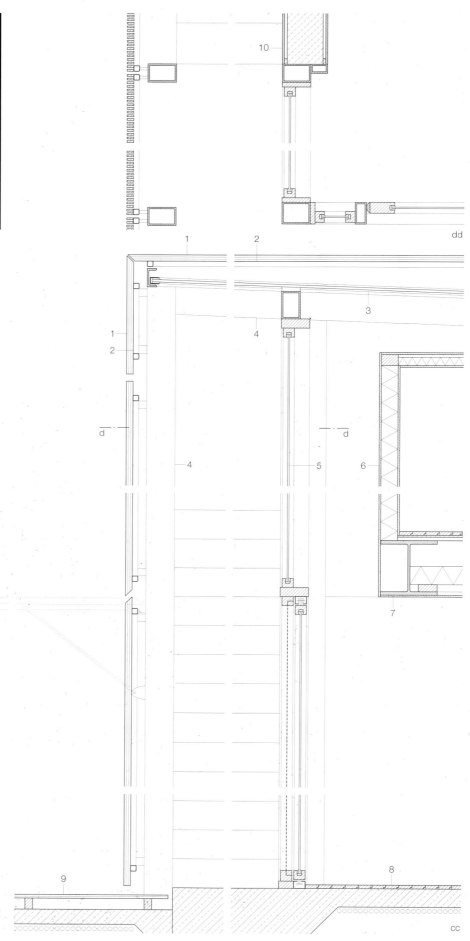

Administration Building
in Reutlingen

Allmann Sattler Wappner, Munich

The administrative headquarters of an employers' federation for metalworking trades in Germany comprises three distinct volumes. With their characteristic double-pitched roofs, similar eaves heights, facade widths and depths, they are typologically well integrated into the existing small-town environment. The unusual design of the building skin strikes a different note, however. Drawn over the facades and roof is a homogeneous, seamless layer of bead-blasted steel sheeting. The tactile and visual qualities of the resulting surfaces seem unfamiliar: the material adopts the colours of the sky and the surroundings, reflecting them and lending the outer skin an intangible depth. Even

the individual volumes are difficult to apprehend, since nowhere is there an indication of the material thickness – not at the corners, the eaves or verges, nor around the window openings. The casements, without visible frames, are set back slightly in a second plane behind the metal facade and are shaded by centrally controlled perforated elements. In a closed position, the windows seem to fit flush with the facade. They are opened by sliding the two halves upwards and downwards behind the outer metal skin. Even the linings to the entrance doors are integrated into the facade pattern of the plinth zone so as to be scarcely noticeable outside opening hours.

The striking three-metre-high plinth storey is clad with square steel sheets in which large-scale leaf motifs have been cut. The sheets also extend as pavings across the open spaces around and between the three buildings. As a result, the ground seems to fold upwards at the foot of the blocks, determining their position on the site like metal sleeves. Behind the perforations in the sheeting, the glazed ground floor facades and the interiors of the buildings are vaguely perceptible. Green vegetation sprouts through the areas cut out of the plates on the ground. Where access is provided to the outdoor realm, the openings are closed off with concrete.   DETAIL 7/8 2003

Site plan
scale 1:2000
Sections · Floor plans
scale 1:750

1 Canteen
2 Entrance hall
3 Store

4 Basement garage ramp
5 Continuous floral pattern over 3,164 stainless-steel sheets
6 Office
7 Discussion space

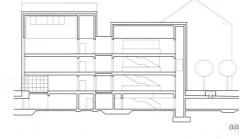

aa

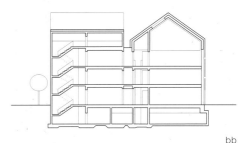

bb

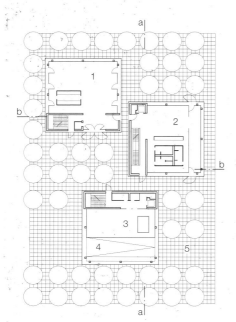

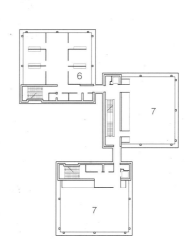

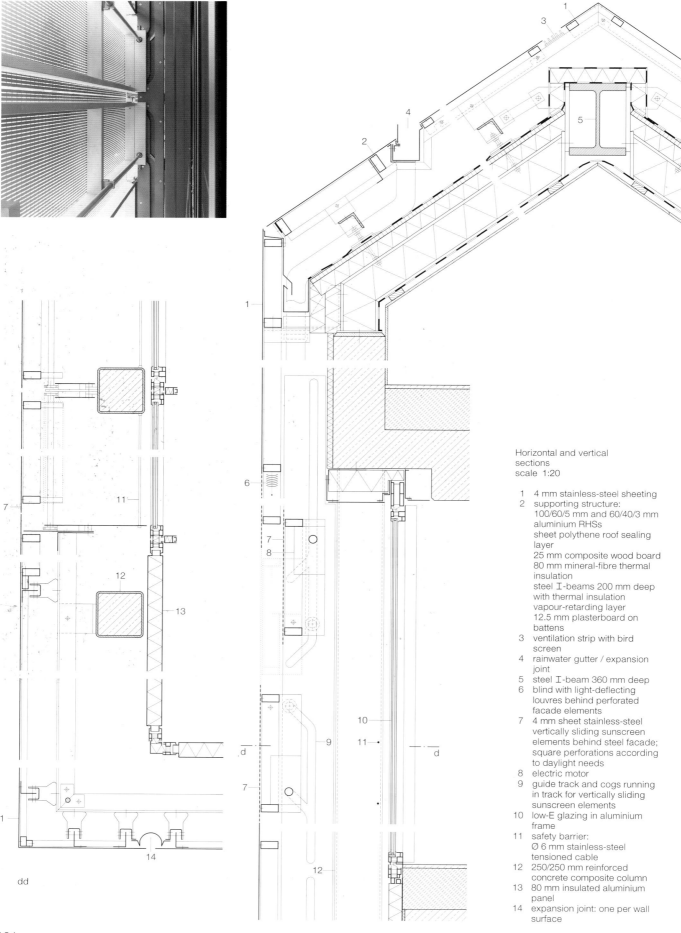

Horizontal and vertical
sections
scale 1:20

1 4 mm stainless-steel sheeting
2 supporting structure:
  100/60/5 mm and 60/40/3 mm
  aluminium RHSs
  sheet polythene roof sealing
  layer
  25 mm composite wood board
  80 mm mineral-fibre thermal
  insulation
  steel I-beams 200 mm deep
  with thermal insulation
  vapour-retarding layer
  12.5 mm plasterboard on
  battens
3 ventilation strip with bird
  screen
4 rainwater gutter / expansion
  joint
5 steel I-beam 360 mm deep
6 blind with light-deflecting
  louvres behind perforated
  facade elements
7 4 mm sheet stainless-steel
  vertically sliding sunscreen
  elements behind steel facade;
  square perforations according
  to daylight needs
8 electric motor
9 guide track and cogs running
  in track for vertically sliding
  sunscreen elements
10 low-E glazing in aluminium
  frame
11 safety barrier:
  Ø 6 mm stainless-steel
  tensioned cable
12 250/250 mm reinforced
  concrete composite column
13 80 mm insulated aluminium
  panel
14 expansion joint: one per wall
  surface

dd

1   4 mm bead-blasted stainless-steel sheets
    1,500 mm wide with laser-cut vertical abutments,
    bolted to supporting structure in compression
    joints; milled to mitre at eaves and verge;
    with one large thermal-expansion joint per
    wall surface

2   Ø 6 mm threaded bolt 14 mm long
    welded to 1

3   40/60/3 mm steel RHS

4   5 mm steel plate

5   60/90/6 mm steel angle for hanging facade
    sheeting on 6

6   Ø 14 mm threaded bolt

7   100/100 mm steel angle

8   730/730/5 mm sheet stainless steel blasted
    with special-grade corundum; with laser-cut
    ornamentation

9   60/60 mm steel SHS with 40/5 mm steel flat
    insert for fixing ornamental sheets

10 facade bracing / abutment piece for
    lightweight partition

Details of sheet abutment   scale 1:5
Sections through plinth storey   scale 1:20

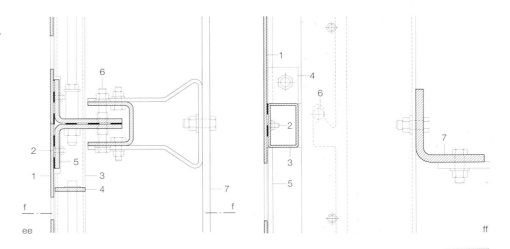

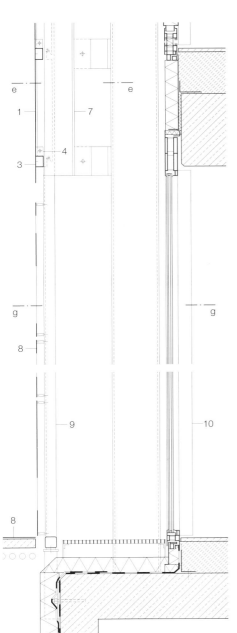

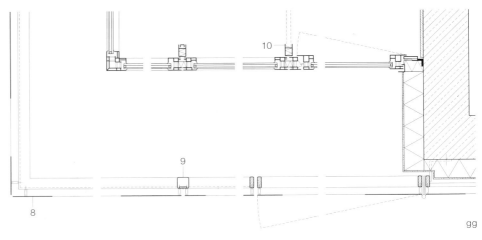

Production Building for Large-Scale Printing Technology in Grosshöflein

querkraft architects, Vienna

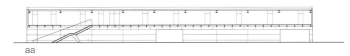

aa

Section
Floor plans
scale 1:750

1 Parking area
2 Store
3 Printing shop
4 Manufacturing area
5 Car hire
6 Entrance
7 Reception
8 Staff offices
9 Management
10 Staff room

How does a company that prints large-scale banners for cultural events and advertising purposes present itself to the world? For its new works building in Austria, the Trevision concern deliberately chose a location next to an autobahn. Coming from the direction of Vienna at night, one sees the 300 m² rear-lit image of a mountain panorama projected on to a translucent screen, while the rear face of the building bears the 60-metre-long slogan "Unoverlookable" printed on a net covering that can be illuminated from above. Completed in June 2002, the structure was conceived outwardly as an illuminable box. In view of the bold appearance thus created, a further company logo was regarded as un-

necessary. At the instigation of the client, the operation of the lighting effects was to form part of an international art project organized by the Museum in Progress in Vienna. The motifs are designed by modern artists and are changed every year.

Just as important as the external appearance, of course, was an optimum functioning of the production process, with short routes and scope for flexibility and future change. Access to the office area is via a concrete staircase element of sculptural appearance, while the flow of materials on the ground floor follows a circular route.

Since the high-frequency welding process can result in surge voltage that might affect

the sensitive printing machines, it was necessary to separate the two areas functionally and acoustically without marring the sense of spaciousness. This was achieved by drawing a scarcely perceptible transparent plastic sheet across the width of the hall. The easternmost bay of the building is divided off by a metal panel wall and forms a discrete unit that can be leased out separately. The open layout allows the available space to be adapted to the changing needs of the concern. The building still stands alone on an open site. When further structures are erected in the future, restricting the view out from the interior, the screen-like, filtering effect of the net facade will reveal its true significance.   DETAIL Konzept 9/2003

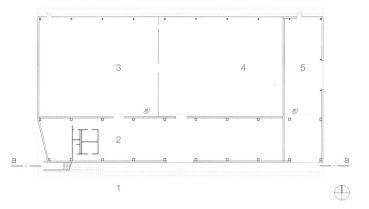

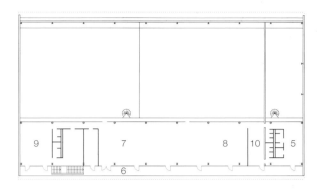

The Client's View

My concept for the new works building was clear from the start. It was to have a striking appearance that would distinguish it from the usual corrugated-metal box form; and employees working in the production hall were to enjoy the same status as those in the offices. I visited several established architects with an initial sketch, but the concepts they presented were so conventional that we decided to invite a number of younger architects to submit proposals. The querkraft office surprised us at first with the many questions it asked relating to the functions and needs of the concern, which in turn stimulated a lively discussion among the staff. At

a certain point, it became clear that querkraft was not going to design a run-of-the-mill building. We therefore clarified certain issues with the local authority and with neighbours long before actually submitting the scheme for approval. This greatly eased later negotiations and the process of gaining building permission. Once the basic design decisions had been made, we gave the architects a free hand in the detailing, without losing sight of cost parameters, of course. The mechanical services were minimized for economical reasons. Suction apparatus was installed directly next to the printing machines to remove vapours. Ventilation is effected via windows and roof lights in the

hall and via flaps over the office doors. No heat-load calculation was made, and the interior heats up more than expected on warm afternoons. To overcome this, we shall install additional small, decentralized appliances in the facade. The relatively small radiatiors, on the other hand, have proved to be wholly adequate. The outcome has fully confirmed our expectations. Not only has productivity increased; the building has evidently made quite a mark publicly, judging by the client's prize it was awarded in 2002 and the numerous requests we receive to view it.

Heinz Wikturna, the author, is senior head of the Trevision company.

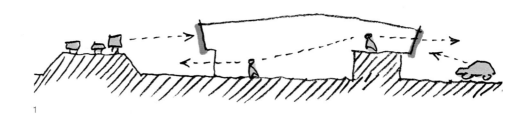

1

The Search for an Efficient Performance Profile

At our first meeting with the client, he presented us with a layout sketch for a new works building. It comprised a head structure for the administration and an adjoining production hall. Although we had no previous experience of industrial construction, our identification with the project soon earned us the client's trust. As the name Trevision implies, there is a dominant visual aspect to the products made at the works. The sight lines within the hall and to the outside world were, therefore, of central importance (ill. 1). By accommodating all departments beneath a single roof, we also resolved any contradiction that may have existed between the goal of achieving social equality among the various sections of the staff, and the creation of a separate head structure for the administration. The height of the hall was fixed at seven metres. This is higher than necessary for present production purposes, but it facilitates future growth and extensions and increases the value of the building by providing scope for other uses. The basic outline and layout of the building and the accommodation of the working processes in the architectural form were resolved in close collaboration with the client (ill. 2).

The preliminary design foresaw a 7-metre construction grid with a vertical poster area in front of every structural axis, creating a rapidly changing, staccato-like sequence of images for vehicles passing on the autobahn. To the rear of this, a planted strip within the hall was to filter the view to the road (ill. 2a). Access was to be via one of the end faces. The concept underwent various stages of development. The axial grid dimension was increased to 8 m for the submission in August 2001 (ill. 2c), and the changes that followed were so drastic that, after completion of the work, it was necessary to redraw the scheme entirely in order to obtain final planning approval. During the bills of quantities phase, we abandoned the idea of an additive tubular access route and accommodated the circulation behind a net screen in the main section of the building (ill. 2d).

Changes to the grid dimensions were still being made during the negotiation of contracts, since different manufacturers worked with systems of different unit sizes. A grid dimension of 6.20 m was finally determined. One way of ensuring efficiency in the cross-sectional form is to accommodate a number of functions in each part of the building. This can save space and money by eliminating the need for additional structures.

The cantilevered element over the deliveries area provides protection against the weather, accentuates the entrance situation and creates a covered recreational area for the staff. It is also a means of sunshading the glazed office facade, and it supports the

nets that act as a visual screen. Last, but not least, it forms an effective piece of corporate design. An internal counterpart to the mesh is the walkway between the administration tract and the production hall. Fixed on the underside of this strip, are cable runs. The main functions of the walkway, though, are to provide a short route between the offices and the hall areas, and to allow the effects of the large printed objects to be judged from a greater distance.

1   View from the director's office to the vehicle approach zone and into the hall
2   Optimization of the cross-section

The authors are Jakob Dunkl, Gerd Erhartt, Peter Sapp and Michael Zinner, querkraft architects.

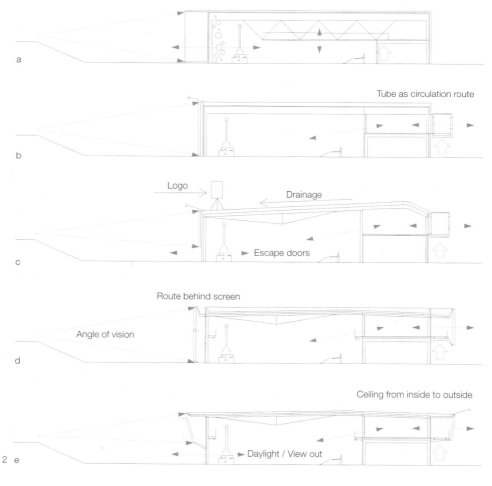

a

Tube as circulation route

b

Logo   Drainage

Escape doors

c

Route behind screen

Angle of vision

d

Ceiling from inside to outside

Daylight / View out

2 e

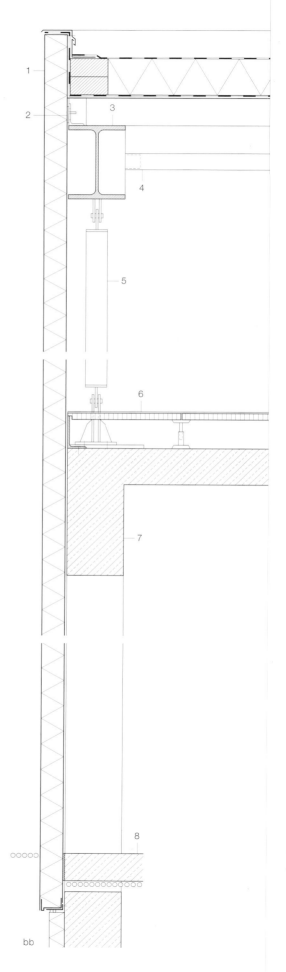

bb

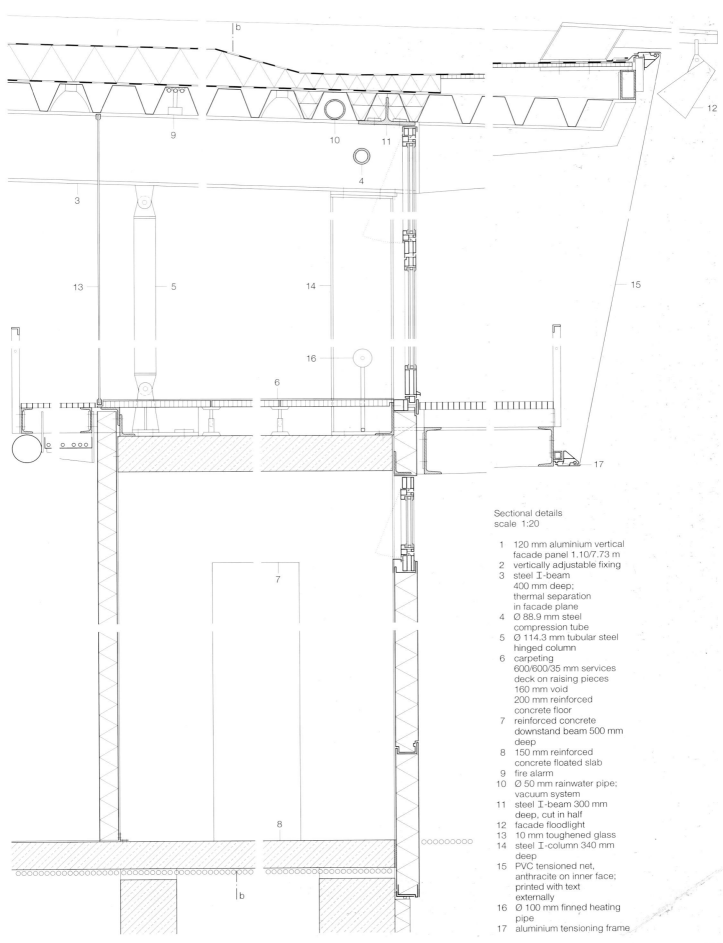

Sectional details
scale 1:20

1   120 mm aluminium vertical
    facade panel 1.10/7.73 m
2   vertically adjustable fixing
3   steel I-beam
    400 mm deep;
    thermal separation
    in facade plane
4   Ø 88.9 mm steel
    compression tube
5   Ø 114.3 mm tubular steel
    hinged column
6   carpeting
    600/600/35 mm services
    deck on raising pieces
    160 mm void
    200 mm reinforced
    concrete floor
7   reinforced concrete
    downstand beam 500 mm
    deep
8   150 mm reinforced
    concrete floated slab
9   fire alarm
10 Ø 50 mm rainwater pipe;
    vacuum system
11 steel I-beam 300 mm
    deep, cut in half
12 facade floodlight
13 10 mm toughened glass
14 steel I-column 340 mm
    deep
15 PVC tensioned net,
    anthracite on inner face;
    printed with text
    externally
16 Ø 100 mm finned heating
    pipe
17 aluminium tensioning frame

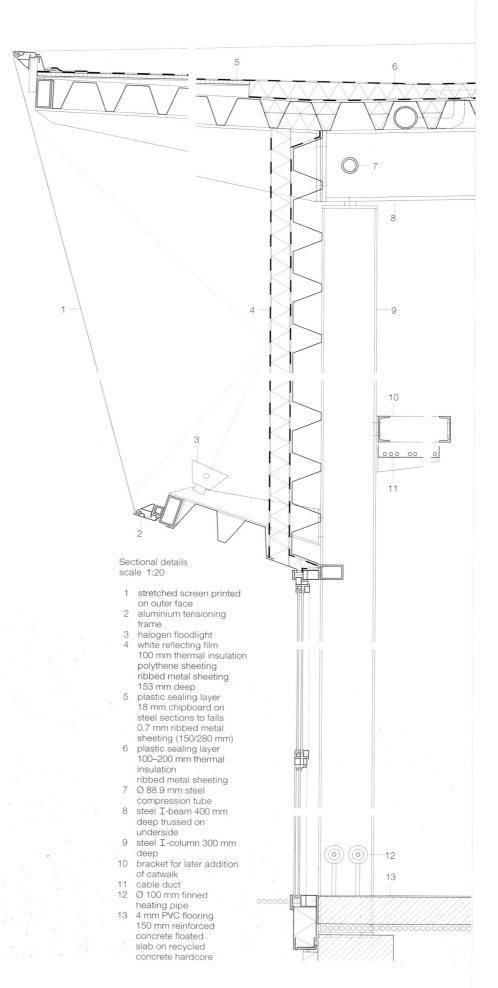

Transparency and Cost Management – the Facades

The printed translucent screen facing the autobahn is indirectly lighted by halogen lamps shining on a white reflecting layer on the wall of the hall. To avoid causing glare for drivers, the maximum illuminance is 100 lux. In order to create the requisite visual links and a sense of open space, the glazing had to be as transparent as possible.

The division between the offices and the hall is in toughened glass as a safety measure for the walkway on the hall side. Jointed with silicone, however, the glazing is scarcely perceptible. The printed net to the south facade filters the view out to the landscape in a soft-focus manner. Only when seen from an oblique angle is the net visible (ill. p. 110). A reinforced concrete structure was specified to provide an economical form of fire resistance (1 1/2 hours). The load-bearing columns are visible only through the upper clerestory window strips. By setting the column axes at 6.20-metre centres, the structural strength of the ribbed metal sheeting was exploited to the full, thereby avoiding the need for secondary beams. Other savings included the omission of additional metal angles and bracing tubes in fixing the windows. For the closed facade areas, we also specified the cheapest metal panels on the market. The cost limits were, in fact, so tight that we had to use standard coloured panels instead of the pure white ones originally proposed. The number and size of the domed roof lights were also reduced to save costs. Even cheap building materials, however, can be used in an architecturally satisfying way, with minor modifications sometimes leading to quite individual solutions. The omission of the cover strips, for example, and the special treatment of the sheet abutments and corner details helped to create a building skin of distinctive character. Additional costs were incurred for the hall flooring, where it was necessary to lay PVC instead of leaving the concrete with a smooth finish as originally planned.

Erwin Sattler, a freelance assistant with querkraft architects, was the project architect for the Trevision scheme.

Sectional details
scale 1:20

1   stretched screen printed on outer face
2   aluminium tensioning frame
3   halogen floodlight
4   white reflecting film
100 mm thermal insulation
polythene sheeting
ribbed metal sheeting
153 mm deep
5   plastic sealing layer
18 mm chipboard on steel sections to falls
0.7 mm ribbed metal sheeting (150/280 mm)
6   plastic sealing layer
100–200 mm thermal insulation
ribbed metal sheeting
7   Ø 88.9 mm steel compression tube
8   steel I-beam 400 mm deep trussed on underside
9   steel I-column 300 mm deep
10   bracket for later addition of catwalk
11   cable duct
12   Ø 100 mm finned heating pipe
13   4 mm PVC flooring
150 mm reinforced concrete floated slab on recycled concrete hardcore

Extension of the Albertina in Vienna

Erich G. Steinmayr & Friedrich H. Mascher,
Feldkirch / Vienna

The ensemble of buildings known as the Albertina, an urban palace dating from the 18th century, houses one of the largest collections of graphic art in the world. Over the past ten years, the complex has been extended and has undergone a comprehensive restoration. A new exhibition hall, a store and an adjoining study building with workshops and a library have been inserted in the listed ensemble between the Burggarten and the Hofburg in a form that is scarcely visible from the outside. The elevated position of the Albertina on the city bastions was exploited to accommodate the large new volume. By sinking the extension structures four storeys into the ground, it was possible to leave the historical silhouette of the complex unchanged. The former fortifications in front of the Albertina were removed, and in their place an underground exhibition hall and store were built. The study building opens on to a newly excavated internal courtyard. The courtyard facade – the only visible face of the new structure – differs on each of its three storeys in accordance with the internal uses. The face of the in-house study hall at courtyard level comprises room-height transparent panes of glass. On the floor above, fixed sunshading elements in front of the set-back line of the glazing prevent direct insolation of the restoration workshops. The top floor, containing the study hall for external visitors, receives additional light via roof lanterns, which alternate with aluminium louvres to create a clearly articulated roof area. The study building is divided in the middle by a three-metre-wide glass-covered light well that extends over the four storeys of this tract and allows daylight to penetrate to the library at the lowest level. Adjoining the study building is the store with an automatically operated high-bay system. The third new element, the exhibition hall, is directly linked with the Albertina Palace by escalators. These lead to the Albertina Court, a glass-covered central space that serves as a circulation area between the main entrance, the historical rooms, the exhibition hall and the café and museum shop.

DETAIL 10/2003

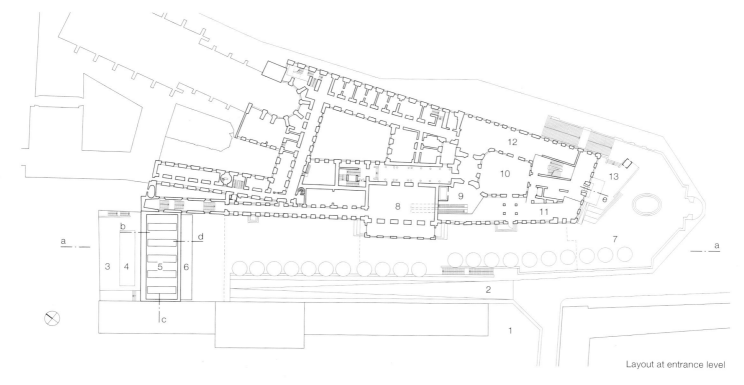

Layout at entrance level

Layout plans · Section
scale 1:1250

1	Burggarten	5	Study building	9	Escalators to new exhibition hall
2	Pedestrian ramp	6	Light well in study building	10	Albertina courtyard
3	Courtyard	7	Bastions	11	Café
4	Water pool	8	Existing exhibition hall	12	Museum shop

13	Entrance to Albertina	16	High-bay store
14	Film museum	17	Store for large-scale works
15	Study hall for visitors	18	Exhibition hall
		19	Access for visitors

	to study hall	
20	Restoration workshops	
21	Study hall	
22	Library	

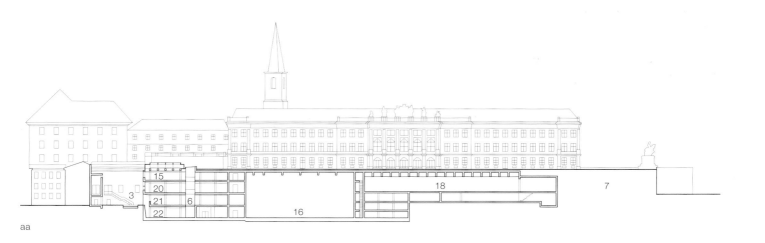

aa

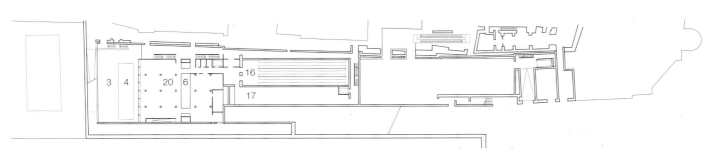

First basement level

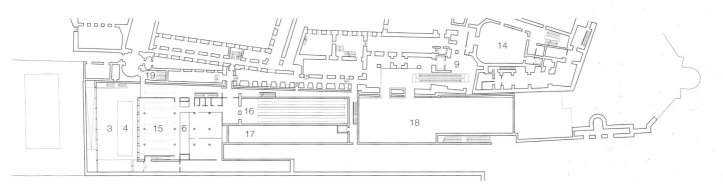

Second basement level

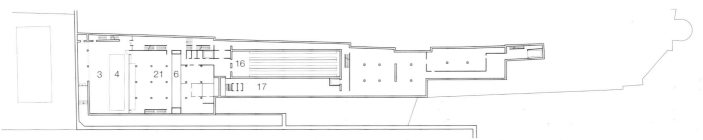

Third basement level

Section through
courtyard facade
scale 1:20

1   3 mm black-anodized aluminium sheeting
2   120 mm insulated aluminium panel
3   double glazing: 6 mm toughened glass + 8 mm
    cavity + 6 mm toughened glass with enamelled
    inner face
    100 mm thermal insulation
    2 mm aluminium sheeting
4   low-E glazing (U = 1.1 W/m²K): 6 mm toughened
    flint glass + 24 mm cavity with sunblind + 6 mm
    toughened flint glass
5   60/150 mm natural-anodized aluminium RHS
    post-and-rail structure; 60/15 mm black-anodized
    aluminium cover strips
6   3 mm natural-anodized aluminium fascia to
    air-conditioning plant
7   25 mm natural-anodized aluminium cellular
    sunshading with black-anodized aluminium
    anti-reflection sheeting on side exposed to sun
8   30 mm natural-anodized aluminium sunshade
    grating
9   slide-down, push-out aluminium casement:
    6 mm low-E laminated flint glass with black
    enamel edge + 16 mm cavity + 6 mm laminated
    flint glass adhesive fixed
10 3 mm natural-anodized sheet-aluminium
    light deflector
11 3 mm natural-anodized sheet-aluminium
    light-deflector fin with integrated lighting

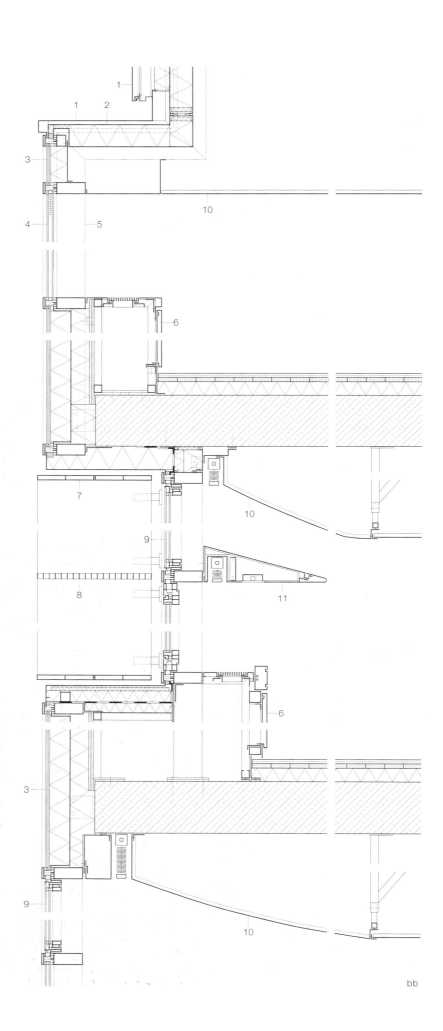

bb

116

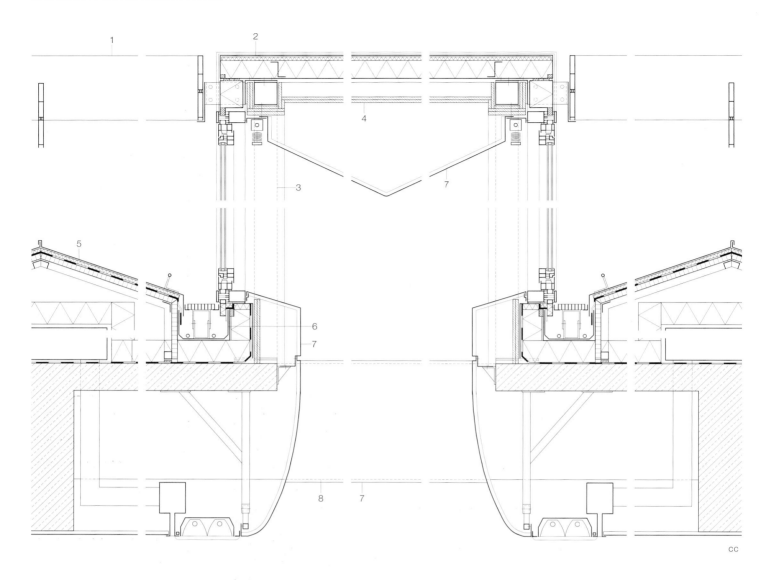

Vertical sections
through roof lantern
and light-well facades
scale 1:20

1   350/25 mm grey-coated aluminium cellular
    sunshading louvres
2   120 mm black-anodized insulated aluminium panel
3   120/120/5 mm steel SHS lantern structure
4   2x 15 mm gypsum sheeting (1 1/2 hr. fire resistance)
5   3 mm natural-anodized sheet aluminium
    1 mm anti-drumming mat
    24 mm PVC rigid-foam insulation
    plastic sealing layer; 30 mm three-ply lam. sheeting
    40/40/4 mm steel SHS bearers
6   0.8 mm stainless-steel gutter with heating
7   3 mm natural-anodized sheet-alum. light deflector
8   350/650 mm reinforced concrete beam
9   double glazing: 10 mm toughened flint glass +
    12 mm cavity + lam. safety glass (2× 8 mm)
10 glass fin bearer: 3× 10 mm toughened glass in
    60/50/4 mm aluminium channel
11 Danube limestone coping, bush-hammered
12 60/110 mm aluminium post-and-rail construction
    (1/2 hr. fire resistance)
13 fire-resisting double glazing (1/2 hr.):
    6 mm toughened flint glass + 15 mm fire-resisting
    gel + 6 mm toughened flint glass
14 fire-resisting double glazing (1/2 hr resistance) to
    balustrade and edge of floor: 6 mm toughened flint
    glass + 15 mm fire-resisting gel + lam. safety glass
    (2× 6 mm) with 2× matt-white films
15 glass floor: 3-layer lam. safety glass (36 mm) with
    matt-white films; upper layer with non-slip surface
    60/120/5 mm steel RHS supporting structure
    fire-resisting glazing to underside (1/2 hr.):
    6 mm toughened flint glass + 15 mm fire-resisting gel
    + lam. safety glass (2× 6 mm) with matt-white film

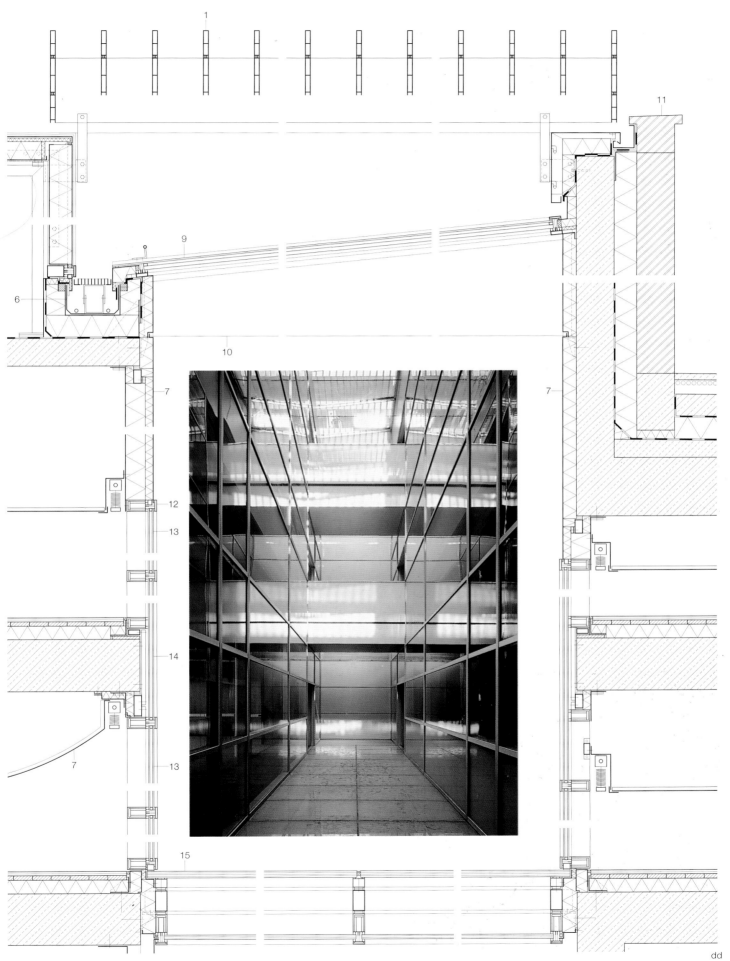

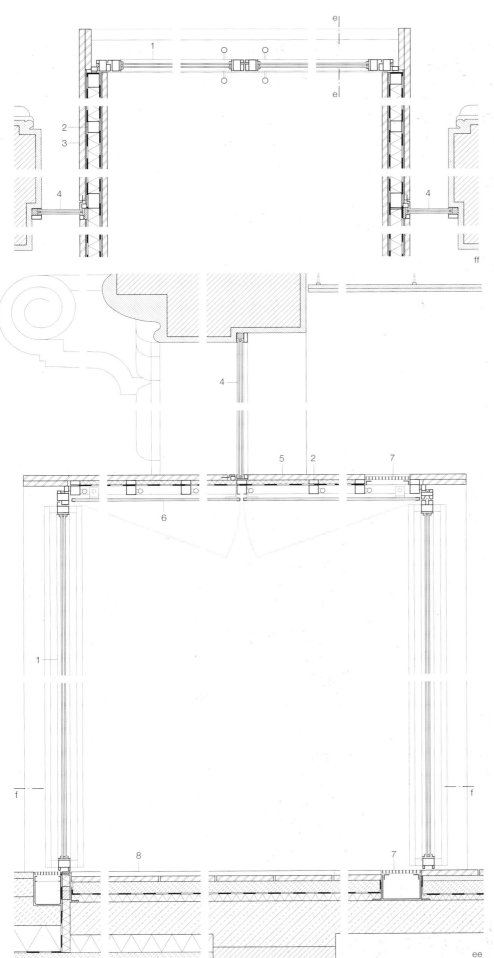

Horizontal and vertical sections
through draught-excluding lobby
scale 1:20

1 glass door in black-burnished stainless-
    steel frame:
    double glazing: 8 mm lam. safety glass +
    16 mm cavity + 6 mm toughened glass
    Ø 30 mm black-burnished stainless-steel tubular
    door pull
2 70/70/4 mm steel SHS
3 30 mm travertine cladding 900/300 mm
    polythene sealing layer
    90 mm rock-wool insulation
    30 mm Rosso Lepanto marble cladding
    2,600/900 mm
4 fixed double glazing: 8 mm lam. safety glass +
    16 mm cavity + 6 mm toughened glass
5 30 mm travertine lining
6 light-diffusing soffit:
    lam. safety glass (2× 3 m) with satin finish
7 2,000/200 mm stainless-steel ventilation grating
8 16 mm mesh dirt trap
    20 mm stone paving
    57 mm reinforced mortar bed
    10 mm bituminous sealing layer
    50 mm polystyrene rigid-foam thermal insulation
    180 mm reinforced concrete floor slab

Studio Extension in Olot

Jordi Hidalgo + Daniela Hartmann,
Barcelona

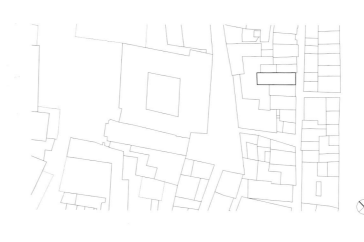

The scheme involved the refurbishment of a small rear courtyard in the old town centre of Olot in north-eastern Catalonia, Spain. Over the years, the 6 × 5 m area had become cluttered with various structures that had to be removed before the extension could be inserted. The measures comprised the construction of a flat glass roof over an existing gym to provide natural lighting, and the erection of a studio and sauna on top. In addition, a small private patio was to be created between the existing living quarters and the extension. The greatest problem was that the work had to be executed within a period of two months, and it was not possible to use a crane. The load-bearing structure and the roof over the extension were constructed first. The courtyard was provisionally covered and the roof light installed over the gym. Only then was it possible to begin removing the old accretions hand in hand with the erection of the new elements. The contrast between the puristic, glazed studio and the neighbouring buildings could hardly be greater. Nevertheless, the extension, with its smooth glass surfaces and simple metal roof, is well integrated into the surroundings. DETAIL 10/2003

aa

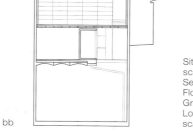

bb

Site plan	1	Existing
scale 1:2000		building
Sections	2	Patio
Floor plans	3	Roof light
Ground floor	4	Washroom
Lower ground floor	5	Sauna
scale 1:250	6	Studio

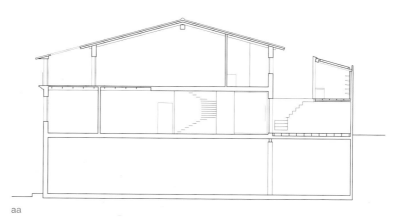

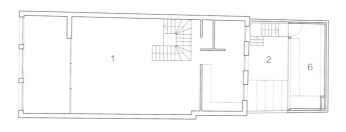

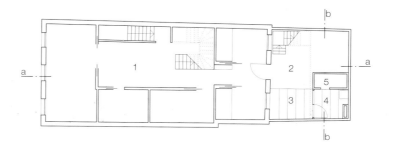

Diagrams
A Initial state
B Development process
during construction
C Finished state

A

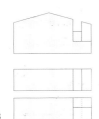

B

C

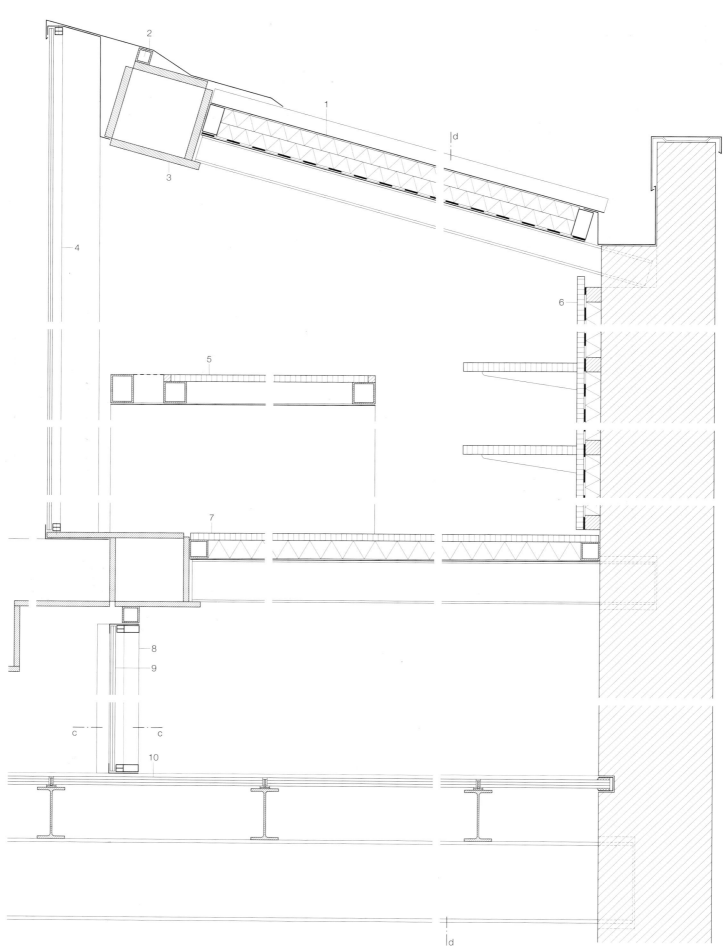

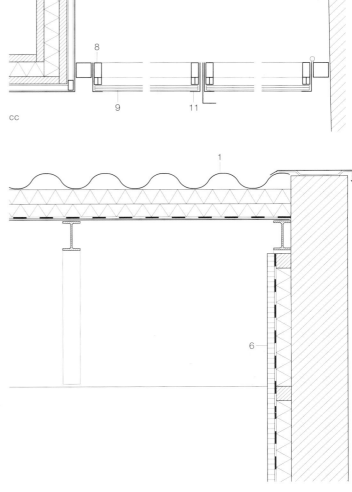

cc

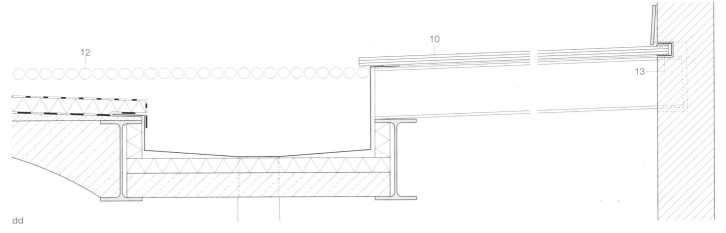

Vertical sections
Horizontal section
scale 1:10

1 0.6 mm corrugated galvanized
steel sheeting
80 mm thermal insulation
vapour barrier; 2 mm sheet steel
steel I-beams 80 mm deep
2 40/40/1.5 mm steel SHS
3 hollow section:
20 mm steel plates
4 2× 20/10/2 mm steel RHSs
5 19 mm medium-density
fibreboard
50/50/2 mm steel SHSs and

80/50/2 mm steel RHSs with
2 mm sheet steel
6 19 mm MDF on vapour barrier
40 mm insulation between battens
existing wall
7 19 mm chipboard
50 mm thermal insulation between
50/50/2 mm steel SHSs
2 mm sheet steel, painted
steel I-beams 120 mm deep
8 40/20/1 mm steel RHS
9 lam. safety glass (2× 6 mm)

10 lam. safety glass (3× 6 mm) with
25/25 mm steel T-sections on
steel I-sections 140 mm deep
11 2 mm sheet steel bent to shape
12 layer of gravel; geotextile layer
40 mm insulation
EPDM sealing layer
screed finished to falls
(max. 50 mm)
concrete composite floor slab with
steel I-beams 220 mm deep
13 40/40 mm steel channel section

dd

House in Mont-Malmédy

ARTAU SCRL, Malmédy
Norbert Nelles, Luc Dutilleux

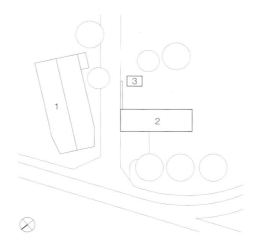

Situated on the outskirts of a village near a nature reserve in the Ardennes, Belgium, this house was built as a second home for a family of six. It stands opposite an old farmhouse and was designed to look like one of the outbuildings. By using simple forms and a minimum of materials, however, the narrow, elongated structure has its own bold and quite distinctive character.

The random rubble outer skin consists of locally quarried reddish schistose sandstone. Various other features add to the sense of rhythm and the lively appearance of the building envelope. These include the wall in the same stone extending from one of the narrow ends of the house; the small, deeply recessed windows; the untreated concrete surfaces around the sliding copper gate; and the steeply pitched copper-covered roof. In time, the copper and the sandstone will gradually colour the concrete. With its through-driveway and garden wall, the building reflects many elements of the local rural style. These are arranged to form a sheltered courtyard flanked on the opposite side by a small outhouse. In contrast, the extensive glazing in the double-height living-dining area opens the interior to the extensive grounds. The other rooms are grouped on two levels around this central space. The fluid transitions to the more private parts of the house are achieved without doors: the various realms are separated by partitions and by flights of stairs, which also extend the floor finish from the living area to the upper storey. Further zoning is achieved

through the size and depth of the window openings: the more private the space, the smaller and deeper they are. In this way, an exciting contrast is established between the rough-textured exterior of the house and the smooth, white interior, which radiates a sense of security.   DETAIL 11/2003

Site plan	1	Old farmhouse	Kitchen
scale 1:1000	2	New house	6 Master bedroom
Section •	3	Store	7 Bedroom
Floor plans	4	Bathroom/WC	8 Void
scale 1:250	5	Living room/	9 Gallery/Lounge

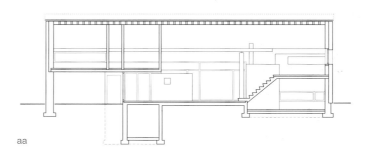

aa

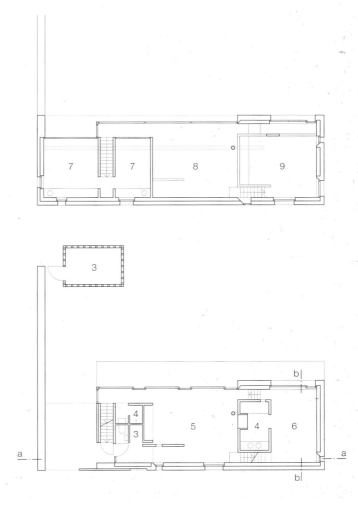

House in Mont-Malmédy

Section   scale 1:250
Vertical sections
scale 1:20

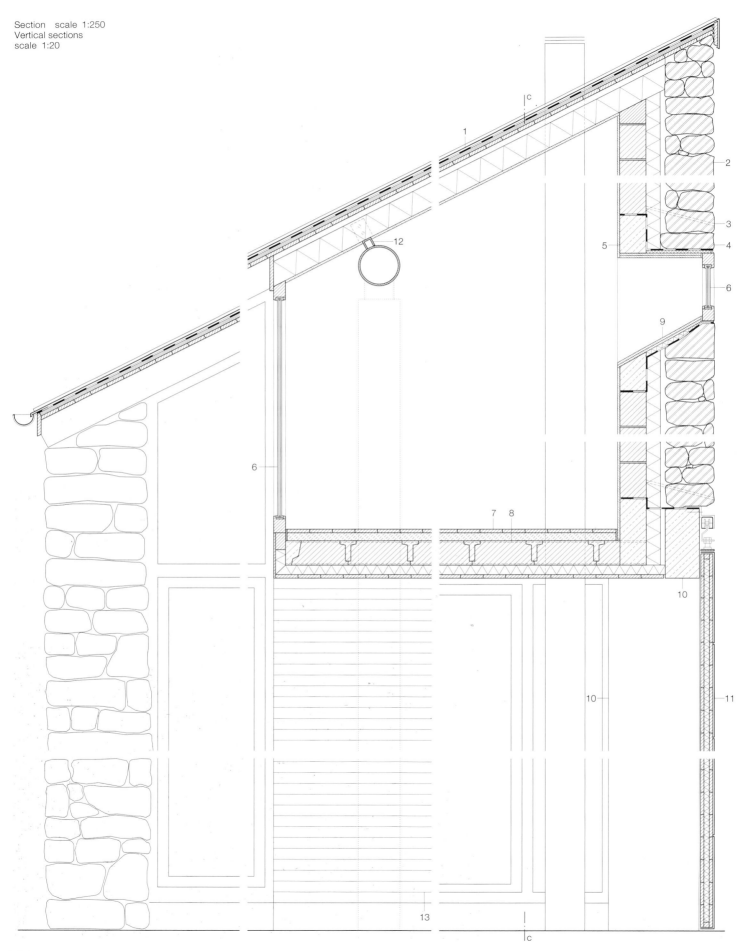

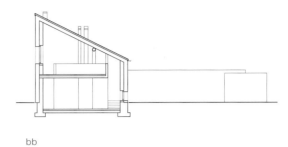

bb

1 sheet-copper roofing with welted seams
roof sealing layer
battens and counter-battens
120 mm thermal insulation between
70/150 mm rafters at 400 mm centres
12.5 mm plasterboard
2 260 mm sandstone rubble walling
25 mm ventilated cavity
75 mm thermal insulation
140 mm blockwork
15 mm plaster
3 wall tie
4 rubble stone lintel
5 reinforced concrete lintel
6 double glazing in cedar frame
7 20 mm untreated fir boarding on pugging
120 mm hollow clay blocks
50 mm rock-wool thermal insulation

20 mm wood soffit boarding
8 steel I-beam 160 mm deep
9 2× 12.5 mm plasterboard
30 mm polyurethane thermal insulation
separating layer
10 untreated exposed concrete surface
11 sliding gate:
copper sheeting
18 mm boarding
40 mm supporting structure with
rock-wool thermal insulation
18 mm boarding
12 50/50 mm steel channel section welded
to Ø 219.1/7.1 mm tubular steel beam
13 untreated fir cladding on supporting
structure
14 40 mm foamed-glass thermal insulation
on bed of mortar

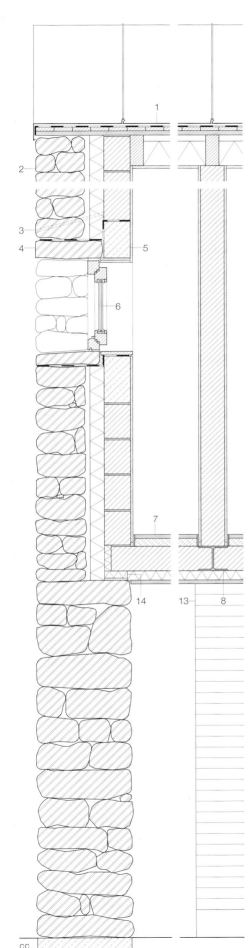

Representation of the States of Brandenburg and Mecklenburg-West Pomerania in Berlin

Gerkan, Marg und Partner, Hamburg

After the fall of the Berlin Wall, plans were made to put the area formerly known as the "Ministerial Gardens" north of Leipziger Platz to a new use in keeping with its political tradition. After the war, this heavily bombed site lay on the border between East and West Berlin. It was cleared in 1961 and redeveloped on the eastern side in the 1980s with blocks of housing in concrete panel construction. In 1993, new planning proposals were drawn up for the area: the representations of all 16 German Länder were to be accommodated in 12 separate structures on the southern part of the site.
Some of the states subsequently took up residence in older buildings in Friedrich-

stadt, but new structures were erected for the other missions. The building for the states of Brandenburg and Mecklenburg-West Pomerania was laid out in the form of two offset L-shaped tracts linked by a common central hall with a glass roof. On the west side, a lower volume containing a space for meetings and lectures extends out into the garden. Open terraced areas punctuated by stakes for climbing plants mediate between the gardens and the building. The ground floor discussion spaces at the two ends are glazed over their full height and appear almost to have been carved out of the solid structure. The various functions of the complex are clearly articulated from storey

to storey, with the offices of the two state missions housed above ground floor level. This clear layout allows good public access in spite of security requirements. The two restaurants on the lower ground floor can be reached from the hall and from the gardens. The facades of the two main tracts are clad in natural-cleft slate slabs arranged in a strict pattern, with the wood casement elements forming a lively contrast. The position of the marine-plywood panels varies according to the function to the rear. The horizontal lines of the parapet wall to the roof and the bands of stone over the edges of the floor slabs are set off against the vertical articulation of the concrete hall structure.   DETAIL 11/2003

1	Basement garage	8	Foyer		of Mecklenburg-
2	Restaurant	9	Hall		West Pomerania
3	Kitchen	10	Caretaker	13	Records office
4	Services	11	Offices	14	Executive offices
5	Changing room		of State of	15	Departmental
6	Store		Brandenburg		offices
7	Discussion space	12	Offices of State	16	Administration

Sections · Floor plans
scale 1:750
Basement
Ground floor
First floor

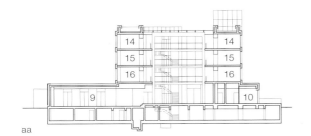

aa

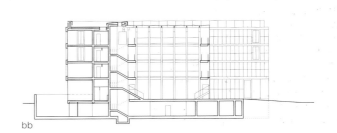

bb

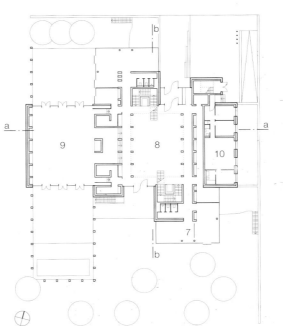

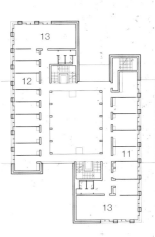

131

Vertical section
scale 1:20
Sectional details
scale 1:5

1 0.8 mm titanium-zinc sheet
   covering
2 40 mm natural-cleft slate slabs
   40 mm ventilated cavity
   120 mm rigid-foam thermal
   insulation
   300 mm reinforced concrete
   parapet wall
3 40 mm concrete paving slabs
   on bed of stone chippings
4 meranti window element with
   low-E glazing: 2× 6 mm float
   glass + 16 mm cavity

5 40 mm natural-cleft
   slate slabs with
   elastically sealed joints and
   stainless-steel anchors
   90 mm ventilated cavity
   120 mm mineral-wool insulation
6 burglar-resistant double
   glazing:
   12 + 30 mm laminated safety
   glass + 16 mm cavity
7 60/8 mm stainless-steel fixing
   strip with stainless-steel screws
8 2 mm sheet aluminium fascia
9 120/57/8 mm galvanized
   steel angle, welded in place
   after adjustment
10 recessed soffit fixing with
   anthracite coating

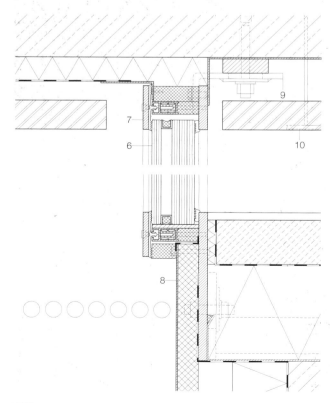

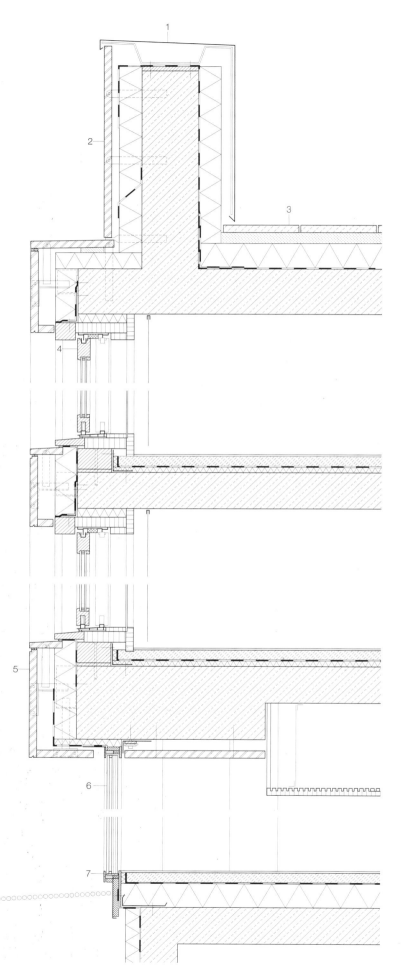

Isometric of slate cladding (not to scale)
Vertical and horizontal sections through facade
scale 1:10

1 40 mm natural-cleft slate slabs
   adhesive fixed at mitred arris
2 106/95 mm meranti strip
3 curtain strip
4 meranti lifting-sliding window
   with low-E glazing:
   2× 6 mm float glass + 16 mm cavity
5 10 mm laminated safety glass barrier
6 160/30–40 mm meranti sill, splay cut
7 170/30–40 mm slate window sill,
   splay cut
8 38 mm veneered composite wood
   board

9 shelf recess
10 12 mm marine plywood
   panel, with ventilated
   cavity to rear
11 external wall construction:
   40 mm natural-cleft slate slabs
   90 mm ventilated cavity
   120 mm mineral-wool insulation
   200 mm reinforced concrete wall
   74 mm bearers
   12.5 mm plasterboard
12 stainless-steel angle with
   anchor supports

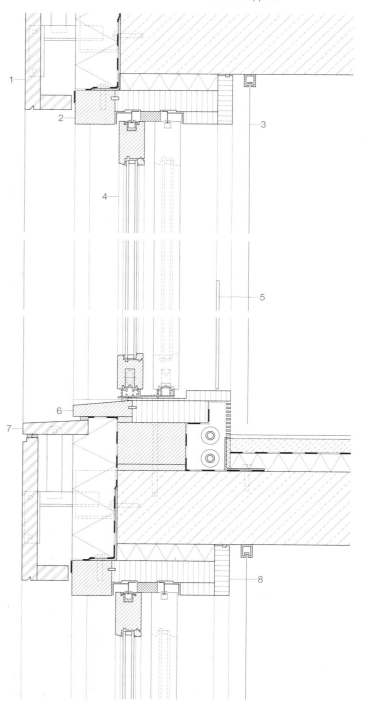

School Building in Zurich

Patrick Gmür Architects, Zurich

Increasing numbers of schoolchildren and the need to integrate new, team-oriented educational concepts into existing structures have forced the city of Zurich to enlarge the capacity of its schools. The Scherr school complex, situated on the Zürichberg, consisted of a central building dating from 1865 and two later sports halls erected in 1916 and 1973. With a compact extension in area and height at one corner of the 70s' gym, additional classrooms and common rooms have been created that double the teaching space of the original school building. The dense spatial layout of the new volume, into which the existing structure has been carefully integrated, has resulted in a reordering

and improvement of the urban situation. With its restrained appearance, supported by the facade design, the building now forms a counterpoint to the listed Oberstrass church nearby, without impinging upon it in any way. Internally, the spatial organization is based on urban models. The heart of the complex is no longer the playground, but a new central space, conceived as a kind of forum. The stairs and corridors laid out about this space are in the nature of indoor streets that widen to forecourts in front of the classrooms. In this city within a city, the boundary between public and private space is indicated by lighting and coloration. The calm design of the classrooms in white and grey

is contrasted with the bold pink, orange, yellow and blue of the corridors and stairs. The coloration, which reaches its climax in the central hall, lends the building a special identity. The architects and the artist sought to invent a pictorial world for children based on a unity of architecture and colour. To attain the expressive force of a picture, the colour space was built up – as in a painting – in layers that reveal not only the material quality of the concrete and the irregularities of the shuttering, but the brushwork as well. The concrete itself was not homogeneously coloured. Traditional acrylic-based Lascaux materials were applied on a white ground to achieve an intense coloration and great

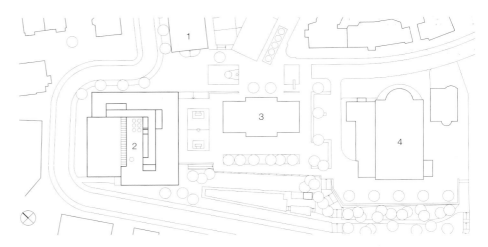

radiance. The tonal quality thus attained
is accentuated by the incidence of daylight,
which enters, sometimes indirectly, via the
numerous roof lights in the hall, accentuating
and changing the effects of the colours
and the character of the space. The compact external form of the building is thus
contrasted with the richness of the interior,
which is generated by the interplay of
space, colour and light.   DETAIL 12/2003

Site plan   scale 1:1500
Section • Floor plan
scale 1:750

1   Gymnasium (1916)
2   Gymnasium/School
    (1973/2003)

3   School building
    (1865)
4   Oberstrass church
5   Existing gymnasium
6   Hall
7   Classroom
8   Group room

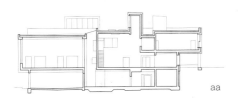

aa

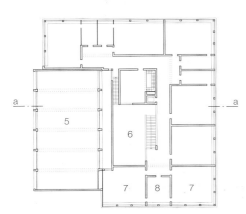

Housing and Commercial Block in Zurich

Marcel Meili, Markus Peter
Architects, Zurich, with Zeno Vogel
Astrid Staufer & Thomas Hasler
Architects, Frauenfeld

This centrally located building combines high-quality urban dwellings with cultural amenities. Set above a café and two cinemas are 14 spacious flats. The rendered facades are in the same style as those of the neighbouring buildings, but they are contrasted in colour and have a multilayered surface. The rich yellow or red outer coat of rendering was applied over a composite system of thermal insulation and brushed in different directions from bay to bay to create a varied surface texture. Finally, a unifying grey glazing coat was applied that tones down the intensity of the colours. The bold yellow of the window frames and reveals forms a striking contrast with the facade. The dwelling layouts seek to recreate the spatial sequences of rooms found in grand buildings of the past, while the lofts are designed in an open style. Situated on the street face are the large living rooms; the smaller working spaces and bedrooms are on the courtyard side. The kitchens and bathrooms reveal a new interpretation: here, the cooking areas and bathtubs are located in internal recesses.   DETAIL 12/2003

Site plan
scale 1:3000
Floor plans
scale 1:500

1   Living room
2   Study/Bedroom
3   Roof terrace
4   Café/Lounge
5   Box office
6   Void over foyer
7   Cinema

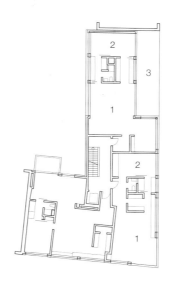

Third floor

Roof storey

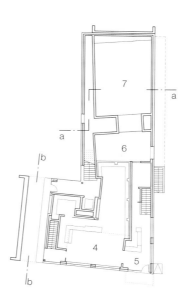

Ground floor

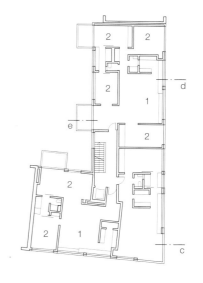

First and second floors

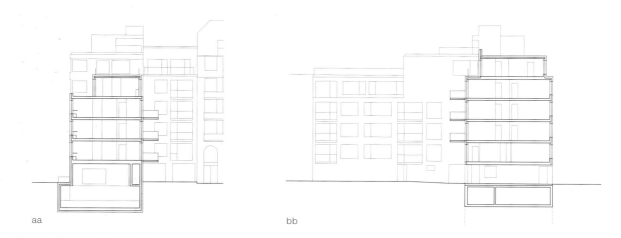

aa   bb

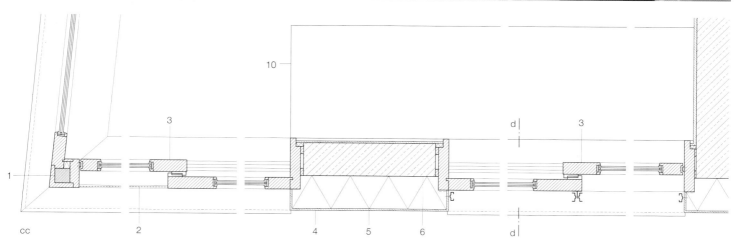

cc   2   4   5   6   d

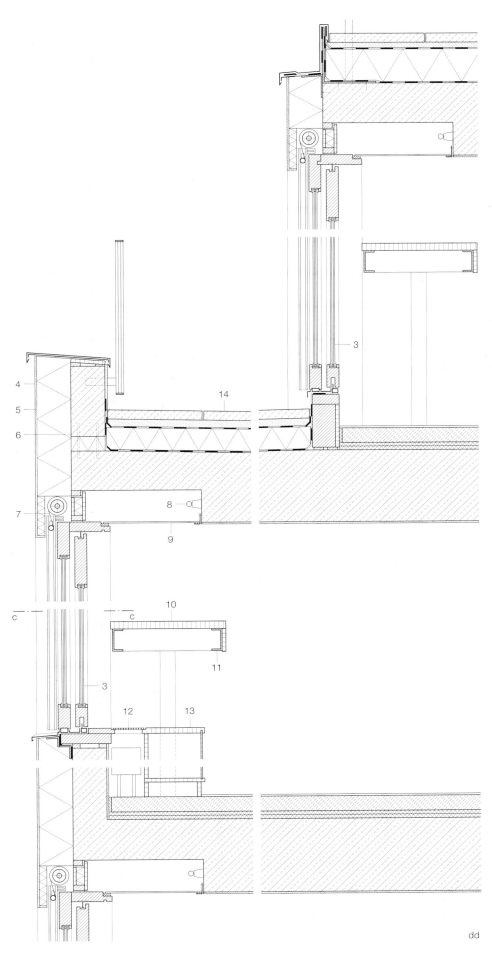

Sections
scale 1:500

Horizontal section
Vertical section
scale 1:20

1   80/80 mm steel column
2   safety barrier: stainless steel mesh
3   sliding door with softwood frame and
    double glazing: 2× 6 mm toughened
    glass + 16 mm cavity (U = 1.0 W/m²K)
4   5 mm rendering:
    grey silicone-resin glaze coat applied
    with roller
    finishing coat of plastic-modified mineral
    plaster (1.5 mm grain), coloured red and
    yellow in alternate bays; horizontally and
    vertically brushed
    glass-fibre mesh fabric reinforcement
    in mortar
5   180 mm polystyrene rigid-foam
    thermal insulation
6   180 mm reinforced concrete wall
7   fabric roller sunblind
8   fluorescent tube
9   6 mm white-opal perspex on
    60/30/50/2 mm natural-anodized
    aluminium angle
10 30 mm three-ply laminated sheeting:
    solid African mahogany strips, oiled
11 120 mm steel channel section
12 expanded-steel mesh radiator cover,
    painted
13 upstand fitting:
    20 mm MDF sheeting, painted
14 inverted roof construction:
    40 mm pigmented concrete paving
    slabs 700/500 mm
    50 mm bed of stone chippings (3–6 mm)
    moisture-diffusing plastic separating
    layer
    120 mm extruded polystyrene rigid-foam
    thermal insulation
    two-layer bituminous sealing membrane
    430–400 mm reinforced concrete slab
    to falls
    10 mm gypsum plaster, painted white

dd

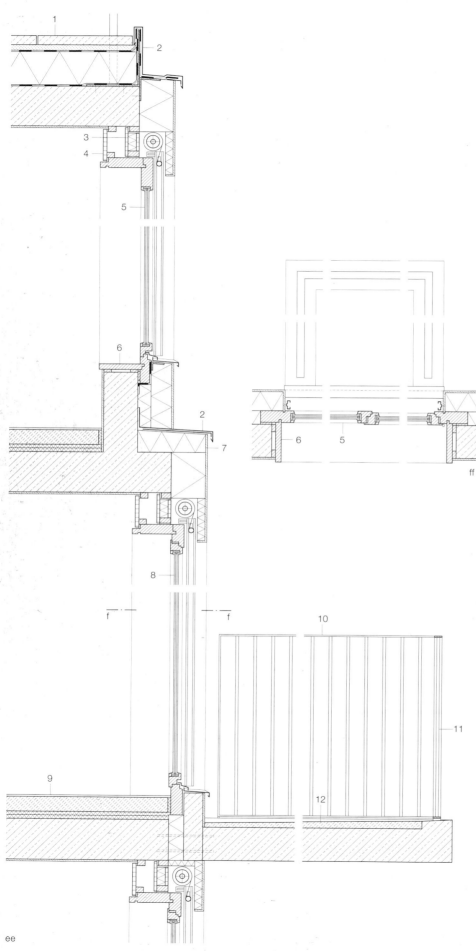

Sections through courtyard facade
scale 1:20

1 inverted roof construction:
   40 mm pigmented concrete paving
   slabs 700/500 mm
   50 mm bed of stone chippings (3–6 mm)
   moisture-diffusing plastic separating
   layer
   180 mm extruded polystyrene rigid-foam
   thermal insulation
   two-layer bituminous sealing membrane
   430–400 mm reinforced concrete slab
   to falls
   10 mm gypsum plaster, painted white
2 stainless-steel sheeting
3 sandwich slab: polystyrene rigid-foam
   slab between 20 mm composite wood
   boards
4 20 mm composite wood board
5 fixed double glazing in softwood frame:
   2× 6 mm toughened glass +
   16 mm cavity (U = 1.0 W/m^{2}K)
6 220/25 mm softwood sill painted yellow
7 foamed-glass insulation splayed on top
8 door with double glazing in softwood
   frame: 2× 6 mm toughened glass +
   16 mm cavity (U = 1.0 W/m^{2}K)
9 floor construction:
   3 mm poured coloured polyurethane
   finish
   80 mm screed
   20 mm impact-sound insulation
   20 mm polystyrene rigid-foam
   thermal insulation
   400 mm reinforced concrete floor slab
10 40/8 mm galvanized steel flat handrail
11 15/15 mm galvanized steel balusters
12 balcony slab:
   45–25 mm granolithic paving to falls
   180 mm reinforced concrete

ff

ee

technology

High-Performance Concretes

Wolfgang Brameshuber

Improved performance

Concrete technology has undergone a constant process of development over the past 50 years. Today, it provides engineers and architects with a broad range of possibilities in terms of both structural and formal design. In office construction, for example, high-strength concrete offers scope for saving space by reducing the dimensions of the load-bearing structure and thereby increasing the rentable floor area. This type of concrete also allows the construction of building elements that have a great resistance to weathering, that are durable and that, in certain circumstances, can protect the environment against harmful liquids. Today, new types of concrete are available that mark a considerable advance on normal concrete in terms of their strength and ductile behaviour. It has been possible, for example, to increase the compressive strength by a factor of 10. In addition to purely technological developments, there has also been a great increase in the use of cementitious elements in composite forms of construction. Of special interest in this respect is the creation of fibre-reinforced and textile-reinforced concrete. Fibre-reinforcement, for example, has helped to improve the ductile properties of concrete. Indeed, in certain situations, such as load-bearing walls in housing construction, fibres can replace conventional steel rod reinforcement. Glass-fibre-reinforced concrete is mostly used for slender constructional elements, e.g. roof coverings, shell structures, facade slabs and sunshading fins.

Textile-reinforced concrete is a logical development of glass-fibre-reinforced concrete, since it allows the direction of the load-bearing reinforcement to be controlled, in contrast to the random arrangement of reinforcing fibres. With textile-reinforced concrete it is possible to create extremely thin and lightweight elements, which have a great potential in architectural design. The development of self-compacting concrete marks a quantum leap in processing techniques. The properties of this type of concrete afford virtually unlimited scope for design in terms of unit geometry and surface treatment.

Costs

The materials used in high-performance concrete usually mean that it is considerably more expensive than normal concrete. Depending on the application, an increase in the cost of the initial constituents ranging from 50 to as much as 200 per cent or more may be expected. These figures are related to a cubic metre of concrete, however, so that the additional costs may be offset in part by reductions in the cross-sectional dimensions of elements and the resulting increase in rentable space. Furthermore, additional sealing measures may become superfluous with dense types of concrete; and in the case of self-compacting concrete, there will be savings in the amount of processing and subsequent treatment and in remedial work, such as making good small defects. A calculation of the additional costs and savings should be made in each individual case. Only with a sustainable approach can an objective analysis of the ultimate costs can be obtained.

High-strength concrete

High-strength concrete has a long tradition both at home and overseas. With extremely low water/cement ratios (below 0.4) and with the addition of pozzolana, highly reactive additives such as powdered silica or metakaolin, a compressive strength of up to 150 N/mm^2 can be achieved in practice (compared with a strength of 20–50 N/mm^2 for standard concrete). The potential reduction in the cross-section of a member through the use of high-strength concrete instead of standard concrete is shown diagrammatically in ill. 2. Assuming the same amount of reinforcement and the use of C70/85 concrete, the cross-section could be reduced by 30 per cent. In many situations, a reduction in the amount of reinforcement may be required instead, in order to facilitate the execution of the work (ill. 2). In most cases, however, a solution will be sought

1 Slender members of a bridge in reactive-powder concrete, Quebec, Canada [1]
2 Potential reductions through the use of high-performance concretes (strength grades C35/45 and C70/85, in accordance with German standards)
3 Seonyu footbridge, Seoul: ultra-high-strength, self-compacting, prestressed concrete with steel fibre reinforcement; heat treatment of formwork; VSL-INTRAFOR Group, Subingen, Switzerland
4 Section through footbridge, scale 1:70; the superstructure is only 30 mm thick
5 Optimization of wall thicknesses in an office building, using high-strength concrete (shaded black)

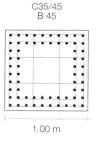
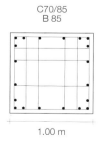
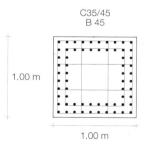
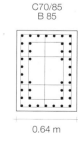

C35/45 B 45	C70/85 B 85	C35/45 B 45	C70/85 B 85
1.00 m	1.00 m	1.00 m	0.64 m
max. N = 21 MN μ = 4.0 % 64 È 28	max. N = 21 MN μ = 1.23 % 20 È 28	max. N = 21 MN μ = 4.0 % 64 È 28	max. N = 21 MN μ = 4.0 % 40 È 28

2

between these two extremes. A situation in which high-strength concrete can be used in optimum form is shown in ill. 5, where the design study for an office building with a mushroom-shaped form is shown. Only by using this type of concrete was it possible to keep the thickness of the walls on the lower floors within reasonable limits. With concrete of standard strength, a wall thickness of about 2 m with a very large amount of reinforcement would have been necessary. It was possible to reduce the thickness to roughly 1.40 m and to use only a moderate amount of reinforcement. Nevertheless, for walls of this thickness, it is necessary to reduce the cement content to well below normal levels and to add pulverized fuel ash (PFA) to the mix. Preliminary trials allowed the appropriate combination of cement and PFA to be determined in order to avoid deleterious cracking through the discharge of the heat of hydration. In Germany, solutions of this kind require a special certification from the relevant state planning authorities. Even with the use of an optimum concrete mix, however, newly constructed concrete elements still need appropriate subsequent curing to prevent heat escaping too quickly. In view of the very low water/cement ratio and the use of pozzolanic additives, high-strength concrete is not only strong, but also dense. Both properties can be exploited in areas like bridge-building, where highly

durable concrete is required to ensure long life as well as slender cross-sectional dimensions. Increasingly slender superstructures continue to enhance the impressions of bridges.

Where harmful liquids are used in buildings such as clinics, hospitals or chemical laboratories, additional measures will be necessary to protect the ground and groundwater from contamination. Dense concrete mixes have proved particularly suitable in such cases. The advantages of high-density concrete slabs include their greatly reduced permeability in comparison with standard concrete, and their higher tensile strength. In slabs of smaller area (up to a maximum dimension of 15 m), their greater strength means that they are not subject to cracking. Cracks in construction elements are especially critical in buildings where water-polluting organic liquids are used. With the use of high-density concrete, it is often possible to do without an additional protective coating. As far as performance of cementitious building materials is concerned, new developments have taken place in recent years that will considerably extend the use of concrete in this area. This applies in particular to high-strength concretes with compressive strengths of up to 800 N/mm^2 (in comparison with standard applications of about 300 N/mm^2). Considerable reductions in the cross-sections of reinforced and prestressed

concrete members can be achieved with this type of concrete. Slender elements also mean a lower overall weight, as well as a more sustainable form of construction through the conservation of resources. New methods of construction are also emerging through the use of so-called "reactive-powder concrete", as can be seen in the bridge constructed by Bouyges in Quebec, Canada, in 1997 (ill.1). In the meantime, this technology has been applied to other structures, such as the footbridge in Seoul, South Korea (ills. 3, 4).

Fibre- and textile-reinforced concrete
Fibre-reinforced concrete is a relatively long-established composite material. The fibres used may be of plastic, glass or steel.

Plastic fibres
Plastic fibres (ill. 6) are mostly used to reduce cracking as a result of early shrinkage in concrete, but they also serve to increase fire resistance; for example, in high-strength concrete. Polypropylene fibres, which are most commonly used for this purpose, vaporize at high temperatures; although the precise mechanism involved has not been finally established, an increase in the available pore space for the release of the steam developing at higher temperatures may be responsible for the improved fire resistance of the concrete building elements.

3

4

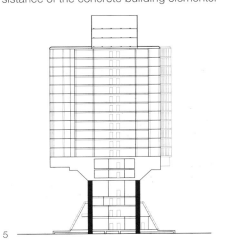

5

Glass fibres

Glass fibres are used to reduce cracking in setting concrete, but they also have a structural function in smaller building elements (ill. 7). In addition, they provide an alternative to asbestos, which was widely used as a means of reinforcing cement-bonded elements in the past. In view of its ductile properties, its high strength and durability, glass-fibre concrete has a wide range of applications, including semi-finished products and other elements.

Steel fibres

The use of steel-fibre-reinforced concrete is also possible in the field of engineering (ill. 8); for example, in precast reinforced concrete floor elements or for load-bearing walls without additional steel reinforcement. It is also used in industrial floor finishes or for securing excavations in tunnel construction. Steel-fibre-reinforced concrete has very specific functions due to its flexibility of form and stability.

Like steel rod reinforcement, steel fibres have a structural relevance. In terms of architectural design, however, their use poses certain problems, since any fibres that lie on or near the surface of the concrete of external building elements will be subject to corrosion when exposed to moisture and oxygen. In terms of the load-bearing capacity and durability of the concrete, this is not a

problem, but the brown discoloration of the surface to which corrosion gives rise is normally unacceptable aesthetically. Even in internal building elements this form of unsightly corrosion may occur when the construction phases were very extended, allowing moisture to come in contact with the interiors.

Textile-reinforced concrete

Textile-reinforced concrete is a logical development of fibre-reinforced concrete. Textile-like structures allow the alignment of the load-bearing reinforcement to be controlled and facilitate an economical exploitation of the material. In conventional reinforced concrete construction, the concrete has the additional function of protecting the reinforcement against corrosion. The use of engineering textiles made of glass or carbon means that the concrete cover can be reduced, thereby allowing the construction of thin-walled, three-dimensionally shaped elements.

The use of textile-reinforced concrete is conceivable in many areas, even for complex load-bearing shell structures. Used in precast elements as a kind of "integrated formwork" in combination with in-situ concrete, it offers a number of advantages. As permanent formwork, it does not have to be removed from the building component; the concrete surface requires no subsequent

treatment; and the load-bearing capacity of the "formwork" can be included in calculations for the overall strength of the element. Last, but not least, it serves to increase the fire resistance of structural members. Ill. 11 shows a formwork element developed in the past few years, constructed in such a way that it functions as a continuous beam. Through a careful selection and combination of the desired textile and concrete properties (in this case, fine-grain concrete with coarse aggregate of very small maximum size), the load-bearing capacity and deformation behaviour of textile-reinforced concrete can be precisely controlled. Ill. 13 shows the outcome of uniaxial tension tests carried out with various types of textile-reinforced concrete. The choice of the appropriate kind of concrete resulted in an increase in the load-bearing capacity in normal use (and in the residual load-bearing capacity at the point of failure) by a factor of 2.

The versatility of textile-reinforced concrete is yet to be realised. Various applications are possible today, including the construction of facade panels with simple geometric forms, and the creation of formwork components integrated in to compound wall and floor systems. An example of these innovative processes can be seen in ill. 9, where a new type of yarn (friction-spun hybrid yarn) is shown. In Ill. 10, one can see a section of the three-dimensional textile itself. The friction-

6

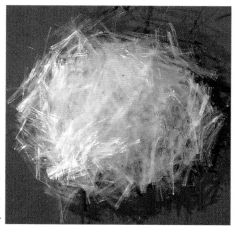

7

8

6 Plastic fibres (polypropylene)
7 Glass fibres
8 Steel fibres
9 Friction-spun hybrid yarn (under electron microscope)
10 "Pile" spacing fabric
11 Textile-reinforced concrete formwork element integrated into compound building component
12 Diagram showing noise levels at vibration tables in a precast concrete works
13 Stress-strain diagram of textile-reinforced concrete; upper curve = reactive-powder concrete (MW RPB-2E-3ARG); lower curve = fine-grained concrete (reference mix MW PZ-0899-01)

11

spun hybrid yarn consists of a number of glass threads that can be fusion-coated individually and in their entirety. The relation between the core material (usually glass fibres) and the coating (e.g. polypropylene) can be precisely determined and varied at will, allowing careful control of the properties of the yarn.

The knitted fabric consists of two load-bearing layers – with a space between them – tied together with "pile" threads. These threads may also be load-bearing, or constructed of simple polypropylene connected together and simultaneously spaced as desired. The spacing between the layers depends on structural requirements. Production processes need to be developed that will allow the economical manufacture of various building components with these materials. One possible application for textile-reinforced concrete lies in the creation of finely dimensioned forms that would allow the actual load-bearing behaviour to be visualized. Obviously the properties of textile-reinforced concrete are highly dependent upon the textile itself; new yarns and textile production techniques being under continual modification. As far as the surface design is concerned, similar scope exists with this type of concrete as with self-compacting concrete. The fine-grain concretes used in conjunction with textile-reinforcement have a high fluidity and are usually self-compacting

Noise emission in dB (A)

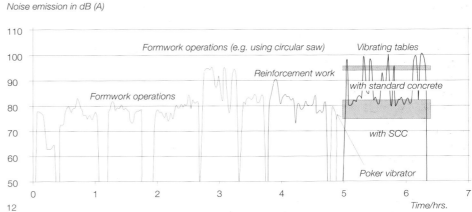

12

Tensile stress in N/mm²

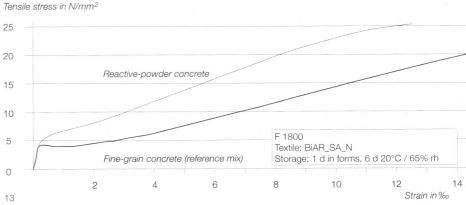

F 1800
Textile: BiAR_SA_N
Storage: 1 d in forms, 6 d 20°C / 65% rh

13

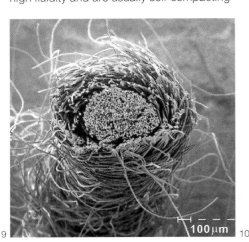

9

10

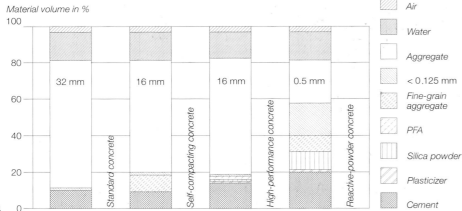

Material volume in %

Standard concrete — 32 mm
Self-compacting concrete — 16 mm
High-performance concrete — 16 mm
Reactive-powder concrete — 0.5 mm

Air
Water
Aggregate
< 0.125 mm
Fine-grain aggregate
PFA
Silica powder
Plasticizer
Cement

14

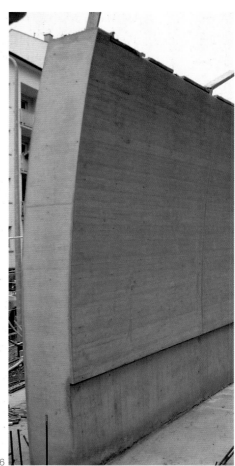

15

(see next section). New design opportunities exist in the field of surface finishes both for facade elements and elements used as formwork as part of a system-integrated wall skin. It is possible to create finely delineated contours of all kinds without blemishes or defects. Since the elements are extremely thin, it is economically viable to obtain coloured surfaces through pigmentation, thereby obviating the need for colour coating or painting. Textile-reinforced concrete has a high load-bearing capacity, even with comparatively small cross-sectional dimensions. It is, therefore, a sustainable form of construction, since the use of raw materials is relatively low, thus helping to conserve resources. The high performance of textile-reinforced concrete is shown by the construction of carving skis, which have been tested and function well.

Self-compacting concrete (SCC)
The greatest step forward in concrete technology in recent years is certainly the development of self-compacting types of concrete. A material that flows like honey offers fantastic opportunities for creating building components with complex forms and surface effects.

Fine-grain aggregate content
Self-compacting concrete differs from vibrated concrete in that it contains a greater proportion of cement and fine-grain aggregate. The concrete acquires its self-compacting properties in conjunction with high-performance additives. Examples of various mixes for the types of concrete, including self-compacting concrete, described here are shown in ill. 14. Roughly 30 per cent of the volume of standard concrete consists of the cement-paste matrix. The maximum diameter of the aggregate may be 8, 16 or 32 mm. The largest constituent is the aggregate, which makes up more than 70 per cent of the volume. Depending on the water/cement ratio, the volume of water will probably be slightly less than 20 per cent. Self-compacting concrete differs from standard forms of concrete in

that it generally contains aggregate with a maximum diameter of 16 mm. The aggregate again accounts for about 60 per cent of the overall volume. What is decisive in this context is the considerably higher proportion of fine-grain material; consisting of cement and additives – mostly PFA or powdered limestone. The fine-grain material, half of which is cement, makes up about 20 per cent of the mix by volume. In other words, the cement content is roughly the same as that in standard concrete, as is the water content.

High-strength and high-density concretes
In high-performance concrete (i.e. high-strength and high-density concrete) there is a considerably greater proportion of cement. The fine-grain material is generally formed by cement and microsilica. In most cases, the coarse-grain aggregate will also have a maximum diameter of 16 mm (as in self-compacting concrete), but the water content will be somewhat lower. In view of the much greater proportion of bonding agent, the water/cement ratio will also be somewhat lower, compared with standard and self-compacting concretes.

Reactive-powder concrete
The column at the right-hand end of ill. 14 shows an example of the composition of so-called "reactive-powder concrete". Here, too, the water content is roughly the same as that for standard concrete, but there are considerable quantities of additional fine-grain material, silica powder and cement required. The proportion of "coarser aggregate" (albeit with a maximum grain diameter of 0.5 mm) is just over 25 per cent and thus significantly lower than that for all other types of concrete.

Testing methods for self-compacting concrete
With a very precise composition, it is possible to prevent the coarser aggregate from sinking in the fluid matrix. The rheological properties of self-compacting concrete are, therefore, described in terms of flow times, flow dimensions and sedimentation stability.

Self-compacting concretes usually have a slump value of between 600 and 800 mm, which provides some indication of the yield point of this type of concrete. The run-out time from the conical discharge funnel – which as a rule lies between 10 and 20 seconds – is an indirect measure of the viscosity of the concrete, this range being desirable in relation to the required rheological properties. The combination of these two values determines the consistency of the self-compacting concrete. Tests also have to be carried out to determine whether self-compacting concrete can flow between the reinforcement. So-called "block ring tests" have been developed for this purpose. The

16

148

17

18

References:
[1] Company brochure Bouygues, France
[2] Brameshuber, W.: Selbstverdichtender Beton: Spezialbetone vol. 5, Verlag Bau + Technik, 2003
[3] Guthardt, W. et. al.: Selbstverdichtender Beton – Innovation am Beispiel »PHAENO«, Science Centre in Wolfsburg, Beton-Information Spezial 3/2002

14 Various concrete mixes
15,19 "PHAENO" Science Centre, Wolfsburg; completion date: 2004 [3]; architect: Zaha Hadid, London, in collaboration with Mayer/Bährle, Lörrach
16 In-situ concrete wall in self-compacting concrete
17 Testing process with block ring
18 Precast concrete elements: self-compacting concrete (above); standard concrete (below)

spacing of the bars should be coordinated with the maximum size of the aggregate. In the example of self-compacting concrete shown in ill. 17, there is a danger of serious blocking. The two values mentioned above do not help to determine the sedimentation stability. For this purpose, therefore, another testing pro-cess has been developed – which can also be carried out on the building site together with the slump test and the coni-cal discharge test – in which a sample of the concrete is filled into a tubular vessel on site and stored without jolting or vibration until the following day. The tube is then cut apart in the middle, and the concrete is inspected to see whether the coarse aggregate remains homogeneously distributed in the material or has sunk to the bottom. Like compressive strength trials, this process serves as a pre-liminary test for the acceptance of concrete. As the concrete pour has been completed by the time of testing, these tests serve as a control of the specified properties.

Professional techniques
When working with self-compacting con-crete, the temperature during the hydration process is critical. In comparison with stan-dard concrete, it has a much greater rheo-logical influence on the material. Tempera-tures that are either too low or too high (up to 30 °C) can result in sedimentation and ex-cessive rigidity or fluidity. It is important, therefore, that the concrete manufacturer is aware of the possible effects of tempera-ture on the rheological properties of self-compacting concrete. The choice of the appropriate mix proportions and the pro-duction of self-compacting concrete pre-suppose specialist knowledge in this field.

Sharp Edges
Although it is not necessary to use vibrators with self-compacting concrete, it is possible to achieve sharply delineated forms and sur-face textures. An example of the design po-tential this offers may be seen in ill.16. With self-compacting concrete it is in fact pos-sible to form a negatively curved surface free from defects and with sharply visible timber graining. The Science Centre in Wolfsburg (ills. 15,19), probably the most well-known example in Germany, demon-strates further the architectural design scope offered by self-compacting concrete today.

Self-compacting concrete in prefabrication
This material is particularly relevant in the field of prefabrication, where there is also a social dimension to this form of construction, in relation to labour conditions. Vibration tables are among the noisiest appliances in the building sector. The use of self-compacting concrete obviates the need for this equip-ment, thus eliminating the associated health hazard, e.g. loss of hearing. Ill. 12 shows the noise levels measured in the production of a precast concrete element. During the vibra-tion process, they can be as high as 115 dB(A). The use of self-compacting concrete reduces this burden to an acceptable level. As far as surface quality is concerned, the same rules apply as for in-situ concrete. Two precast elements in self-compacting concrete may serve as examples (ill. 18). The picture shows the difference between the two types of slab – in self-compacting concrete (above), and in standard concrete (below). The voids in the vibrated concrete are clearly visible.   DETAIL 4/2003

The author is head of the Institute for Building Research at Aachen University.

19

Metal Facade Finishes

Stefan Schäfer

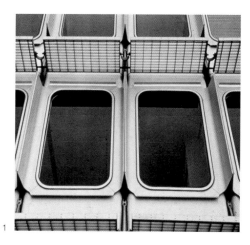

The significance of Jean Prouvé's use of metal as a facade material might be compared with the contribution Joseph Paxton made to iron and steel construction with the erection of his Crystal Palace in London in 1851. Prouvé, a trained blacksmith, explored numerous innovative techniques in the course of his life and did much to further the cause of advanced building skins. Using machines he had developed himself in part, he was able to apply metal casting and processing methods to large-scale construction and the creation of new building components. As a result of his experience in furniture manufacture, artefacts and wrought-iron production, Prouvé developed a great variety of different building elements, like moveable sunshading fins and post-and-rail facades. The materials he used most frequently were steel, aluminium and stainless steel, and sometimes brass and copper. One of his greatest achievements was to apply metals in areas where timber, glass and mineral materials had been used hitherto. The curtain-wall facades Prouvé developed at the end of the 1950s introduced a new age in the use of metals (ill. 1). The advantages of metals as facade finishes lie in the ease with which they can be worked, the low maintenance they require and the scope they offer for individual design. As a rule, surfaces of this kind are robust, have a long life and can be economically manufactured.

General construction techniques

The main factors to be considered in determining the appropriate working techniques and dimensions of metal facade finishes are wind suction and the degree of thermal expansion and contraction to which elements will be subjected. Constructional measures such as the correct spacing of joints and fixings that allow for movement in the sheeting can help to avoid strains in the material. Increased incidence of wind suction loads on edges and corners of buildings in particularly affected regions require extra constructional detailing. Consideration of the individual fixing-point strengths gives rise to the allowable spacing of these fixings.

The insulating property of thin metal sheeting is usually not very great. For that reason, it is mostly used in multilayer composite forms of construction in which only the outer skin is of metal. Other requirements with respect to the building physics of an enclosing skin will be met by the supporting structure. With few exceptions, the metallic outer layer will merely provide protection against the weather, corrosion and various mechanical forces. Functionally, a distinction can be made between ventilated and non-ventilated forms of construction. In the former case, the outer skin and the supporting structure are separated by a cavity through which air flows. Here, it is important to provide adequately dimensioned air inlets and outlets (> 1/500 of the ventilated area). The movement of air through the cavity ensures that vapour escaping from the interior of the building will be removed before it can condense. With non-ventilated forms of construction, there is no cavity. The advantages of this are the smaller depth, the elimination of ventilation openings, and a simpler form of construction. In this case, however, an effective, correctly positioned vapour barrier will be necessary.

Stabilizing and jointing

Metallic surfaces usually have a membrane-like thickness and are inherently unstable. Some form of structural bracing will therefore be necessary for large sheets. This can be achieved, for example, by bending up the edges, which may also serve as a means of fixing. Other forms of bracing include the application of stiffening angles to the rear face of metal sheets or the manufacture of composite elements with adequate rigidity. One can distinguish between fixings that penetrate the sheet and are visible on the outer face, and those that do not penetrate the sheet (invisible fixings). All fixings should be reversible to allow for subsequent maintenance and replacement work. Thermal expansion can cause friction between the surfaces of metal components that are in contact with each other and lead to unpleasant noises. One solution to this problem is the use of plastic washers to separate the two

surfaces. Classical forms of jointing the individual strips of metal cladding include standing seams (ill. 2, 3a) and batten roll seams. These allow loads to be transmitted without restricting movement within the individual sheets. The number of fixings required will depend on the transmission of vertical loads and the calculated wind-suction forces. Numerous other jointing techniques are available where structural aspects play a subordinate role. For one building project, a metal roof covering with recessed joints was developed. The principle of this system (ill. 3b) was based on the use of prefabricated metal sheets with longitudinally bent edges, which were clipped into position on site without the use of special tools. The interaction of pretensioning, geometry and jointing pattern created a homogeneous surface appearance that would also lend itself to use in facades. Depending on the type of metal used, various jointing techniques are available: both discrete fixings (screws, bolts, rivets, clips) and linear methods (brazing, soldering, welding, adhesives). Ideally, however, metal panels should be clipped together or suspended.

Surfaces

In addition to visual design aspects, an important consideration in determining the surface quality of sheet metal is its long-term resistance to corrosion. Steel-based materials are especially critical in this respect. In such cases, protection may be provided in the form of metallic or non-metallic coatings. Some metals have their own natural surface protection. Aluminium, stainless steel, zinc, tin, copper and titanium, for example, have a natural resistance to corrosion and, under normal weather conditions, will require no additional protection. The natural, regenerative, passive coatings these metals form can sometimes be artificially induced more rapidly and in a more precise way. The anodizing of aluminium – often in combination with coloration – is one example of this. Steel surfaces can also be chemically treated to create a brown, oxidized protective layer. Protective metal coatings can be applied through an electro-chemical process (galva-

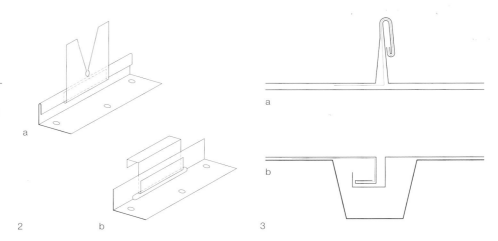

Stefan Schäfer is an architect in Stuttgart and professor for structural design and building construction at the University of Technology, Darmstadt.

1   Facade consisting of prefabricated metal panels:
    UNESCO building, Paris, 1969;
    architect: Jean Prouvé
2   Expansion clips:
    a for hand-formed seams;
    b for preformed metal sheets
3   Seam forms:
    a standing seam;
    b downstand seam
4   Liner Museum, Appenzell;
    architects: Gigon/Guyer, Zurich;
    material: chromium-steel sheet

nizing), through a vapour metallizing process, or in the form of plating. Weak acidic or alkaline solutions are used as the electrolytic bath for galvanizing; for example copper-plating of brass objects will normally take place in a solution of copper sulphate ($CuSO_4$), while the anodes are usually of the same material as the original base metal. The application of extremely thin coatings (e.g. in a vacuum process) is gaining in importance. Among the most familiar and reliable forms of surface coating are enamelling and galvanizing. Enamelling comprises the application of a thin vitreous layer, such as silicon oxide, by dipping, spraying or powdering the surface and then stoving it at a temperature of approximately 800 °C. Enamel powder can be applied in thicknesses between 80 and 200 μm. Surfaces treated in this way are acid- and alkali-resistant, electrically non-conductive and shock resistant. Zinc-galvanizing is carried out by dipping steel elements for a few minutes in a bath of liquid zinc at a temperature of 450 °C. The coating will be about 0.1 mm thick. The original metal is no longer visible but, due to the thinness of the protective coating, highly susceptible to mechanical damage, particularly at the edges, at perforations and at welding seams. To increase the resistance to corrosion, the zinc coating can be chromed, oiled or covered with a further coating of plastic. Freshly galvanized surfaces require further treatment before colour coatings can be applied; alternatively, they should be exposed to weathering for some months before painting. Non-metallic surface coatings include transparent or opaque paint, and calendered foils of various thicknesses. Polyester is commonly used for this purpose. Electrostatic powder coating is based on the principle that particles with opposite electrical charges attract each other. All thermally stable substances can be treated in this way. An electrostatically charged layer of powder is evenly sprayed on to the earthed object and then subjected to a fusion and setting process at 160–200 °C. The thickness of the surface coating will be roughly 30–500 μm. Vitrified or stove-enamelled coatings are produced when

Material Chemical Symbol	Titanium Ti	Steel	Iron Fe	Stainless Steels	Nickel Ni	Aluminium Al	Copper Cu	Zinc Zn	Tin Sn	Lead Pb
Density [g/cm³] at 25 °C	4.51	7.8	7.87	7.9	8.9	2.7	8.96	7.13	7.29	11.34
Light Metal (LM)/ Heavy Metal (HM)	HM	HM	HM	HM	HM	LM	HM	HM	HM	HM
Elasticity [GPa]	110	210	211.4	195	200	65	70	69.4/104.5	45.8/16.1	58.2/49.9
Thermal Expansion Coefficient [x 10⁻⁶/°C]	9	11.7	12.1	17.3	11.4–14	21–24	16.2–20	31	29	23.5
Thermal Conductivity [W/(mK)]	22	65	80.4	14	15 [90.9]	160	150	116	35.3	66.8
Melting point [°C]	1668	1510	1538		1455	660.32	1084	419.5	231.9	327
Boiling point [°C]	3287	3000	2861		2913	2519	2562	907	2602	1749
Geological Deposit [mg/kg]/[%]	0.6		4.7		0.008	8.1	0.007	0.012	0.00022	0.001
Toxic	no	no	no	no	no	no	no	no	no	yes
Price [€ per Tonne]	40–50,000	2600–3000 (Mild Steel)	150		7100	1450	1540	870	4400	500

5

polyester and melamine resins react and chemically fuse together at high temperatures (80–350 °C). They result in a shiny, mechanically robust and corrosion-resistant surface film. They are an important aspect of the industrial treatment of metal surfaces (e.g. for car bodies, household appliances, etc.). Applied coatings play a major role in the realm of building physics. Anti-drumming coatings as sound protection and vibration-reducing coatings are examples of this. Today, industrially applied, tough varnished coatings are available that can withstand the subsequent shaping of the element in question (see table 11). Other forms of surface treatment allow visual and functional changes to be made to the surface quality. Stucco effects can be created through impressed microstructures that significantly increase the stability of sheet metal. As a means of cleaning, refining or strengthening metal elements, the surfaces can be blasted with stainless steel or corundum granules, glass or ceramic beads. Areas that are inaccessible to mechanical treatment can be electrically polished, to smooth and clean welding joints, for example; and fine ornamental surface textures can be applied by brushing.

Corrosion protection
Where metals with different chemical valencies are used adjacent to each other, care must be taken to avoid galvanic corrosion caused by oxidation acids. Rainwater must not be allowed to flow from metals of higher valency to those of lower valency. Where an area of copper is situated above an area of zinc, for example, the zinc would be subject to corrosion damage. Where aluminium, stainless or galvanized steel are above zinc, however, there will be no corrosion damage, although rust lines may appear due to the oxidization of any raw cut edges. Similarly, in combination with moisture, mineral products like cement, gypsum or lime can have an aggressive effect on metals. Where this is likely to occur, separating layers will be necessary.

Transport and storage
The surfaces of all metal components should, in principle, be protected. This applies to every stage of their transport, storage and assembly. Special transport pallets and specifically developed lifting equipment should be used. Metal panels are usually delivered face to face, thereby protecting each other. Where they are to be stored over a longer period of time, moisture penetration should be avoided. In order to allow moisture run-off, a gentle incline when in storage is recommended. Enclosed storage facilities are an even better solution. Self-adhesive protective foils should, however, be removed on site as soon as possible, due to any possible residue. Individual manufacturers' storage recommendations should be strictly complied with.

Visual effects
In addition to its purely functional role, perforated metal cladding can be used to create diaphanous effects. Seen from a distance externally, it has the appearance of a closed, metallic skin, with various possible surface textures. From inside the building, it can be virtually transparent (ill. 6). High-gloss metal surfaces create an effect of great plasticity (ill. 7); and metal fabrics can be used to achieve a state of semi-transparency (ill. 8). Finely perforated metal sheets provide good solar screening, while again allowing a high degree of transparency from within. Grids or gratings permit direct (orthogonal) views into and out of a building, while restricting oblique views. Metal facade elements are also ideally suited for suspended external sunshading and light-deflecting functions.

Metals for facade elements
As chemical elements, metals belong to the basic substances of our earth. Their deposits are subject to change through the agency of man and nature. Transformation processes, like leaching for example, assist in local chemical enrichment. All metals undergo a natural circulation. For example, four times more copper is moved annually as a result of biological cycles – through the fall of leaves and the sprouting of plants – than through human activity. Some metals, like iron, are even necessary for human nutrition. Only a

6

7

8

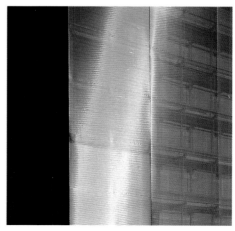

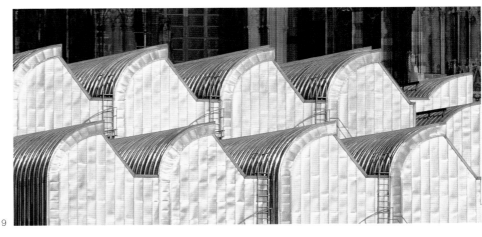

9

few heavy-metal compounds, such as cadmium and mercury, are ecologically harmful and potential health hazards. Metals with a density of < 4.5 g/cm³ are referred to as "light", those metals with densities above this are defined as "heavy metals" (see table 5). Combinations of various metals are known as alloys. These may have quite different properties from their component elements. Most metals used in building are, in fact, alloys.

Steel
Steel differs from iron in its smaller content of undesirable secondary elements such as carbon, phosphorus and sulphur. The material described here is fine sheet steel which is not used in a pure form; i.e. without some form of surface protection. Among low-alloy steels, some quickly acquire an oxidized surface, but then cease to rust further (e.g. Corten® steel). The corroded surface forms a weather-resistant coating for the steel beneath, provided that the building skin is able to dry out completely. These constructions must be particularly well detailed to avoid continued oxidation and unsightly corrosion blemishes on adjacent elements. Steel is a reasonably priced, durable material, the use of which is ecologically unproblematic.

Stainless steel
High-quality, rustproof stainless steel is produced by alloying steel with other metals such as chromium (at least 10.5 per cent) or manganese. Today, more than 120 varieties of this durable alloy are produced for use in many different situations. Although stainless steel is categorized as rustproof due to its regenerative, insoluble, passive coating, corrosion cannot be entirely excluded, especially under aggressive environmental conditions. A greater proportion of other metals such as chromium, nickel, molybdenum, manganese or copper can improve the resistance to corrosion, but in many cases they also change the character of the material. Stainless steels are much more expensive than normal steel because of their content of chromium and nickel, but require no additional corrosion protection and are extremely durable. They are normally used only in thin sheet form, for fasteners or in smaller cross-sections.

Aluminium
After oxygen and silicon, aluminium is the third most commonly found element in the earth's crust (8.1 per cent content). This silvery-white, ductile, lightweight metal is a good electrical conductor, but, as with all commercially used metals, it does not exist in a pure form in nature. It is extracted at a temperature of over 2,000 °C, which means that the costs of its production are very high. The largest deposits are to be found in Australia, West Africa, the Caribbean and South America. It can be used in a pure state or in alloys and is available in sheet, rolled and foil form and in various cross-sections. Its natural, regenerative oxidized surface makes it resistant to environmental influences. Aluminium is extremely robust and durable. Its great resilience means that it is ideally suited for clip fixings avoiding perforations in a variety of elements. In view of its high production costs, this metal cannot be regarded as environmentally sustainable, but its use is economically viable in situations where long life is required.

Zinc
Zinc is a bluish-white brittle metal, shiny on freshly cut surfaces, and can be rolled at a temperature of 120 °C. The zinc content in the earth's crust is estimated at 0.012 per cent. It is commonly available in a low-alloy form (with copper and/or titanium). Because of the natural surface coating it forms, zinc requires no further treatment to protect it against corrosion. In fact, it is one of the cheapest protective coatings for other metals. Exposed to aggressive moisture (e.g. acid rain), however, it can suffer damage in the long term. Zinc is non-toxic, compared with some heavy metals; run-off rainwater containing zinc residues is, therefore, not a health hazard. In the form of titanium-zinc, its mechanical and technical properties are greatly enhanced. Zinc scrap can be practically 100 per cent recycled. Zinc sheeting can be easily worked even at

10

11

Organic Coatings			
Coating Material	Abbreviation	Coating thickness µm	Corrosion protection class (DIN 55928-8)
Paint systems			
Polyester	SP	10	II
Polyester	SP	25	III
Polyurethane	PUR	25	III
High-durability polymers	HDP	25	III
Polyvinylidene fluoride	PVDF	25	III
Polyvinyl chloride (Plastisol)	PVC (P)	100–200	III
Film systems			
Polyvinyl chloride	PVC (F)	100–200	III
Polyvinyl chloride	PVF (F)	40	III

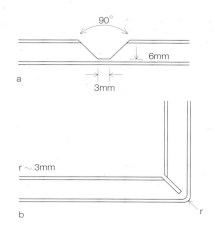

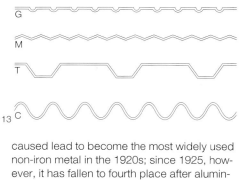

12   Milled edges of metal plates with plastic core:
    a milled V-shaped groove for folding the sheeting
    b 90° bend
13   Sheet metal cross-sections:
    F = flat   L = linear recessed
    G = grooved   M = micro-profile
    T = trapezoidal section   C = corrugated
14   Table: electrochemical (reactivity) series for
    metals compared with hydrogen

low temperatures. Zinc is a widely used material due predominantly to its inherent stability, economy of use as a corrosion protecting metal and lack of health issues.

Titanium
This silvery-white, extremely ductile metal, the 22nd element in the periodic table, is the tenth most common element in the earth's crust (0.6 per cent). A reliable method of extraction was introduced in the 1950s. Titanium is now produced in two basic forms: as pure titanium (> 99.2 per cent titanium, plus oxygen, carbon and iron) in four strengths ranging from 290 to 740 N/mm²; and as titanium alloy (80–98 per cent titanium plus aluminium, vanadium, tin, chromium, etc.) with strengths exceeding 1,200 N/mm². The various strengths of pure titanium are determined by their oxygen content. Alloyed with palladium and nickel-molybdenum, titanium has a much greater resistance to corrosion. Titanium is 42 per cent lighter than steel of equivalent strength, but is considerably more expensive. Due to its corrosion resistance, high strength combined with low weight, and stable mechanical and thermal properties; it is popular in many different areas, particularly aviation and space technology.

Copper
Copper is a glossy, red, heavy metal; relatively soft, robust, highly ductile and, second only to silver, an excellent conductor of electricity and heat. It makes up 0.007 per cent of the earth's crust with a deposit incidence between 3 and 290 mg/kg. Copper forms a natural oxidized protective coating on its surface when exposed to the atmosphere; depending on environmental conditions, roof geometry, etc., it can assume a green patina (copper carbonate) over the course of time. Due to the improved air conditions over the last 20 years, the rate of decay of copper surfaces has decelerated; in Europe, the rate of run-off has been reported to be between 0.7 and 1.5 g/m²/year. In spite of the higher costs involved in its production, its extremely long life makes the use of this material economically viable. Copper is manufactured in wire, rod, sheet and tubular form, and is also used for various fittings.

Lead
This bluish-grey, soft, malleable, slightly toxic heavy metal is shiny on freshly cut surfaces and forms a protective oxide coating when exposed to the air. The content of lead in the earth's crust is calculated to be about 0.002 per cent. The largest deposits are to be found in the USA, Australia, Russia and Canada. As a result of its excellent recycling qualities, the demand for lead has annually decreased. Lead (Lat.: plumbum) has been in use since 2500 B.C., but was first widely used by the Romans for plumbing. Continued demand caused lead to become the most widely used non-iron metal in the 1920s; since 1925, however, it has fallen to fourth place after aluminium, copper and zinc. The available world supply of lead is estimated to be approximately 200 million tonnes. It is extremely resistant to hard water, but tends to dissolve in soft water with a high CO_2 content, which is one reason why it is no longer used for water pipes. Lead has neglible qualities as a thermal and electrical conductor. It is mainly used in building today to form connections and as a shield against radiation. The lead alloys still found in construction (drips, flashings, etc.) present no health hazard.

Tin
Tin is the 30th most common element (0.0035 per cent). The largest geological deposits are to be found in Australia, Malaysia, Indonesia, Bolivia, Thailand, Nigeria, the Congo and Zaire. In its pure form, this silvery-white, somewhat soft heavy metal has a relatively low melting point. It assumes three modified forms, changing its crystalline structure at 13.25 °C and 162 °C. At room temperature it is covered with a grey protective oxide coating. More than a third of the tin used today is a product of recycling. As a technical material, aluminium is increasingly being used as a substitute. Almost half the tin produced today is applied as a durable, silvery coating to other metals (tin plate).   DETAIL 1/2 2003

Metal	Symbol	Normal potential (V)
Gold	Au	+ 1.50
Mercury	Hg	+ 0.85
Silver	Ag	+ 0.80
Copper	Cu	+ 0.35
Hydrogen	H	0
Lead	PB	− 0.12
Tin	Sn	− 0.14
Nickel	Ni	− 0.23
Cadmium	Cd	− 0.40
Iron	Fe	− 0.44
Chromium	Cr	− 0.56
Zinc	Zn	− 0.76
Manganese	Mn	− 1.05
Aluminium	Al	− 1.68
Magnesium	Mg	− 2.34
Potassium	K	− 2.92

References:

Deutsches Kupfer-Institut: Beschichten von Kupfer und Kupfer-Zink-Legierungen mit farblosen Transparentlacken; Deutsches Kupfer-Institut, Berlin, 1991
Franqué, O. V.: Wechselwirkungen zwischen Kupfer und Umgebung; Deutsches Kupfer-Institut, Berlin, 1986
Geyer, C.: Einschalige Dachkonstruktionen mit Kupfer; DBZ 11/93 pp. 1905–1908
Haselbach, M.: Kupfer im Hochbau; Deutsches Kupfer-Institut, Berlin, 1987
Koewius, Gross, Angehrn: Aluminium-Konstruktionen. Aluminium-Verlag, Düsseldorf, 1999
Liersch, K.: Belüftete Dach- und Wandkonstruktionen, Bauverlag, Wiesbaden and Berlin var. vols. since 1981
Moritz, Karsten: Membranwerkstoffe im Hochbau. Detail 6/2000, pp. 1050–1055, Institut für internationale Architektur-Dokumentation, Munich

Schäfer, Stefan: Neuartige metallische Dacheindeckung. Detail 5/2000, pp. 880–882, Institut für internationale Architektur-Dokumentation, Munich
Schittich, Christian (ed.): Gebäudehüllen – Konzepte, Schichten, Material. Institut für internationale Architektur-Dokumentation, Munich 2001
Schulitz, Sobek, Habermann: Steel Construction Manual, Institut für internationale Architektur-Dokumentation, Munich 1999
Schunck, Oster, Barthel, Kiessl: Roof Construction Manual, Pitched Roofs. Institut für internationale Architektur-Dokumentation, Munich 2002
Sulzer, Peter (ed.): Jean Prouvé – Meister der Metallumformung, Das neue Blech 15, Verlagsgesellschaft Rudolf Müller GmbH, Cologne, 1991

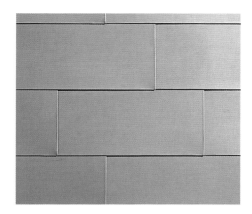

Sheet titanium-zinc

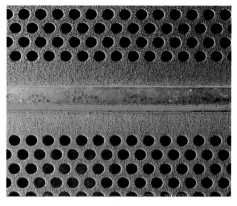

Oxidized steel with round perforations

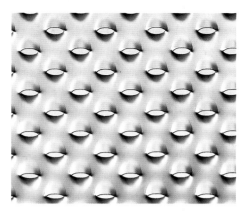

Stainless steel with lenticular dimpled perforations

Metal shingles, plates and sheets
Classically, metal cladding or roofing is in the form of bands of sheet metal with welted, standing or batten seams, which result in a characteristic banded structure. The great resistance of metal coverings to weathering allows roofs with a slope of < 15° to be realized. In view of the high proportion of manual work involved, only soft metals such as copper or zinc are suitable. Cladding systems with preformed, shingle-like flat sheets have also enjoyed increased usage in recent years, allowing various patterns of articulation to be created. Systems of this kind are easy to joint – usually by means of concealed clips fixed to the supporting structure.

Perforated metal sheeting
Perforations between < 1 mm and roughly 500 mm in diameter and with various spacings can be punched in thin metal sheets by a number of processes and in combination with computerized numeric control (CNC). As a rule, the diameter of the perforations should not be less than the thickness of the sheet. Perforations can be in straight lines or in an offset pattern; they can be round, square, slit-like or in various ornamental forms. A common feature of all punching processes is the wave-like deformation of the metal sheets caused by the energy released. This deformation has to be corrected subsequently before the sheets are cut to size.

The spacing of the perforations at the edges of the sheets should also be considered carefully. Metal thicknesses should be between 0.5 mm and 6 mm. For perforated sheets more than 6 mm thick, a soft material is preferable. Standard sheeting is available in sizes up to 1.6 × 4.0 m, and in coils up to 1.25 m wide and up to 2 mm thick. Special sizes can be manufactured to order. Perforated sheeting is widely used in trade fair and interior construction, for facade cladding, sunshading louvres and balustrades. Ease of handling, highly industrialized production methods, a wide range of surface textures and its light weight make this form of sheeting an economical and versatile building material.

Stainless steel, embossed

Expanded steel mesh

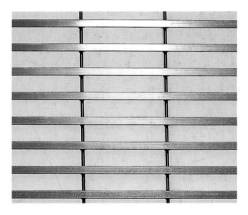

Stainless steel strip grating

Embossed metal sheeting
Embossed metal sheeting is manufactured in a similar process to that used for perforated sheeting. The sheet is not punched through its thickness, however; the surface is subjected to a process of deformation to create various protrusions and patterns. The depth of the embossing will depend on the thickness of the material. The embossed area should be rectangular and cover the entire sheet, with the exception of edge strips, which may be bent. Embossed sheets are commonly used internally – where non-slip finishes are required, for example. Great reservations still exist towards the use of these materials for facades, however.

Expanded metal mesh
Expanded metal mesh is a semi-finished product with a planar structure and openings in various forms. No waste is incurred in its manufacture: the sheets are merely cut and drawn to shape. The process can be applied to iron, steel, aluminium and lightweight alloys, as well as to copper, brass, nickel, bronze and zinc. Light forms of expanded metal mesh are used as a base for plaster. The great stability of this material and its relatively light weight allow the creation of extremely resilient facade elements. Expanded metal mesh is also used as a translucent "curtain" to large openings and for grilles, suspended soffits and visual screening.

Metal gratings
Gratings are commonly made from steel, stainless steel or aluminium and consist of slotted bearing bars and filler strips, pressed together in an industrial process and/or electrically welded. The orthogonal grid of bars can be manufactured to various spacings. The edges of gratings are enclosed in and stabilized by a frame-like surround. To avoid any confusion in determining the load-bearing direction, square gratings should not be used where they have to carry foot traffic. Gratings can be made with non-slip and various other surface qualities. They can also be used as facade and soffit elements. Gratings are available in all sizes and depths.

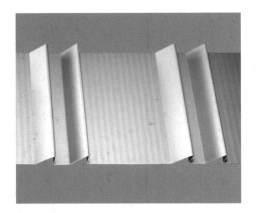

Ribbed aluminium panel

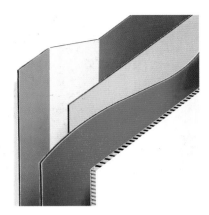

Multilayer aluminium sheet

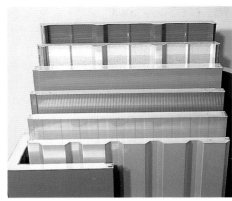

Thin-steel sandwich panel

Ribbed metal sheets and coffered panels
Ribbed metal sheets can be cold-rolled to various geometries and to lengths up to roughly 4 m. Sheeting of this kind can be used in single- or multilayer forms of construction for load-bearing planar floor structures or for wall elements. A wide range of cross-sections and surface textures are available. The thickness of the metal is normally between 0.5 mm and roughly 1.5 mm (coffered panels: ca. 1.0–1.5 mm). The most common material used for this purpose is thin steel sheeting with a corrosion-resistant surface coating applied at the works. In many roof systems, the edge sections are industrially preformed for clamp or press fixing.

Multilayer sheets
Composite or multilayer (laminated) elements usually consist of a plastic core with lightweight metal sheeting on both faces. They are supplied as slabs or panels with the surface finish often covered with a protective foil layer. Slabs with maximum dimensions of roughly 1.50 x 5 m are available and with metal thicknesses between 2 mm and max. 10 mm. Sheet abutments can be screwed, bolted, riveted, or fixed with adhesives or clips. Although multilayer sheets are relatively expensive, their great stability and low weight simplify operations on site and reduce the cost of the supporting structure, allowing precise and economical facade solutions.

Sandwich panels
Sandwich panels are prefabricated composite elements, consisting of two shear-resistant steel sheets and a multifunctional insulating core of polyurethane foam. Panels are available with various surface textures and cross-sections. They can be simply fixed in position with preformed interlocking seams. Sandwich panels require little maintenance and are extremely robust. They are also capable of transmitting substantial loads. An 80 mm thick standard wall panel can span a distance of 5–6 m; while a similar roof element with a ribbed profile on top and a beaded underside (and a weight of roughly 11–18 kg/m^2) can span a distance of 4–6 m.

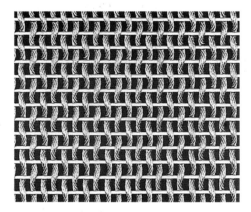

Stainless steel fabric: cable warp and rod weft

Stainless steel fabric: warp chains and weft rods

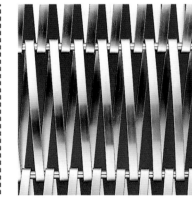

Stainless steel fabric: loops and round rods

Metal fabrics
Round or flat wires, bands or cables can be woven to form various kinds of metal fabric. Commonly used materials include stainless steel, titanium, chromium-nickel steel and even copper and brass. Where the individual wires or strands have a diameter of more than 3 mm, their wavelike profile should be preformed (without pretensioning). Using various classical weaves, fabrics up to 8 m in width can be produced. Metallic fabrics are available in a natural form or with various surface treatments: painted, anodized, pickled, etc. They have great stability and can be used over large areas without intermediate seams or connecting elements. Metal fabrics

can be obtained in roll and panel form, or cut to size. In recent years these materials have been increasingly used in architecture. The scope for rolling them makes them suitable for sunshading and visual screening purposes. They are also used for filter heads, safety barriers, infill panels, windbreaks and even partitions. Materials of this kind require little maintenance and can be readily cleaned. The fact that they can be built in as pretensioned elements has the structural advantage of a load-bearing function combined with low weight. Special fixing details have to be developed to ensure an efficient load transfer at the points of support. In addition to fabrics, grilles and gratings can be formed. Structures

of great strength can be created by welding or pressing the wires together at their points of intersection. A wide range of products is available in a variety of mesh dimensions, wire thicknesses and metals, including galvanized and ungalvanized steel, aluminium and stainless steel. Large-mesh wire structures are used for fences and enclosures. Woven wire-mesh materials are also employed in mountain regions as safety nets to withstand snow or avalanches. In building, wire netting can be used in conjunction with other materials to stabilize dry stonework. The flexibility, stability and extreme lightness of wire mesh makes it suitable for large-span structures such as aviaries.

Metal Mesh Facades

Stefan Schäfer

1

2

Today, a great selection of diaphanous metal materials is available to architects, ranging from perforated sheets, gratings and expanded mesh to net-like, woven and knitted fabrics. The desire to achieve greater transparency in building has been met by glass. Now planners and designers are seeking ways to create building skins with a range of effects between transparency and opaqueness. Not only simple products from the realms of industrial building and scaffolding are being used for this purpose; more sophisticated elements have also been developed, as can be seen in many prestigious modern structures. Similarly, the ongoing improvement of manufacturing techniques is resulting in materials and products with special properties that offer new scope for design, especially in the context of building skins.

Diaphanous metal building skins
Perforated layers can result in interesting visual effects that vary with the distance of the observer from the surface structure. From afar, one will have the impression of a practically closed metal skin, while from another perspective, it may seem almost transparent. The changes caused by light and shade, sun and rain, and the differences between day and night will enliven the surface and lend the structure a diverse range of effects. Views into the building will vary according to the angle of incidence of light. Depending on one's position, the surfaces may appear opaque or transparent. Sheet metal with very fine perforations, and grating-like components also allow a high degree of sunshading without seriously impeding the view out of a building. The term "skin" itself suggests a sense of lightness and permeability, as well as a certain variability in appearance. This state of openness is an essential characteristic of these semi-finished products, which have their origins in industrial filter and screening technologies. A new understanding of spatial demarcation and enclosure was necessary, however, before the scope of fabric-like materials could be discovered for build-

ing. With the introduction of stitch-like, perforated metal products for use in facade construction, it became possible to cover buildings with light, fabric-like materials in the nature of a curtain. Metal meshes with a textile character can be manufactured to cover large areas. The advantages of metal fabric facades lie in their comparatively easy assembly and treatment, the low level of maintenance they require, and the scope they offer for individual design. In addition, they are usually robust and can be economically produced.

Metal fabrics
Metal fabrics consist of round or flat wires, strands or cables. The metals used include untreated iron, galvanized steel, stainless steel and chromium-nickel steel. Aluminium, bronze, copper, brass, titanium and tin can also be specified if desired. As with woven textiles, the longitudinal wires (warp) in the fabric strip can be woven in a variety of forms with the lateral wires (weft). Metal fabrics are produced on special weaving looms. The most important weave forms are described below.

Plain weave (ill. 4a)
This is the most common form of weave used for metal fabrics. It allows a high degree of precision and the most even spacings. To achieve a better positioning of the

warp and weft wires, a strong curvature of the wires is necessary at the points of contact. This, in turn, results in a rough surface texture. The greater the ratio between the aperture of the mesh (w) and the diameter of the wire (d), the more subject to displacement the mesh will be. A ratio of less than 3:1 (w:d) is, therefore, recommended.

Plain Dutch weave (ill. 4b)
A special form of plain weave is where the warp wires are considerably thicker than the weft wires. The tight alignment of adjoining weft wires results in what is known as a "zero mesh". The almost triangular openings created with this kind of weave are visible when viewed from the side and result in a homogeneous appearance. By subjecting the finished mesh to a rolling process (calendering), the surface roughness can be reduced. The mesh can be easily bent to shape about the axis of the thick warp wires.

Twill weave (ill. 4c)
Twill weave results in less stress in the wires during the weaving process. The geometry of the weave means that the radii of curvature of the wires are only half as great as those in plain weaves, so that the strains at the crimps are much smaller. Fine-mesh fabrics are manufactured almost exclusively with this weave, which allows the use of rel-

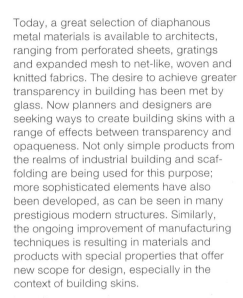

3

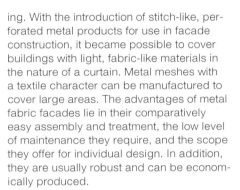

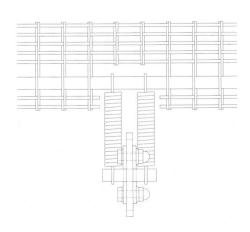

1 Parking block at Cologne-Bonn Airport
  architects: Murphy/Jahn, Chicago
2 Post Office Tower, Bonn
  architects: Murphy/Jahn, Chicago
3 Facade fixing: lower fixing with tension springs
4 Types of weave for metal mesh fabrics

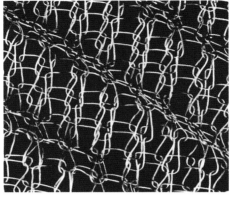

Stainless steel mesh: long meshes/double wires

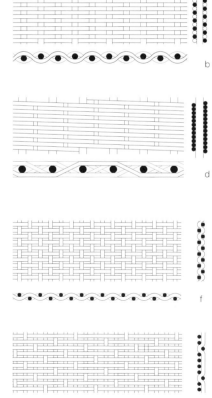

Stainless steel knitted fabric: corrugated round wire

atively large wire gauges. With increasing cohesion (the number of wires crossed in one weave), the precision of the mesh decreases, but the surface smoothness increases.

Twill weave (ill. 4d)
Closely aligned weft wires are woven in a twilled type of weave and pressed together. There is always a weft wire over and under every warp wire. Where the wire diameters are the same, twice as many weft wires are used as in the normal ribbed weaving. The outcome is a very dense, mechanically resilient weave with an extremely smooth, stable surface and fine, pore-like openings.

Reverse plain Dutch weave (ill. 4e)
This type of weave is a reversed form of plain Dutch weave. The closely aligned warp wires have a much smaller diameter than the strong weft wires. The very precise mesh formed with this type of weave is distinguished by fine openings oblique to the surface plane. The fabric itself has a remarkably high mechanical strength and can be readily shaped about the axis of the thicker wires.

Long-mesh weave (ill. 4f)
With a mesh ratio of 1:3, this type of weave has great cohesion. If one reverses the direction of the weave, one speaks of a broad-mesh weave. To achieve greater stability, wires of different thicknesses may be used for warp and weft.

Multiplex weave (ill. 4g)
In this type of mesh, groups of five parallel wires are woven together in both directions to produce a very smooth, easily cleaned surface in the form of a regular chequered pattern.

Five-heddle twill weave (ill. 4h)
This is a special form of weave consisting of a four-strand arrangement. Strands of single wires are laid out parallel to each other in both directions to form a large number of tiny, pore-like openings.

Metal fabric quality
As a means of determining the quality of metal fabrics in Germany, the following criteria are defined (in DIN 4189)
• Aperture (opening) (w)
  The clear space between adjoining wires is defined for both the warp and weft directions.
• Wire diameter (d)
  The wire diameter is defined prior to weaving. Slight changes in diameter can occur during the fabrication process.
• Mesh
  This is defined in terms of the number of meshes per inch measured between wire axes.
• Open sieve area (A_o or F_o)

The area of mesh spacings is given as a percentage of the entire mesh area.
• Number of stitches (mesh/cm²)
  The number of stitches or meshes is stated per square centimetre.
• Fabric thickness (D)
  The thickness of the fabric dependent upon the wire diameter.

Fabric properties
There are six fabric quality level, which are denoted with numbers from 0 to 5. At the upper end of the quality scale, resistance to the displacement of wires is greater. Technically speaking, metal mesh materials are extremely efficient and versatile. In addi-

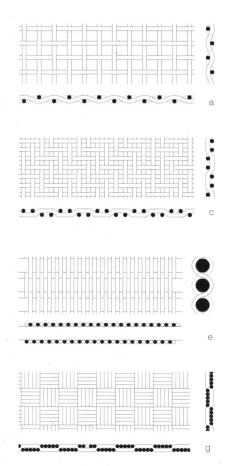

4

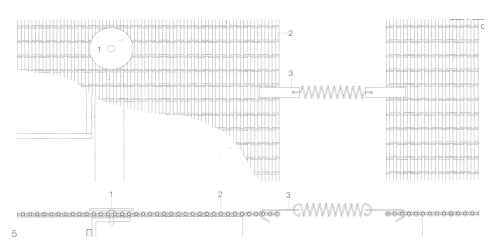

5 Velodrome in Berlin: view from above and section
  through tensioning of metal fabric on roof
  scale 1:5
  1 Ø 84.3 mm stainless steel disc
  2 stainless steel fabric
  3 110×30×2 mm steel plate with Ø 2.8 mm
    tensioning spring
  architects: Dominique Perrault, Paris, in
  collaboration with APP, Berlin;
6 "Five Courtyards" shopping and commercial
  development, Munich;
  architects: Herzog & de Meuron, Basle;
  material: folded sheet tombac (brass alloy
  with a high proportion of copper)

tion to their industrial uses – as filters, sieves and for sound absorption – they now have a wide range of applications in architecture; especially in facade construction, as wall and soffit linings, and in forming partitions. There is even scope for the use of fine-mesh stainless steel products as floor finishes – as matting that requires no preliminary sub-floor measures. The material is virtually maintenance free, of unlimited durability and completely recyclable. In addition to the production of small, medium and large batches, many firms are prepared to manu-facture individual elements to order.

Metal grilles and knitted fabrics
Wire-mesh products are complemented by a range of other materials, including flat-strand products (e.g. metal grilles and grat-ings) and knitted fabrics. Thanks to simple industrialized mass production, products of this kind are very reasonable in price. Net materials are a special case in this context. Typologically, they are single-layer mesh products, consisting of parallel steel cables joined together at offset nodes. Nets of this kind possess great three-dimensional flexi-bility and mesh stability and are of minimal weight. As a result, they are especially suitable for wide-span open structures such as aviaries.
Knitted metal fabrics consist of a virtually endless thread wound in a series of stitches row by row. Knitted fabrics have been ap-plied mainly as internal finishings and in filter technology. They can also be used for sunshading; e.g. in the cavity between panes of double glazing.

Assembly and fixing of metal fabrics
An important factor in the assembly of metal mesh products is the geometry of the fa-cade areas. A logical classification of fa-cade types would be: planar surfaces, sur-faces curved about a single axis, and those curved about two axes. In most cases, how-ever, facades are in the form of flat planes. By pretensioning flat areas of mesh across a facade, negative effects such as vibration, whipping and flapping can be reduced,

but heavy anchoring loads will occur at the points of support. In interior situations, where there is no wind to cause flapping, metal fabrics can be freely suspended to form soffits, wall linings, etc. Mesh sheeting subject to wind loads, however, requires numerous fixings along the "weak" axis. The principle underlying the manufacture of ribbed weaves, with warp or weft wires of large dimensions, facilitates the transmis-sion of loads along a single axis with greater distances between fixings. In such cases, the wires act like a series of closely spaced beams subject to bending. The softer wires along the "weak" axis either carry no loads at all or transmit only tension. Areas curved

about two axes are obviously the ideal structural solution, since the geometry al-lows a simpler transmission of loads to the supporting structure. To avoid complicated intersections and cutting, the appropriate weave with flexible mesh cross-sections should be specified. Fabric mesh products must be fixed in a hanging state, like cur-tains. The dead load is then transmitted through the upper supports and conveyed to the ground.   DETAIL 7/8 2003

Stefan Schäfer is an architect in Stuttgart and profes-sor for structural design and building construction at the University of Technology, Darmstadt.

6

Stone Surface Dressing

Theodor Hugues
Ludwig Steiger
Johann Weber

Theodor Hugues, emeritus professor of the Faculty
of Building Construction and Materials at the University
of Technology, Munich
Ludwig Steiger and Johann Weber, members of the
Prof. Florian Musso Faculty of Building Construction
and Materials at the University of Technology, Munich

1 Bush hammer with interchangeable heads

New mechanical tools and techniques allow stone to be dressed much more easily and quickly. This, in turn, has led to an increased demand for "craft-worked" products. The many different textures of stone mean that a great range of treatments can be applied. It is possible not only to bring out the specific properties of the material, but to exploit various effects of light and shade. The choice of surface finish, however, will depend on the type of stone, its hardness, the effects that can be achieved, and the situation in which an element is to be used. The strength of the stone is an important factor in determining which finish to apply. Every working process demands a minimum material thickness in order to withstand the tooling impact. If properly selected and executed, the treatment can greatly enhance the expressive quality of a building component, although not all forms of dressing can be applied to all kinds of stone. The stoneworking trade distinguishes between "hard" and "soft" materials. Soft stone includes sedimentary rock like limestone and sandstone as well as marble. Hard stone ranges from effusive and igneous rock, such as granite, syenite and basalt, to metamorphic rock like gneiss, quartzite and slate. The surface quality will be determined by the fineness of the treatment applied. Polishing, which produces the finest surface of all, brings out the mineral content, the colour, texture and structure of the stone. Dark stones reveal their true character only through polishing, whereas other, coarser forms of treatment can make the surface appear paler in colour. Conversely, polishing makes lighter-coloured stone appear somewhat darker. Stone can be polished only if it is sufficiently hard and dense, however. Many other aspects have to be considered, too; for example, the fact that rougher finishes are subject to greater soiling, while stone flooring has to comply with non-slip safety requirements. On the following pages, various kinds of surface treatment are described to two types of stone found in Germany: Jurassic limestone from the Altmühl region, and granite from the Bavarian Forest.   DETAIL 11/2003

Type of stone	natural cleft	rough-hewn	pointed / punched / furrowed	bush-hammered (coarse)	bush hammered (fine)	axed	patent axed	plain work	combed	boasted (droved)	quarry faced	rubbed	sandblasted	steel-sawn with sand	cable sawn	diamond sawn	milled	coarse rubbed	fine rubbed	coarse ground	ground	fine ground	semi-polished	polished	flamed
Igneous rock																									
granite	•	•	•	•	•									•		•	•	•	•		•	•		•	•
syenite	•	•	•	•	•									•		•	•	•	•		•	•		•	
diorite	•	•	•	•	•									•		•	•	•	•	•	•	•		•	
gabbro	•	•	•	•	•									•		•	•	•	•		•	•		•	
rhyolite (porphyry)	•	•	•	•	•									•		•	•				•	•		•	
trachyte	•	•	•	•	•									•		•	•				•	•		•	
basalt	•	•	•	•	•									•		•	•	•	•		•	•		•	
dolerite (diabase)	•	•	•	•	•	•								•	•	•	•	•	•		•	•		•	
lava stone	•	•	•	•	•	•			•	•	•			•	•	•	•				•	•			
volcanic tuff	•	•	•			•	•	•	•	•	•	•		•	•	•	•								
Sedimentary rock																									
conglomerate	•	•	•		•						•			•	•	•	•								
breccia	•	•	•		•		•	•	•	•	•	•		•	•	•	•								
sandstone, quartziferous	•	•	•		•		•	•	•	•	•	•		•	•	•	•						•		
sandstone	•	•	•		•		•	•	•	•	•	•		•	•	•	•								
greywacke	•	•	•		•		•	•	•	•	•	•		•	•	•	•								
argillaceous slate	•													•	•	•	•								
limestone	•	•	•		•		•	•	•	•	•	•		•	•	•	•				•	•	•	•	
Muschelkalk	•	•	•		•		•	•	•	•	•	•		•	•	•	•				•	•	•	•	
travertine	•	•	•		•		•	•	•	•	•	•		•	•	•	•				•	•	•	•	
calcareous tufa	•	•	•											•	•	•	•								
Solnhofen lithogr. limest.	•																				•	•	•	•	
dolomite	•	•	•	•						•	•	•		•	•	•	•					•		•	
onyx														•	•	•	•					•		•	
Metamorphic rock																									
orthoparagneiss	•	•	•										•		•	•	•	•	•		•	•		•	
quartzite	•														•	•	•					•		•	
mica schist	•														•	•	•					•		•	
chloritic schist	•														•	•	•					•		•	
serpentinite			•	•											•	•	•	•	•		•	•		•	
marble	•	•	•	•	•	•	•		•	•	•	•	•		•	•	•	•	•		•	•	•	•	
migmatite	•													•		•	•	•	•		•	•		•	
phyllite	•														•	•	•					•		•	
crystalline schist	•														•	•	•					•			
slate	•														•	•	•				•	•		•	•
granulite	•	•	•	•	•									•	•	•	•	•	•		•	•		•	

• Indicates common forms of surface treatment for the various types of stone, whereby other kinds of surface treatment are not excluded.

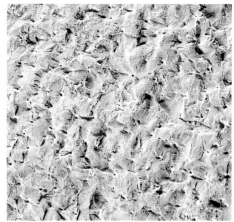

Punched or pointed surface (coarse/fine)

The surface is struck off using a hammer and a tapering, pointed iron. The entire area should be dressed in this way. For finer work, the punching should be evenly spaced and the hammer blows of equal force.

Vertically punched surface

This is a special form of punched or pointed work in which the iron is held almost at right angles to the surface, as opposed to the common form of treatment where the tool is held at an angle of about 45°.

Furrowed or strip-tooled surface

In this special type of treatment, a hammer and chisel are used to create regular parallel tracks to a predefined pattern. Using the same technique, it is also possible to produce special patterns (e.g. herringbone).

Notched-chiselled surface

The claw or toothed chisels used for this type of finish have a 2–5 cm wide tip with between three and five teeth. By applying the chisel in different directions, a variety of effects can be achieved (straight, curved, diagonal).

Boasted or droved surface

A wide range of effects can be achieved using boasting or drove chisels of different widths (ca. 8–15 cm) and by varying the spacing, the angle and direction of working, as well as the force of the hammer blows.

Herringbone boasted surface

With this type of treatment, the desired herringbone pattern can be achieved by using a roughly 3-centimetre-wide chisel and dressing the stone in alternating diagonal directions in parallel strips.

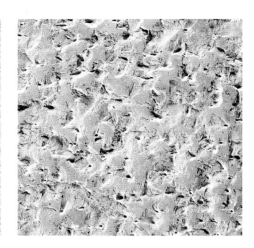

Bush-hammered surface

The interchangeable heads of the bush hammer have pyramidal teeth in various arrangements, depending on the coarseness/ fineness of the work required (see ill. p. 160). The tooth spacings range from 4 to 15 mm.

Fine bush-hammered surface

Using a hammer head or iron with a tooth spacing of 4–5 mm (12 × 12 teeth), a fine bush-hammered surface can be obtained with an even, homogeneous finish. This may also undergo subsequent grinding.

Pointed and ground surface

This type of work involves a combination of two quite different surface treatments. The stone is first punched or pointed, then ground to soften the angular finish achieved through the initial process.

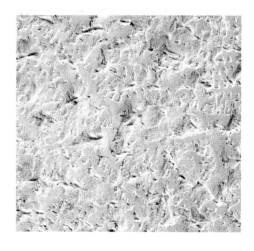

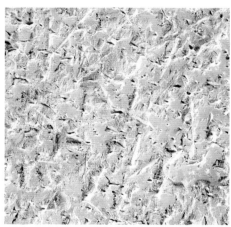

Punched, combed and ground surface

A punched or pointed finish can be reworked with a toothed chisel to remove irregularities and unwanted roughness in the surface. A subsequent grinding process will then provide a more uniform finish.

Punched, bush-hammered, axed and ground

With this kind of treatment, the surface of the stone is subjected to four quite different processes – a combination of enlivening and smoothing effects – which produce a varied and animated texture.

Coarse-punched and combed surface

An extremely lively texture can be obtained by dragging a serrated tool over a coarsely punched surface. In this way, an even, linear combed texture is overlaid on the rougher background treatment.

Bush-hammered, brushed and partly ground

In this case, three mechanical forms of treatment are applied to the surface. In the course of the work, the initially coarse-tooled stone undergoes a gradual process of refinement and smoothing.

Bush-hammered, brushed and waxed surface

The surface of the stone is subjected to two working processes, while the final wax treatment serves to intensify the colour and provides additional protection during subsequent jointing or other work.

Diamond-sawn surface

Diamond-blade saws – used in a horizontal to-and-fro movement, or in combination with circular or drag saws, or disc cutting tools – produce a relatively fine surface finish, although the saw marks remain visible.

Ground surface

Depending on the grain size of the abrasive sand used, coarse or microscopically fine circular marks will be visible in the surface. The work is usually carried out wet. Only small areas of stone can be dry ground.

Laser-treated surface

With laser technology, it is possible to create extremely fine indentations in a polished or smoothly ground surface. The colour brilliance of the stone is retained almost completely with this process.

Polished surface

Polishing is the final refinement applied to ground stone. Small openings in the surface can be filled with epoxy resin or mineral substances. Hard stone is polished mechanically with ceramic or diamond discs.

Finely hewn surface

The face of the naturally cleft stone from the quarry (quarry face) is finely tooled with a 3-cm-wide flat iron. The different angles and depths of the chiselling lend the surface an extremely lively effect.

Bush-hammered surface

The mechanically bush-hammered surface of the granite (hammer with 2 × 2 teeth) indicates the different effects that may be achieved when similar forms of treatment are applied to different types of stone.

Fine bush-hammered surface

In this example of fine bush-hammering, the sawn surface of the granite was mechanically worked with a pneumatic hammer (attachment with 5 × 5 teeth) to produce the desired effect.

Serrated strip treatment

The working technique is similar to that for bush-hammering, although here the surface is articulated into parallel, saddle-shaped strips and combed. The boldness of the striped effect depends on the type of stone.

Sandblasted surface

Sand or synthetic corundum (aluminium oxide) is blasted under great pressure on to the sawn stone to produce an evenly roughened surface. Saw marks remain visible, but a uniform, softened finish is achieved.

Flame treatment

A blowtorch flame is applied to the stone until the surface particles split off, forming an evenly roughened finish that reveals the crystalline structure. Quartz-bearing stone of adequate thickness is required for this process.

From the Molecule to the Finished Building

Jean-Luc Sandoz
Jan-Erik Schmitt

1   Platform for Expo 02 in Neuenburg, Switzerland
    (27,000 m² in O'Portune system)
2   Soffit of floor in O'Portune system
3   Experimental model of D-Dalle system
4   Model section with bonding angle
5   Sheet steel angle used in composite floor
    construction
6   Section through D-Dalle floor system
7   Section through O'Portune floor system

*Ecological considerations in the
21st century*
Safeguarding the environment and preserving the balance of nature are the great challenges facing humanity in the 21st century. With each new climate-related disaster, the concept of sustainable development gains in importance. Higher levels of carbon dioxide in the atmosphere lead to the reflection of infrared radiation and global warming, which in turn results in an intensification of the greenhouse effect. Studies of the development of global temperatures show that a further increase of 1.5–2.0 °C would mean that an average temperature had been attained that last prevailed on earth some five million years ago. That would be equivalent to leaping across 20 ice ages within a period of only 150 years. Climatologists, indeed, predict a mean rise in temperature of 2–6 °C, extreme in geological terms.

Nature and construction
Building construction and the use of the built environment are two major factors in the worldwide emission of CO_2. By this is meant the production of building materials on the one hand, and the heating and air-conditioning of buildings on the other. In view of the natural properties of wood, timber construction provides scope for ameliorating this situation. As part of their growth, trees absorb carbon dioxide, which is stored in the timber cut from them. A cubic metre of oak, for example, contains one tonne of CO_2. By specifying timber in building, when this is accompanied by reforestation, one not only stockpiles carbon dioxide by using timber; one also reduces CO_2 emissions by curbing the production of steel, concrete and other materials. Timber is thus ecologically beneficial, as long as it is used more or less in its natural state; i.e. in solid form without chemical treatment and the use of glues, and without long transport routes. Timber is also superior to other construction materials at the end

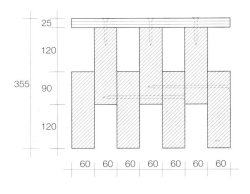

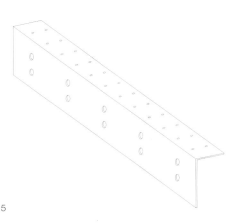

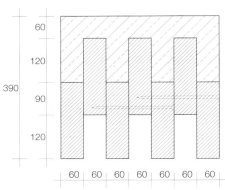

8

9

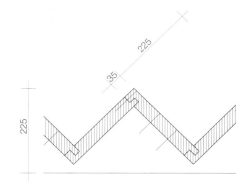

10

of its useful life, as a clean organic heating fuel. Timber structures also possess extremely good properties with respect to building physics. This is attributable to the great porosity of the material. With a density of 0.42 (420 kg/m³), spruce has a 73 per cent porosity, for example. With nearly three-quarters of its volume in the form of voids, this timber is an excellent insulating material and an efficient hydrothermal regulator in buildings. These qualities serve to minimize heating needs in winter and cooling needs in summer.

From single element to complete building
Throughout history, timber jointing tech-

niques have developed from the simplest connections of round pegs and scantlings, via iron ring fixings, to the nails and screws of the industrial revolution. The 20th century witnessed the development of laminated timber elements. Synthetic adhesives were employed in place of the mechanical fixings (as designed by the architect Philibert Delorme in the 16th century) between solid boards in similar forms of construction. These synthetic adhesives enabled the development of new forms of manufacture and assembly of structural elements to previously unimagined new dimensions. In order to achieve environmentally friendlier and more economical solutions, and to im-

prove the status of timber in comparison with steel and concrete, a number of research projects have been undertaken at the Swiss University of Technology in Lausanne (EPFL). These have focused on the development of new constructional principles and the realization of pilot schemes, as well as on the serialization of products. All the systems discussed below have one thing in common: they consist to more than 80 per cent of simple timber boards of commonly available dimensions. These were applied to timber stuctural systems requiring large spans, self-supporting wall elements, or composite timber and concrete slabs. The remaining 10–20 per cent are accounted for by technologically advanced timber products that serve to increase the economic efficiency of the concepts.
The simple timber board is multiplied to form a complete building. It fuses into a new, grander structure; just as glucose bonds to form cellulose in order to create timber in the first place.

O'Portune flooring element
In the 1980s, supported by investigations initiated by Prof. Julius Natterer at the EPFL, new paths were explored in the construction of solid timber slabs. Floor slabs of face-nailed boards on edge can be constructed to fit into any existing or planned construction. Spans of up to about 5 m can be bridged with this system. Elements of this kind also act as an effective buffer against moisture. The main problem of this form of construction is its relatively high cost: one cubic metre of timber is required to cover an area of only 5–6 m². A new concept was sought, therefore, that would use less timber and span greater distances. The outcome of the research was the O'Portune floor element, which represents an optimization of the face-nailed board system. Again, the boards are fixed together on-edge, but in this case, alternate members are vertically offset. With the same quantity of timber, therefore, it is possible to achieve a greater structural depth and rigidity. The individual boards are screwed rather than nailed to-

11

12

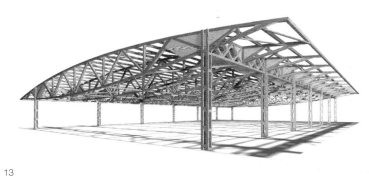

13

gether, whereby each screw passes through up to three shear joints.

For medium spans of between 5 and 8 m, O'Portune beams are used instead of continuous slabs. The beams occupy between half and a third of the overall floor area, and the system functions like a conventional beam structure with planar elements (oriented-strand board, plywood, etc.) between the downstand members. The aesthetic contrast between the beams and the panels can be utilized as desired.

For spans of between 9 and 11 m, the O'Portune beam system would cover the entire floor area. The fluting on the underside also ensures a considerable improvement to acoustic properties.

To bridge even greater spans (up to 18 m) or to carry greater loads, the timber floor can be incorporated in a composite form of construction with concrete. The system is based on the use of timber as a reinforcing element in the tension zone, with a concrete topping to resist compression. This serves to increase the load-bearing capacity of the slab. The offset timber boards provide an ideal means of anchoring the connecting members: sheet steel angles, perforated to achieve a better connection, are inserted at right-angles to the line of the boards (ills. 4,5).

"Wenus" slab element

The concept underlying such slab elements is based on studies of non-timber systems like corrugated cardboard, a material that is light and nevertheless robust on account of its internal corrugations. The translation of this idea into timber construction resulted in a W-shape (wave) cross-section 15 cm deep, which allows the use of 20-cm-wide boards. The rigidity of the final cross-section is 15 to 20 times greater than that of the original (horizontal) cross-section of the boards, using roughly the same quantity of timber.

The "Wenus" slab, as it is known, is a simple, self-supporting system. To facilitate assembly, the boards are screwed into position on a prefabricated construction template, which determines the wave structure,

at the ends and at intermediate points to create rigid elements. In this way, a minimum of timber is used per square metre of floor area. In addition, the slab element has a multi-functional character, since it is possible to leave the load-bearing structure exposed. Used as a wall element, it provides an aesthetically pleasing form of cladding (ill. 11); as a horizontal slab, with spans of up to 5.50 m, it provides a visually attractive exposed soffit. The inclination of the surfaces also lend it good acoustic properties. Flooring can be applied in a traditional manner with a floated screed and finishes, or in the form of floated parquet flooring on a layer of sound insulation. To improve the acoustic insulation even further, the slab elements can be partially filled with sand.

Ariane truss

The Ariane truss, which was designed to span distances of more than 50 m, can be formed with boards of up to 5 m in length. The principle of the truss is that the cross-sections of the beams are made up of a number of smaller cross-sections, similar to the composition of a rope (hence the allusion to Ariane or Ariadne from Greek mythology). The individual boards are screwed or nailed together to form the final cross-section. Junctions between the ends of the boards are staggered to avoid weak points. This system allows elements of theoretically unlimited length to be created. This technique is analogous to timber mast construction in boat building.

The various members of the truss are joined by means of internal gusset plates (ill. 12). These consist of laminated timber sheeting, which thus avoids the use of metal plates or cast steel elements. The diagonals can be directly bolted to the gusset plates, greatly simplifying assembly. All the timber members of a truss are drawn with the aid of CAD programs, and the data is finally transmitted to a carpentry works near the site, where the various parts are cut to size. Site assembly can then be carried out by carpenters from the area. In this way, local resources are used, both as labour and

materials, and transport routes are kept to a minimum, thus conserving energy.

Conclusion

Sustainable development demands a new approach to, and harsher judgement of, the technical achievements of the 20th century. Environmentally and economically speaking, alternative construction methods with reduced CO_2 levels must be developed.

As an organic carbon material used in construction, timber is ideally suited to maintaining the cycle of nature. All new ideas in building should be based on a concept of "molecular architecture", in which the individual constructional elements form the "basic molecules". Using traditional techniques in combination with new technology, concepts of this kind are already being implemented today to realize large-span open structures, or to form panels as shear-resistant elements for walls and floors. These concepts can be infinitely refined to comply with the requirements of architects and clients.

The systems described above, based on the use of nailed or screwed boards, without adhesives or additional chemical treatment of the timber, mark a small step towards a comprehensive concept of sustainable development – from the molecule to the finished building.   DETAIL 1/2 2004

8   Prefabricated Wenus elements
9   Wenus element forming cantilevered slab
10 Section through Wenus system
11 Wenus elements forming self-supporting, bracing wall
12 Ariane system gusset plate
13 Equestrian hall in Arezzo with a span of 45 m

Jean-Luc Sandoz was professor for timber construction at the EPFL in Lausanne from 1993 to 1998. Today, he teaches at various universities in Europe. Since 1998 he has also been in charge of the engineering consultancy CBS-CBT in Switzerland and France. (www.cbs-cbt.com)

Jan-Erik Schmitt studied building engineering in Karlsruhe, specializing in structural engineering. For two years he has been an assistant in the CBT engineering consultancy for timber construction in St Sulpice near Lausanne.

appendix

Design and construction teams • Contractors and suppliers

page 28
Media Library in Vénissieux
Avenue Marcel Houel
F-69631 Vénissieux

• Client:
Stadt Vénissieux
• Architects:
Dominique Perrault, Paris
Guilhem Menanteau (project architect),
Jérome Thibault, Eve Deprez,
Antoine Weygand (assistants)
• Structural engineer:
Guy Morisseau, Paris
• Consultants:
BERIM 17, Vénissieux

• Main contractor:
Lamy-Nallet, Givois
Tel.: +33 4 72492380
Fax: +33 4 78071980
• Structural steelwork:
Viry SA, Remiremont
Tel.: +33 3 296445-45
Fax: +33 3 296445-49
• Facade construction:
Atem, Mérignac
Tel.: +33 5 579200-92
Fax: +33 5 579200-90
• Facade construction:
Wicona, Bonneuil sur Marne
Tel.: +33 1 451380-00
Fax: +33 1 451380-20
• Roofing:
Sarec, Floirac
Tel.: +33 5 56866202
Fax: +33 5 56408265
• Furniture:
Forum Diffusion, Paris
Tel.: +33 1 43806200
Fax: +33 1 43807690

page 32
Museum in Kalkriese
Vennerstrasse 69
D-49565 Bramsche-Kalkriese GmbH

• Client:
Varusschlacht im Osnabrückerland
Museum und Park Kalkriese GmbH,
Bramsche-Kalkriese
• Architects:
Annette Gigon, Mike Guyer, Zurich
Volker Mencke (project architect),
• Structural engineers:
Gantert + Wiemeler Ingenieurplanung,
Münster
• Mechanical services:
Jager + Partner GmbH, Osnabrück
• Electrical planning:
H.-P. Wallenhorst, Osnabrück
• Landscape planning:
Zulauf Seippel Schweingruber
Landschaftsarchitekten, Baden
• Construction management:
Pbr Planungsbüro Rohling AG,
Osnabrück

page 38
Secondary School in Vienna
Heustadelgasse 4
A-1030 Vienna

Competition:	November 1998
Start of construction:	April 2000
Completion date:	May 2002
Type of school:	federal secondary school with various courses and levels
No. of classrooms:	32 for 900–1,000 pupils (years 1–8)
Special classrooms	10
No. of storeys:	2
Library:	153 m²
Central assembly hall:	458 m²
Multi-purpose space:	156 m²
Sports hall:	1225 m²
Courtyard:	30x40 m
Sports areas:	2,070 m²
Site area:	17,000 m²
Footprint:	5,550 m²
Net floor area:	11,450 m²
Gross volume:	57,500 m³
Parking spaces/ basement garage:	31
Construction costs:	€ 14,171,200

• Client:
BIG Bundesimmobilienges. mbH,
Vienna
• Architects:
Henke and Schreieck, Vienna
• Structural engineers:
Manfred Gmeiner, Martin Haferl, Vienna
• Mechanical services:
ZFG-Project GmbH / Eipeldauer GmbH,
Baden
• Building physics:
Walter Prause, Vienna

• Lettering:
Ingeborg Kumpfmüller, Vienna

• Contractor:
Strabag GmbH, Vienna
Tel.: +43 1 21728-0
Fax: +43 1 21728-146
• Facade construction:
Schüco International KG, Bielefeld
Tel.: +49 521 783-0
Fax: +49 521 783-451
www.schueco.de
• Facade construction:
Aluet Fassadentechnik GmbH, Vienna
Tel.: +43 1 616743-0
Fax: +43 1 616743-2
• Stonework:
NMP GmbH, Tribuswinkel / Baden
Tel.: +43 2252 46565-55
Fax: +43 2252 46565-65
horn@natursteinmontage.com
• Heating/Ventilation/Sanitary installation:
HTG GmbH, Vienna
Tel.: +43 1 8043548-61
Fax: +43 1 8043548-46
helmut.brandt@htg-austria.com
• Glass:
Petschenig glastec GmbH,
Lepoldsdorf
Tel.: +43 2216 2266
Fax: +43 2216 2266-44
• Dry construction system:
Stuck & Innenausbau Wilhelm Höger,
Vienna
Tel.: +43 1 2902972
Fax: +43 1 29029724
• Acoustic ceilings:
Hoesch Bausysteme GmbH, Vienna
Tel.: +43 1 61546-40
Fax: +43 1 61546-30
www.hoesch.at
• Joinery work:
KTB GmbH, Graz
Tel.: +43 0316 491224
Fax: +43 0316 491504
ktb.graz@utanet.at
• Sports equipment:
Erste Österr. Turn- und Sportgeräte-
fabrik GmbH, Wiener Neudorf
Tel.: +43 2236 63182-0
Fax: +43 2236 63186
office@atmos-platurn.at
www.atmos-platurn.at
• External / Sports facilities:
Swietelsky, Linz
Tel.: +43 0732 6971
Fax: +43 0732 6971-240

page 46
Museum of Soviet Special Camp in Sachsenhausen
Strasse der Nationen 22
D-16515 Oranienburg

• Client:
Ministry of Finance, Brandenburg
• Architects:
Schneider + Schumacher, Frankfurt
Nadja Hellenthal (project architect),
Gunilla Klinkhammer (assistant),
Simone Walser (project planner),
Volker Kilian, Jörg Böttcher, Nicolas
Schrabeck (competition)
• Structural engineers:
Bollinger + Grohmann, Frankfurt
• Mechanical services:
Brendel Ingenieure AG, Berlin
• Electrical planning:
Brendel Ingenieure AG, Berlin
• Landscape planning:
schneider + schuhmacher, Frankfurt
• Construction manager:
Christian Jähnig, Berlin

• Structure / Prefabricated facade:
Hering Bau GmbH & Co. KG
Hochbauen, Burbach
Tel.: +49 2736 27-0
Fax: +49 2736 27-256
www.bvmb.de
• Steelwork / Glass roof:
STS Stahltechnik GmbH, Delmenhorst
Tel.: +49 4221 6855-270
Fax: +49 4221 6855-279
www.sts-stahltechnik.de
• Exhibition facilities:
Stefan Haslbeck, Fulda
Tel.: +49 661 25090-95
Fax: +49 661 25090-93

page 50
Laboratory Building in Utrecht
Uithof
NL-Utrecht

• Client:
Universität Utrecht
• Architects:
UN Studios, Ben van Berkel, Caroline
Bos, Amsterdam
Ludo Grooteman, Walther Kloet, Harm
Wassink, Remco Bruggink, Jeroen
Kreijnen, Aad Krom, Laura Negrini,
Marc Prins, Marion Regitko, Henri Snel,
Paul Vriend, Jacco van Wengerden,
Mark Westerhuis (assistants)
• Structural engineers:
ABT Engineer, Velp
• Mechanical services:
Smits van Burgst, Zoetermeer
• Landscape planning:
West 8, Rotterdam

• General contractor:
Ballast Nedam N.V., Nieuwegein
Tel.: +31 30 285-3333
Fax: +31 30 285-4875

page 54
Primary School in Au
Walzenhauserstrasse
CH-9434 Au

• Client:
Primarschulgemeinde Au
• Architect:
Beat Consoni, Rorschach
Daniel Frick (assistant)
• Structural engineers:
Zoller AG Bauingenieure,
St. Margrethen
• Mechanical services:
Enplan AG, St. Gallen
• Electrical planning:
Projekt AG, Heerbrugg
• Sanitary planning:
Tomaschett, Rorschach
• Construction manager:
Frankhauser Brocker Architects
AG, Au

• Main contractor:
Dittadi AG, Au
Tel.: +41 744 1669
Fax: +41 744 1769
• Metalwork / Windows / External doors:
Strub, Au
Tel.: +41 744 2455
Fax: +41 744 2450
• Metalwork / Roofing:
HWT Haus- und Wassertechnik, Au
Tel.: +41 744 1559
Fax: +41 744 6058
• Sunshading:
SWEMO AG, St. Gallen
Tel.: +41 278 6033
Fax: +41 278 6083
• Heating systems:
Hälg & Co. AG, St. Gallen
Tel.: +41 243 3838
Fax: +41 243 3840
• Ventilation systems:
Schenk, Bruhin & Co. AG, Sargans
Tel.: +41 81 723 0261
Fax: +41 81 723 7646
• Joinery work:
Zomoform, Au
Tel.: +41 744 1633
Fax: +41 744 6841
• Wall elements:
Rosconi AG, Villmergen
Tel.: +41 56 622 9430
Fax: +41 56 621 9844
• Stone floor coverings:
Castratori Baukeramik, Au
Tel.: +41 744 4848
Fax: +41 744 5588
• Luminaires:
Tulux AG, Tuggen
Tel.: +41 55 445 1616
Fax: +41 55 455 1920

• Wall panels / Projection wall:
Hunziger AG, Thalwill
Tel.: +41 722 8111
Fax: +41 720 5629
• Lifts:
Köppel Aufzüge AG, Au
Tel.: +41 747 4780
Fax: +41 747 4781

page 58
Restaurant in Brighton
Bartholomew Square
GB-Brighton, Sussex

• Client:
Moshi Moshi, London
• Architects:
dRMM, de Rijke Marsh Morgan, London
Alex de Rijke, Michael Spooner,
Satoshi Isono (assistants)
• Structural engineers:
Michael Hadi Associates, London
• Landscape planning:
dRMM, London
• Furniture design:
dRMM, London
• Construction manager:
Guildprime Ltd., Rayleigh

• Translucent facade:
Kalwall, USA-Manchester
Tel.: +1 603 6273861
Fax: +1 603 6277905
www.kalwall.com
• Weathered copper (facade):
TECU, Osnabrück
Tel.: +49 541 321-4323
Fax: +49 541 321-4030
info-tecu@kme.com
www.tecu.com
• External timber paving:
HLD Ltd, Gainsborough
Tel.: +44 1427 611800
Fax: +44 1427 612867
technical@hld.co.uk
www.hld.co.uk
• Furniture:
Lloyd Loom Ltd., Spalding
Tel.: +44 1775 712111
Fax: +44 1775 710571
info@lloydloom.com
www.lloydloom.com
• Fluorescent ceiling paint:
Bristol Paints Ltd., Bristol
Tel.: +44 20 7624 4370
tech.sales@bristolpaint.com
www.bristolpaint.com
• Catering facilities:
Trak Conveyor Systems Ltd., Merseyside
Tel.: +44 151 549-1010
Fax: +44 151 549-1212
sales@trakhupfer.co.uk
www.trakhupfer.co.uk

page 63
Wine Tavern in Fellbach
Cannstatterstrasse 13/2
D-70734 Fellbach

• Client:
Markus Heid, Fellbach
• Architect:
Christine Remensperger, Stuttgart
Johannes Michel (assistant)
• Structural engineers:
Dieter Seibold, Fellbach
• Building physics:
Jürgen Horitmann, Andreas Berger,
Altensteig

• Structure:
Homann Rothfurs GmbH, Stuttgart
Tel.: +49 711 23685-91
Fax: +49 711 23685-93
• Windows:
Weber, Ehingen
Tel.: +49 7391 7096-70
Fax: +49 7391 7096-80
• Joinery work / Interior fittings:
B + K Innenausbau, Stuttgart
Tel.: +49 711 530450-5
Fax: +49 711 530450-4
• Floor finishes:
Fußboden Haag, Stuttgart
Tel.: +49 711 13485-0
Fax: +49 711 13485-90
• Tables and chairs:
Sirch und Bitzer, Ottobeuren
Tel.: +49 8338 1060
Fax: +49 8338 933470
• Lighting:
Uli Jetzt Beleuchtungen GmbH,
Backnang
Tel.: +49 7191 3238-0
Fax: +49 7191 3238-2
info@uli-jetzt.de
www.uli-jetzt.de

page 68
Pedestrian Bridge in Boudry
CH-2017 Boudry

• Client:
Kanton Neuchâtel
• Architects:
Geninasca Delefortrie SA,
Architectes FAS SIA, Neuchâtel
Christine Perla (assistant)
• Structural engineers:
Chablais Poffet SA, Esavayer-le-Lac

• Steelwork:
Steiner SA, La Chaux-de-Fonds
Tel.: +41 32 96824-24
Fax: +41 32 96824-54
• Foundations:
Michel Morciano SA, Boudry
Tel.: +41 32 8424486
Fax: +41 32 8425503
• Timber elements:
Tschäppät SA, Cornaux
Tel.: +41 32 7571147
Fax: +41 32 7571943

page 70
Hotel in Groningen
Grote Gang
NL-Groningen

• Client:
Nijestee Vastgoed, Dhr. Renken,
Groningen
• Architects:
Foreign Office Architects, Alejandro
Zaera Polo, Farshid Moussavi, London
Marco Guarnieri, Xavier Ortiz,
Lluis Viu Rebes (assistants)
• Construction planning:
ARTèS, Groningen
• Structural engineers:
Ingenieursbureau Dijkhuis, Groningen
• Mechanical services:
Wolter & Dros Aquatherm, Groningen
• Electrical planning:
Wolter & Dros Aquatherm, Groningen

• General contractor:
Van Wijnen, Groningen
Tel.: +31 50 5414416
www.vanwijnen.nl
• Aluminium facade:
Seedyk Geveltechniek, Buitenpost
Tel.: +31 511 5437-35
Fax: +31 511 5437-85
info@seedyk.nl
www.seedyk.nl
• External steel plates:
TSV Metaalbouw, Nieuw-Buinen
Tel.: +31 599 650778
Fax: +31 599 651060
info@tsv.nl
www.tsv.nl
• Steel stairs:
Stairway, Hengelo
Tel.: +31 74 2503232

• Internal doors:
Bouwprodukten Zomer, Vries
Tel.: +31 592 544114

page 74
House in Dortmund
Kuntzestrasse 71
D-44225 Dortmund

• Client:
Sabine and Martin Ebeling, Dortmund
• Architects:
Archifactory.de, Bochum
• Structural engineers:
Assmann Beraten und Planen,
Dortmund
• Landscape planning:
Archifactory.de, Bochum
• Construction manager:
Archifactory.de, Bochum

• Structure / Earthworks:
Aasee Baugesellschaft mbH, Bottrop
Tel.: +49 2045 4073-38
Fax: +49 2045 4073-39
• Metalwork / Glazing:
Fa. Kremer, Gelsenkirchen
Tel.: +49 209 4080-10
Fax: +49 209 4080-11
info@kremer-metallbau.de
www.kremer-metallbau.de
• Carpentry / Timber engeneering:
Greitemann, Meschede-Erflinghausen
Tel.: +49 291 53131
Fax: +49 291 53263
greitemann.erflinghausen@t-online.de
• Ironmongery:
W. Siegel GmbH, Bottrop
Tel.: +49 2045 4951
Fax: +49 2045 4976
• Plastering / Painting:
Margerka OHG, Recklinghausen
Tel.: +49 2361 184075
Fax: +49 2361 184978
• Ytong blocks:
Hebel AG, Fürstenfeldbruck
Tel.: +49 8141 98-0
Fax: +49 8141 98-324
www.xella.de
• Roof insulation:
DOW Deutschland GmbH, Schwalbach
Tel.: +49 6196 566-0
Fax: +49 6196 566-402
www.styrofoam.de
• Optifloat glass:
Pilkington Deutschland AG, Essen
Tel.: +49 201 1254
Fax: +49 201 1255075
www.pilkington.de
• Museum terrazzo flooring:
Franz Ernst GmbH, Recklinghausen
Tel.: +49 2361 61031
Fax: +49 2361 375457

page 80
Store and Studio in Hagi
J-Hagi-shi, Yamaguchi

• Client:
Kazuhiko Miwa, Yamaguchi
• Architects:
Sambuichi Architects, Hiroshi Sambui-
chi, Hiroshima
Hidenori Ejima, Manabu Aritsuka,
Tsuyoshi Oda, Masataka Maehara
(assistants)
• Structural engineers:
Sadakatsu Nishimura, Hiroshima

• Formwork:
Takemiya Corporation, Yamaguchi-ken
Tel.: +81 832 83 1577
• Sanitary installation:
Toto, Fukuoka
Tel.: +81 93 951 2111
• Lighting:
Nippo, Tokyo
Tel.: +81 3 5703 2181
• Chairs:
hhstyle.com, Tokyo
Tel.: +81 3 3400 3434

page 84
Housing Development in Dornbirn
Sebastianstrasse 6a
A-6850 Dornbirn

• Client:
I+R Schertler GmbH,
Lauterach
• Architects:
Baumschlager-Eberle, Lochau
Harald Nasahl (project architect)
Christine Falkner (assistant)
• Structural engineers:
Rüsch, Diem, Schuler, Eric Hämmerle,
Dornbirn
• Mechanical services:
Peter Diem, Bregenz
• Electrical planning:
Elmar Graf GmbH, Dornbirn

• Landscape planning:
Geringer Gartenpark GmbH,
Ranken
• Building physics:
Lothar Künz, Hard

• Master builder (timber construction)
Schertler-Alge GmbH, Lauterach
Tel.: +43 5574 6888-0
Fax: +43 5574 6888-199
www.schertler-alge.at
• Glazed facade:
Glas Marte GmbH, Dornbirn
Tel.: +43 5574 6722-0
Fax: +43 5574 6722-55
• Metalwork / Roof waterproofing:
Hollenstein Spengler GmbH, Dornbirn
Tel.: +43 5572 23234
Fax: +43 5572 31154
• Electrical installation:
Elmar Graf GmbH, Dornbirn
Tel.: +43 5572 23074-0
Fax: +43 5572 22861
• Heating/Ventilation/Sanitary installation:
Hepp Walter GmbH, Dornbirn
Tel.: +43 5572 24486
Fax: +43 5572 24486-14
• Screeds:
Tschanhenz GmbH, Bludenz
Tel.: +43 5552 69111
Fax: +43 5552 69111-4

page 87
**University for Applied Design
in Wiesbaden**
Unter den Eichen 5
D-65195 Wiesbaden

• Client:
Ministry for Science and the Arts in Hesse
• Architects:
Mahler Günster Fuchs Architects,
Stuttgart
Florian Technau (project architect),
Alexander Carl, Martina Schlude,
Karin Schmid-Arnoldt (assistants)
• Structural engineers:
Fischer & Friedrich, Stuttgart
• Electrical planning:
Paul & Gampe & Partner GmbH,
Esslingen
• Landscape planning:
Taunusfilm Dirk Schelhorn, Frankfurt
• Acoustic planning:
Ingenieurbüro Leschnik, Buxtehude
• Project manager:
Oktavia Galinke, Frankfurt

• Structure:
Hoch- und Tiefbau Schick GmbH,
Bad Kissingen
Tel.: +49 9736 420
Fax: +49 9736 4299

• Facade:
Merk Holzbau GmbH & Co., Aichach
Tel.: +49 8251 9081-20
Fax: +49 8251 9081-03
• Window elements:
Okalux GmbH, Marktheidenfeld
Tel.: +49 9391 900-0
Fax: +49 9391 900-100
www.okalux.de
• Windows:
Schwaiger Fenster, Rohrdorf
Tel.: +49 8032 9545-19
Fax: +49 8032 9545-28
• Glass blocks:
E-Glasbeton GmbH, Oberursel
Tel.: +49 6171 5207577
Fax: +49 6171 581270
• Roof waterproofing:
Bock Industriebedachungen GmbH,
Moringen
Tel.: +49 5554 9922-0
Fax: +49 5554 9922-22

page 92
Laban Centre in London
Creekside, Deptford
GB-London

• Client:
Laban Centre, London
• Architects:
Herzog & de Meuron, Basle
Michael Casey (project architect),
Jayne Barlow, Konstanze Beelitz, Chris-
tine Binswanger, Nandita Boger, Fun
Budiman, Peter Cookson, Irina Davido-
vici, Rita Maria Diniz, Hernan Fierro-
Castro, Alice Foxley, Harry Gugger,
Jacques Herzog, Detlef Horisberger,
Jean Paul Jaccaud, Nick Lyons, Stefan
Marbach, Christoph Mauz, Pierre de
Meuron, Christopher Pannett, Kristen
Whittle
• Structural engineers:
Whitby Bird & Partners, London
• Mechanical services:
Whitby Bird & Partners, London
• IT engineers:
Arup Communications, London
• Landscape planning:
Vogt Landschaftsarchitekten, Zurich
• Acoustic planning:
Arup Acoustics, Winchester

• Facade cladding:
Rodeca GmbH, Mühlheim a.d. Ruhr
Tel.: +49 208 76502-0
Fax: +49 208 76502-11
www.rodeca.de
• Facade construction:
Metallbau Hirsch AG, Biel
Tel.: +41 32 3441711
Fax: +41 32 3417735

page 98
Weekend House in Australia
AUS-Victoria

• Client:
No details
• Architects:
Sean Godsell Architects, Melbourne
Hayley Franklin (assistant)
• Structural engineers:
Felicetti Pty Ltd., Melbourne
• Landscape planning:
Sean Godsell with Sam Cox, Melbourne
• Project management:
Kane Constructions Pty Ltd, Richmond

• Steel facade framing:
Dandenong Steel Pty Ltd., Dandenong
Tel.: +61 3 9793 3348
• Toughened safety glass:
Pilkington Pty Ltd., Victoria
Tel.: +61 3 9212 2222
• Preoxidized steel panels:
BHP Billiton Pty Ltd., Victoria
• Metalworking / steel doors and
windows:
Shush Metal Design, Kensington
Tel.: +61 3 9372 6211
Fax: +61 3 9372 6200
• Jarrah sunshading strips:
Marant Industries, Victoria

page 102
Administration Building in Reutlingen
Schulstrasse 23
D-72764 Reutlingen

• Client:
Verband der Metall- und Elektroindust-
rie Baden Württemberg e.V., Stuttgart
• Architects:
Allmann Sattler Wappner, Munich
Helgo von Meier, Georg Rafailidis, An-
gela Hertel, Bettina Mutzenbach, Sus-
anne Rath (assistants)
• Structural engineers:
Sobek Ingenieure, Stuttgart

• Facade planning:
Fuchs R + R, Munich
• Metal sheets to plinth and
external areas:
Konzeption + Grafik, Roswitha Allmann
Mediendesign, Munich
• Landscape architects:
Realgrün, Munich
• Energy consultants:
TransSolar Energietechnik GmbH,
Stuttgart

Facade construction:
Frener & Reifer Metallbau GmbH,
Bressanone
Tel.: +39 0472 270111
Fax: +39 0472 833550
www.frener-reifer.it
• Floor finishes / Synthetic resin screed:
Sto GmbH, Stühlingen
Tel.: +49 7744 57-0
Fax: +49 7744 572010
www.sto.de
• Lighting (downlights):
Zumtobel Staff GmbH, Dornbirn
Tel.: +43 5572 3900
Fax: +43 5572 390275
www.zumtobelstaff.com

page 106
**Production Building for Large-Scale
Printing Technology in Grosshöflein**
Industriestrasse 1
A-7051 Grosshöflein

Fabricated products / Printed items
Production area: 1,168 m²
Administration area: 508 m²
Total area: 2341 m²
Volume: 12,989 m³
Total costs: € (9000)
Costs/m²: € 466 / m²
Costs/m³: € 84 / m²
Height between
floors (prod.): 7.41 m
Height between
floors (admin.): 3.77 m
maximum height: 7.71 m
External dimensions: 56.3 × 29.7 m
Free span (structure): 20.8 × 8.7 m
Column grid: 6.2 m
Beginning of
construction: Dec. 2001
Completion: June 2002

• Client:
Trevision GmbH, Grosshöflein
• Architects:
querkraft architects, Vienna
• Structural engineers:
Vasko & Partner, Vienna
• Mechanical services:
PME, Ollern/Riedberg

• Lighting design:
Konzept Licht Steindl, Vienna
• Artists:
Trevision GmbH, Grosshöflein

• Main contractor:
Bader Bau GmbH, Horitschon
Tel.: +43 2610 422-01
Fax: +43 2610 422-17
• Steelwork:
Buttazoni GmbH, Sollenau
Tel.: +43 2628 48375
Fax: +43 2628 48375-20
www.buttazoni.at
• Facade:
Brucha GmbH, Vienna
Tel.: +43 1 6670622-0
Fax: +43 1 6678750
www.brucha.at
• Aluminium sections system:
Wicona Bausysteme GmbH, Ulm
Tel.: +49 731 3984-0
Fax: +49 731 3984-241
www.wicona.de
• Roof / Facade:
Gerger Stahlbau GmbH,
St. Michael im Burgenland
Tel.: +43 3327 2430-0
Fax: +43 3327 2430-41
stahlbau.gerger@telecom.at
• Corrugated metal cladding:
Taborsky Dach- und Wandsysteme,
Gramatneusiedl
Tel.: +43 2234 74008
Fax: +43 2234 74008-27
www.wellblech.com
• Glass elements:
Glas Meisl, Graz
Tel.: +43 316 401124-12
Fax: +43 316 401144-18
• Electrical installation:
Radics GmbH, Eisenstadt
Tel.: +43 2682 63556
Fax: +43 2682 63556-16
radics@bkf.at
• Sanitary installation:
Aqua, Theresienfeld
Tel.: +43 2622 72424
Fax: +43 2622 72424-14
schefberger@aon.at
• High-level racking:
Forster Metallbau GmbH, St. Peter
Tel.: +43 7477 401-0
Fax: +43 7477 401-440
www.forster.at
• Partitions:
Kautex Textron GmbH & Co. KG, Bonn
Tel.: +49 228 488-0
Fax: +49 228 488-3710
www.kautex.de
• Industrial flooring:
Regele, Pottendorf
Tel.: +43 2623 72431
Fax: +43 2623 72431
• Lighting:
Trilux-Lenze GmbH & Co. KG,
Arnsberg
Tel.: +49 2932 301-630
Fax: +49 2932 301-510
• Interior fittings:
Stak Living Home International, Vienna
Tel.: +43 1 7136161
Fax: +43 1 7136161
www.stak.at
• Lock systems:
Kaba Gege GmbH, Herzogenburg
Tel.: +43 2782 808-0
Fax: +43 2782 808-5505
www.kabagege.com

page 114
Extension of the Albertina in Vienna
Augustinerstrasse 1
A-1010 Vienna

• Client:
Burghauptmannschaft Österreich, Hof-
burg Säulenstiege und Albertina Vienna
• Architects:
Erich G. Steinmayr & Friedrich H.
Mascher, Feldkirch / Vienna,
Josef Nachbaur-Sturm
(project architect)
Matthias Bauer, Josef Burtschser,
Ulrike Caglar, Christian Dansco, Robert
Dünser, Alfred Fink, Ellen Gehrke,
Helmut Gruber, Stefan Gruber, Bernd
Heger, Benedikt Neuhoeffer, Maja
Lorbek, Daniel Pleikies, Peter Prinz-
Sobre, Philipp Schüssling, Sebastian
Wörter (assistants)
• Structural engineers:
Robert Harrauer & Wolfgang Tötzel,
Vienna
• Mechanical services:
All-Projekt, Vienna
• Lighting design:
Lighting Design Vienna, Eichgraben
• Building physics:
H.-P. Dworak, Vienna
• Project management:
ISP Schickl & Partner, Vienna

• General contractor for earthworks,
structure, interior fittings, excluding
glazing and metalwork:
Porr AG, Vienna
Tel.: +43 50 626-0
Fax: +43 50 626-1111
• General contractor for facade
construction, interior fittings:
ALU Sommer, Stoob
Tel.: +43 2612 42-556
Fax: +43 2612 42-904
www.alu-sommer.at
• Black anodized aluminium components:
BWB Oberflächentechnik Altenrhein
AG, Altenrhein
Tel.: +41 71 85861-64
Fax: +41 71 85861-71
www.bwb.ch
• Natural anodized aluminium
components:
ARGU Oberflächentechnik GmbH,
Gruenburg
Tel.: +43 7257 7696-0
Fax: +43 7257 7696-41
www.agru.net
• Side wall sections:
Alusuisse AG, CH-Neuhausen
Tel.: +41 52 674-9111
Fax: +41 52 674-9676
www.algroup.ch

page 122
Studio Extension in Olot
Valls Vells 9
E-17800 Olot

· Client:
Ruscalleda + Verdaguer, Olot
· Architects:
Jordi Hidalgo + Daniela Hartmann,
Barcelona
Jauhiainen Tuomo (assistant), Helsinki
· Construction manager:
Jordi Hidalgo, Barcelona

· Contractor:
LI-BRA Serveis de Construcció i
Restauració S.L., Olot
Tel.: +34 972 261960
· Metalwork:
Metal.liques Olot S.L., Olot
Tel.: +34 972 269282

page 126
House in Mont-Malmédy
Mont
B-4960 Malmédy

· Client:
De Pauw-Herrmann, Antwerp
· Architects:
ARTAU SCRL, Norbert Nelles, Luc
Dutilleux, Malmedy
Fabienne Courtejoie, Natalie Ries
(assistants)
· Structural engineers:
BCT, Philippe Colson, Liège

· Structure:
Michel Hendrick, Ouifat
Tel.: +32 80 44 55 76
· Roof:
Zanzen Paul Sprl, Sourbrodt
Tel.: +32 80 4402-20
Fax: +32 80 4402-21
· Facade construction:
Carrières de la Warche, Malmédy
Tel.: +32 80 770058

Fax: +32 80 339990
info@carrieres-nelles.com
www. carrieres-nelles.com
· Interior fittings / Furniture:
Jacques Thunus Sprl, Waimes
Tel.: +32 80 444163
Fax: +32 80 445483
· Electrical installation:
Thérer Marcel Sprl, Malmédy
Tel.: +32 80 330337
· Dry construction system:
Dethier & Fils Sprl,
Butgenbach
Tel.: +32 80 678571
Fax: +32 80 679153

page 130
**Representation of the States of
Brandenburg and Mecklenburg-
Western Pomerania in Berlin**
In den Ministergärten 1 and 3
D-10117 Berlin

· Client:
Federal State of Brandenburg, Federal
State of Mecklenburg-Western Pomera-
nia, represented by their respective
Finance Ministries and the Potsdam
Real Estate and Building Department
· Architects:
Gerkan, Marg und Partner, Hamburg
Stephan Rewolle (project architect),
Kemal Akay, Margret Böthig, Annett
Janeczko, Antje Pfeifer, Katja Bernert,
Elke Hoffmeister (assistants)
· Structural engineers:
Köber & Partner GmbH,
Brandenburg a.d.Havel
· Mechanical services:
Bauplan, Schwerin
· Electrical planning:
ITA Ingenieurbüro Technische
Ausrüstung GmbH Potsdam, Bergholz-
Rehbrücke
· Landscape planning:
Wes & Partner, Krafft-Wehberg,
Berlin
· Lighting planning:
Conceptlicht GmbH, Traunreut

· Stone facade:
Natursteinwerk Villmar, Villmar/Lahn
Tel.: +49 6482 9141-0
Fax: +49 6482 9141-25
· Metal windows facade:
Schindler GmbH & Co., Roding
Tel.: +49 9461 409-0
Fax: +49 9461 409-100
· Wooden windows facade:
VHB Vereinigte Holzbaubetriebe,
Memmingen
Tel.: +49 8331 9464-0
Fax: +49 8331 9464-19

· Slates:
Empresa das Lousas de Valongo,
Valongo
Tel.: +351 2 415740-0
· Stone floor coverings:
Saalburger Marmor Werk, Saalburg
Tel.: +49 36647 300-0
Fax: +49 36647 300-30
· Ironmongery:
Hauk Metallbau, Nauen
Tel.: +49 3321 4494-0
Fax: +49 3321 4494-29
· Lighting:
Metallkonstruktion Birke GmbH, Pegau
Tel.: +49 34296 762-41
Fax: +49 34296 762-42
· Plastering:
Knauf, Berlin
Tel.: +49 30 397816-26
Fax: +49 30 397816-30
· Chair lift:
Innocon, Zossen
Tel.: +49 3377 34062-3
Fax: +49 3377 34062-4
· Acoustic walls:
Topakustik, Berlin
Tel.: +49 30 306923-0
Fax: +49 30 3017025

page 136
School Building in Zurich
Stapferstrasse 48/50
CH-8006 Zurich

· Client:
Amt für Hochbauten Stadt Zurich
· Architects:
Patrick Gmür Architects, Zurich
Michael Geschwentner, Franziska
Plüss, Alessandra Boggia, Barbara
Ruppeiner, Katja Albiez, Michèle
Mambourg, Jan Stoos, Diana de
Stopani, Monique Strüby, Anja Hahn
(assistants)
· Structural engineers:
Aerni + Aerni, Zurich
· Mechanical services:
Zünd Heizungstechnik, Zurich
· Electrical planning:
Mehler + Partner AG, Meilen
· Sanitary planning:
Jaques von Moos, Zurich
· Landscape planning:
Raderschall Landschaftsarchitekten
AG, Zurich
· Construction manager:
GMS Partner AG, Zurich
· Artists:
Peter Rösch, Lucerne
· Paint:
Lascauxfarben, Acryl
Barbara Diethelm AG, Brüttisellen
Tel.: +41 1 807414-1

Fax: +41 1 807414-0
www.lascaux.ch

page 138
**Housing and Commercial Block in
Zurich**
Neugasse/Luisenstrasse
CH-Zurich

· Client:
Neugass Kino AG, Zurich
Lifä AG, Zurich
· Architects:
Marcel Meili, Markus Peter Archi-
tects, Zurich with Zeno Vogel
Astrid Staufer & Thomas Hasler
Architects, Frauenfeld
Milan Augustin (project architect),
Peter Althaus, Riet Bezzola, Patrick
Wiesmann, Stefan Deola, Alexander
Albertini, Emil Häberlin (assistants)
· Structural engineers:
Karl Dillier, Seuzach
· Construction manager:
Gianesi + Hofmann, Zumikon
Urs Jöger

· Thermal insulation composite system:
Greutol AG, Otelfingen
Tel.: +43 411 77-77
Fax: +43 411 77-78
www.greutol.ch
· Structure:
Gautschi Bau AG, Affoltern
Tel.: +41 1 761-4747
Fax: +41 1 761-9557
www.gautschibau.ch
· Facade:
Diener AG, Zurich
Tel.: +41 1 253703-0
Fax: +41 1 253703-1
www.diener.ch
· Glass elements:
Pilkington Schweiz AG, Wikon
Tel.: +41 62 745010-1
Fax: +41 62 745010-2
www.pilkington.com
· Floor coverings:
Forbo Repoxit AG, Winterthur
Tel.: +41 52 242-1721
Fax: +41 52 242-9391
www.repoxit.forbo.com

Contractors and suppliers
Details of contractors and suppliers are
based on information provided by the
respective architects.

Photo credits

p. 9:
Duccio Malagamba, Barcelona

p. 10:
ApA© R. Roozen

pp.11/4, 51–53, 21 top right,
58, 60–62, 70–73, 87, 88, 91,
92–93 bottom, 95, 97:
Christian Richters, Münster

p. 11/6:
Klaus Kinold, Munich

pp. 12, 13/5:
MIT Press

pp. 13/3, 13/4:
University of Southern California

p. 14:
Tim Street-Porter, Los Angeles

p. 15:
Scot Zimmerman, Heber City, Utah

pp. 16 top, 17 top right, 20 top, 109,
143, 159, 168:
Frank Kaltenbach, Munich

pp. 16 bottom, 32, 33, 35, 138–142,
151:
Heinrich Helfenstein, Zurich

pp. 17 top left, 19 bottom, 63–67:
Roland Halbe, Stuttgart

p. 17 bottom:
Ralph Feiner, Malans

p. 18 top:
Hisao Suzuki, Barcelona

p. 18 bottom:
Gerrit Engel, Berlin

pp. 19 top, 27, 90, 93 top, 94, 96, 157:
Christian Schittich, Munich

pp. 20 bottom, 38, 39, 41–43,
45 bottom, 117, 120:
Margherita Spiluttini, Vienna

p. 21 bottom:
Dennis Gilbert/View, London

pp. 21 top left, 84–86:
Eduard Hueber, New York

p. 22 top:
from: Kurt Ackermann (editor),
Industriebau, DVA, Stuttgart, 1984

p. 22 bottom:
H. G. Esch, Hennef

p. 23 top:
Archiv Herbert Gunia, Essen

p. 23/5:
Museum für Verkehr und Technik
Berlin, Borsig Archiv

p. 24 top:
from: Colin Davies, *High-Tech
Architektur*, Gerd Hatje, Stuttgart, 1988

p. 24 bottom:
Richard Davies, London

p. 25:
Ken Kirkwood, Northamptonshire

p. 26 top:
Michael Wurzbach, Hamburg

p. 26 bottom:
Jens Willebrand, Cologne

pp. 28, 31:
André Morin / ADAGP, Paris

pp. 29, 30:
Georges Fessey / ADAGP, Paris

p. 34:
Ruedi Baur / Integral, Zurich

p. 36:
Klemens Ortmeyer / architekturphoto,
Brunswick

pp. 46, 47, 48, 49:
Jörg Hempel, Aachen

p. 54:
Michael Egloff, Zurich

p. 55:
Klaus Kinold, Munich

pp. 68–69:
Thomas Jantscher, Colombier

pp. 75–78:
Gernot Maul, Münster

pp. 80, 81, 83:
Shinkenchiku-sha, Tokyo

p. 89:
Ali Moshiri, Zierenberg

pp. 98–101:
Earl Carter, St Kilda / Australia

pp. 102, 104:
Stefanie Friedrich, Munich /
Frener & Reifer, Bressanone

p. 103:
Florian Holzherr, Munich

p. 105:
Jens Passoth, Berlin

pp. 106, 107, 110:
Herta Hurnaus, Vienna

p.114:
Bruno Klomfar, Vienna

pp. 116, 119:
Anna Blau, Vienna

pp. 118, 121:
Christa Schicker, Munich

pp. 122, 123, 125:
Eugeni Pons, Girona
pp. 126–127, 129:
Jean-Luc Deru, Liège

pp. 130–135:
Christian Gahl, Berlin

p. 136 top:
Menga von Sprecher, Zurich

pp. 136 bottom, 137:
Georg Aerni, Zurich

p. 144:
Bouygen company, Paris

p. 145:
VSL-Intrafor Gruppe, Subingen

p. 146:
Gaston Bergerent / AMC, Paris

p. 148:
Beton Marketing Nord, Sehnde

p. 150:
ADMM-ADAGP, Paris

p. 152 bottom centre + right:
Paul Warchol, New York

p. 153:
Marliese Darsow, Krefeld

p. 155 top left:
Rheinzink GmbH & Co. KG, Datteln

p. 155 top right, bottom left:
Heinrich Fiedler GmbH & Co. KG,
Regensburg

p. 155 bottom centre:
Fils S.p.A., Pedrengo

p. 155 bottom right:
AIM, Nürtingen

p. 156 top left:
Corus Bausysteme GmbH, Koblenz

p. 156 top centre:
Alcan Singen GmbH, Singen

p. 156 top right:
Hoesch Siegerlandwerke GmbH,
Siegen

p. 156 bottom:
Gebr. Kufferath GmbH & Co. KG,
Düren

p. 158:
Eckhard Matthäus, Augsburg

Photos for which no credit is given were either provided by the respective
architects, or they are product photos from the DETAIL archives.

Black-and-white photos introducing main sections:

p. 9:   Montessori College Oost in Amsterdam
         architects: Architectuurstudio Herman Hertzberger, Amsterdam

p. 27:   University for Applied Design in Wiesbaden
         architects: Mahler Günster Fuchs, Stuttgart

p. 143: House C Park village in Munich-Unterföhring
         architects: Lauber Architects, Munich

p. 168: M-Preis Grocery in Stuhlfelden
         architects: Holzbox Tyrol, Innsbruck

DETAIL

DETAIL – INTERNATIONAL REVIEW OF ARCHITECTURE AND CONSTRUCTION DETAILS

A subscription to DETAIL: state-of-the-art knowledge delivered to your door

A vision? A promising beginning? But how can one turn visions into reality?

With DETAIL, this is possible: a journal packed with innovative ideas and practical information. International architects and planners show how they have realized their concepts.

Build a valuable archive with DETAIL – the foundation for your personal success.

Choose the subscription that meets your needs. The current publishing programme is shown on the following pages – everything you require for your next project.

Prices as at January 2004

Classic subscription
Model international schemes: a wealth of examples and information on specific construction topics, with extensive keys and true-to-scale detail drawings

€ 109.–

(10 issues a year + p/p + VAT)

Advantages to you:
- DETAIL sent directly to your home
- personal online access at www.detail.de
- € 20 bonus for the Download-Centre in the DETAIL Online Archive at www.detail.de

Student subscription
Special offer for students of architecture: all the advantages of a classic subscription, but at a specially favourable rate. Just send a copy of your student registration form for the current term.

€ 69.–

(10 issues a year + p/p +VAT)

Advantages to you:
- DETAIL sent directly to your home
- personal online access at www.detail.de
- € 20 bonus for the Download-Centre in the DETAIL Online Archive at www.detail.de

Test subscription
To acquaint yourself with DETAIL – Review of Architecture and Construction Details send for a two-issue, no-obligation subscription delivered conveniently to your home address.

€ 22.–

(2 issues, incl. p/p and VAT)

Advantages to you:
- DETAIL sent directly to your home
- personal online access at www.detail.de
- € 20 bonus for the Download-Centre in the DETAIL Online Archive at www.detail.de

Load-bearing structures and building skins

The state-of-the-art reference work on timber construction for architects and engineers

The functional efficiency of modern timber structures is still underestimated. A close collaboration between architects and engineers is necessary in this area – more so than in almost any other field of architecture. The aesthetic quality of exposed timber structures can have a great effect on the architectural form of a building, just as architectural design concepts have a major influence on the form of the structure. Both aspects are treated in depth in this comprehensive standard work.

- **More than 4,000 detail drawings**
- **The main planning principles**
  clearly presented – from building physics to fire protection
- **From simple beam construction to complex lattice shells:**
  a systematic description of structural principles illustrated with many typical details and more than 120 examples
- The wide range of structural systems in use is illustrated by **more than 70 extensively documented examples**

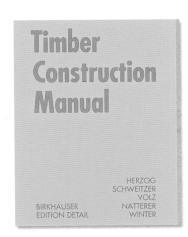

Timber Construction Manual
by Julius Natterer, Wolfgang Winter, Thomas Herzog, Roland Schweitzer and Michael Volz. New, completely revised edition 2003; ca. 380 pp. with approx. 4,000 drawings, 32 colour plates and numerous coloured illustrations; 23 x 29.7 cm, hardback, ISBN 3-7643-7025-4
€ 110 + postage/packing

Leaf through our publications at
www.detail.de

Order now – first-hand knowledge:
Edition DETAIL   www.detail.de

Solar Architecture – indoor-climate design for the 21st century

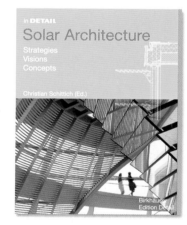

Solar Architecture
Christian Schittich (ed.), 2003;
176 pp. with numerous drawings and photos; 23 x 29.7 cm,
bound, with dust jacket,
ISBN 3-7643-0747-1
€ 65 + postage/packing

**Energy-efficient construction – intelligent solutions for
tomorrow's architecture**

For the first time, a comprehensive treatment of all aspects of
solar construction in a single volume – from urban-planning to
passive and active energy systems and the development of
new insulating materials. *Solar Architecture* presents an over-
view of planning instruments and techniques that allow the
assessment and implementation of the appropriate measures.
The book contains a wide range of innovative solutions, from
single-family houses, office and commercial developments to
settlement models, all presented at a high level of quality and
illustrated with large-scale detail drawings. Sustainable buildings based on holistic concepts in which various aspects of
solar technology are convincingly integrated.

■ **The reference work for climatically respon-
   sive architecture:** for the first time, all areas
   of solar construction in a single volume
■ **Solar architecture as teamwork:** selected
   specialist contributions underline the importance of integrated planning processes
■ **International examples:** technical and
   design solutions presented in a clear, comprehensible documentation of projects

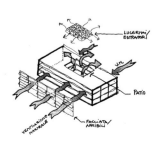

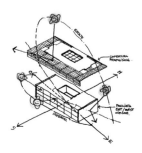

Transparent, translucent, perforated

The modern guide to diaphanous building materials
Translucent materials offer the architect great design scope for a sensitive handling of light and an exciting interplay of indoor and outdoor space that would not be possible with clear glass. Different moods, evoked in the past with stained-glass windows, thinly cut stone slabs or stretched paper, are created in modern forms through the use of special types of glass, plastic sheets, membranes, perforated metal sheeting, etc.

- **Information in compact form**, with a comparison of glass, plastic sheeting, membranes and metal products – all in a single volume
- **Technical properties:** visual screening, protection against glare, thermal and acoustic insulation, fire protection, etc.
- **New materials:** details of when special approval is required for individual design solutions
- **Information on manufacturers**, grouped according to products

Translucent Materials
Frank Kaltenbach (ed.), 2004;
112 pp. with numerous drawings
and photos; 21 × 29.7 cm,
paperback, ISBN 3-7643-7033-5
€ 65 + postage/packing

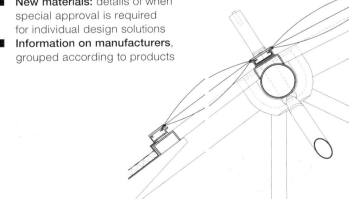

Leaf through our
publications at
www.detail.de

Order form

DETAIL subscription

☐ **Classic subscription** (10 issues per year) starting with issue no. _____
  € 109.– plus postage/packing surface mail + VAT if applicable*

☐ **Student subscription** (10 issues per year) starting with issue no. _____
  € 69.– plus postage/packing surface mail + VAT if applicable* (send copy of student identification)

☐ **Trial subscription** (2 issues)
  € 22.– (€ 16.– + € 6.– postage/packing) + VAT if applicable

Postage/packing 10 issues: € 32.50 European countries/Switzerland; € 29.50 Europe non-EU; € 37.50 oversea
Legal guarantee: DETAIL guarantees that I can cancel all subscription orders in writing within one week.

DETAIL gift subscription

Please mark the type of subscription you require with a cross in one of the squares above.

Address of recipient:

_____ _____
Last name, first name   Street, No.

_____ _____
City, Country   Telephone

Construction manuals

€ 110.– per copy plus postage/packing € 10.30 per copy (outside Germany), plus VAT if applicable.

_____ Copy: Timber Construction Manual   _____ Copy: Steel Construction Manual
_____ Copy: Roof Construction Manual   _____ Copy: Glass Construction Manual
_____ Copy: Concrete Construction Manual   _____ Copy: Masonry Construction Manua

in DETAIL

€ 65.– per copy plus postage/packing € 10.30 per copy (outside Germany), plus VAT if applicable.

_____ Copy: Solar Architecture   _____ Copy: Interior Spaces
_____ Copy: Building in Existing Fabric   _____ Copy: Building Skins
_____ Copy: Single Family Houses   _____ Copy: High-Density Housing
_____ Copy: Japan   (July 2004)

DETAIL Practice

€ 34.50 per copy plus postage/packing € 4,– per copy (outside Germany), plus VAT if applicable.

_____ Copy: Translucent Materials   _____ Copy: Plastering and Rendering,
_____ Copy: Timber Construction   Coatings and Coloration (Sept. 2004)
_____ Copy: Building with Large Clay
        Blocks (October 2004)

From

_____
First name

_____
Last name

_____
Profession

_____
Street, No.

_____
City, Country

_____
Telephone, Fax

_____
E-mail   (L643)

Form of payment

☐ **Credit card**

  ☐ VISA ☐ Eurocard, Mastercard

  Card no. | | | | | | | | | | | | | | | | | | |

  The last three digits of the number
  in the signature strip are | | | |

  Expiry date of card: _____

  Month/Year _____

  Total amount   € _____

☐ **In advance, on receipt of your invoice**

_____
Date/Signature

Tel.: +49 (0)89 / 381620-0
Fax: +49 (0)89 / 398670
E-mail: vertrieb@detail.de

Institut für internationale
Architektur-Dokumentation
GmbH & Co. KG
Postfach 33 06 60
80066 München
GERMANY

www.detail.de

Prices January 2004